nF421209

COPYRIGHT

SPECIAL SALES

For more information about buying this book in bulk quantities, or for special sales opportunities (which may include custom cover designs, and content particular to your business or training goals), please send us an email to support@myexcelonline.com

MYEXCELONLINE ACADEMY COURSE

We are offering you access to our online Excel membership course – The MyExcelOnline Academy – **for only $1 for the first 30 days!**

Copy & Paste this $1 Trial URL to your web browser to get access to this special reader offer: https://www.myexcelonline.com/$1trial

CONNECT WITH US

Website, blog & podcast: https://www.myexcelonline.com

iPhone App: https://www.myexcelonline.com/iphone

Android App: https://www.myexcelonline.com/android

Email Support: support@myexcelonline.com

AUTHOR BIOGRAPHY

John Michaloudis is the Founder of MyExcelOnline.com. John is currently living in the North of Spain, is married and has two beautiful kids. John holds a Bachelor's Degree in Commerce (Major in Accounting) and speaks English/Australian, Greek and Spanish.

Bryan Hong is a contributor at MyExcelOnline.com. He is currently living in the Philippines and is married to his wonderful wife Esther. Bryan is also a Microsoft Certified Systems Engineer with over 10 years of IT and teaching experience!

DOWNLOADABLE PRACTICE WORKBOOKS

Formulas are one of the most powerful features in Excel and learning how & when to use them will make you into an Excel superstar! There are 483 Functions at the time of publishing this book but you only need to know several of these to become efficient at Excel!

To get the most value out of this book, **please download the workbooks below** and practice entering the Function in a cell. Then follow our step by step guide. Make mistakes! That is fine. You may not get it the first time around (we certainly didn't) but when you do, you will be a step closer to Excel stardom!

For the **download link** that has all the workbooks covered in this book, please go to the **last page of the book**.

FREE MICROSOFT EXCEL ONLINE COURSE

As a thank you for your support, we would want to give you a **free Microsoft Excel Online Course** that has 77 video tutorials, 20+ Hours and 10 Modules of different Excel topics such as Excel Functions, Formatting, Tables, Charts, Pivot Tables, Macros, Power Query, Power BI and so much more!

For the **private access link and the password** to this 20+ Hour Excel Course, please go to the **last page of the book**.

Formulas VS Functions

You most probably have heard the words Formulas & Functions both being used in Excel. What is the difference between them?

A **Formula** is an expression which calculates the value of a cell. A **Function** is a predefined formula that is made available for you to use in Excel:

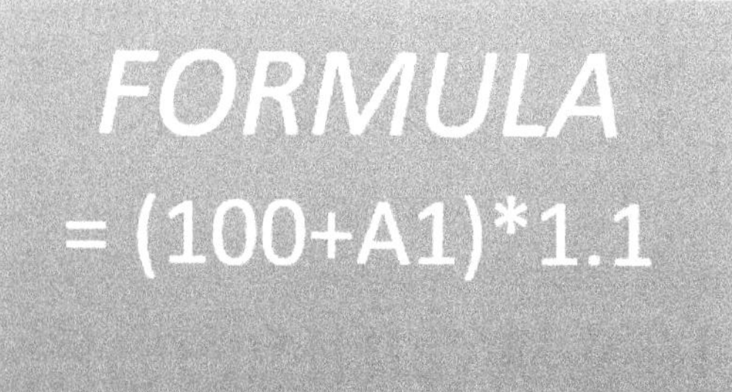

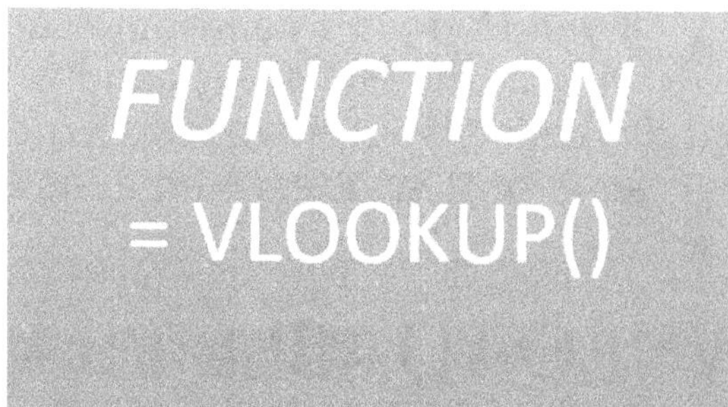

In this book, we use both terms (function and formula) interchangeably.

Here are several **operators** that you can use in a Formula:

OPERATOR	MEANING	EXAMPLE
+ (plus sign)	Addition	=3+3
− (minus sign)	Subtraction	=3-3
− (minus sign)	Negation	=-3
* (asterisk)	Multiplication	=3*3
/ (forward slash)	Division	=3/3
% (percent sign)	Percent	30%
^ (caret)	Exponentiation	=3^3
= (equal sign)	Equal to	=A1=B1
> (greater than sign)	Greater than	=A1>B1
< (less than sign)	Less than	=A1<B1
>= (greater than or equal to sign)	Greater than or equal to	=A1>=B1
<= (less than or equal to sign)	Less than or equal to	=A1<=B1
<> (not equal to sign)	Not equal to	=A1<>B1
& (ampersand)	Connects, or concatenates, two values to produce one continuous text value	="North"&"wind" results in "Northwind"
: (colon)	Range operator, which produces one reference to all the cells between two references, including the two references.	B5:B15
, (comma)	Union operator, which combines multiple references into one reference	=SUM(B5:B15,D5:D15)
(space)	Intersection operator, which produces one reference to cells common to the two references	B7:D7 C6:C8

TABLE OF CONTENTS

FORMULA TIPS

The Function Wizard

What does it do?

If you are unsure on which formula to use in Excel, Excel has you covered! You can use the **Insert Function Wizard** of Excel to find one for your purpose.

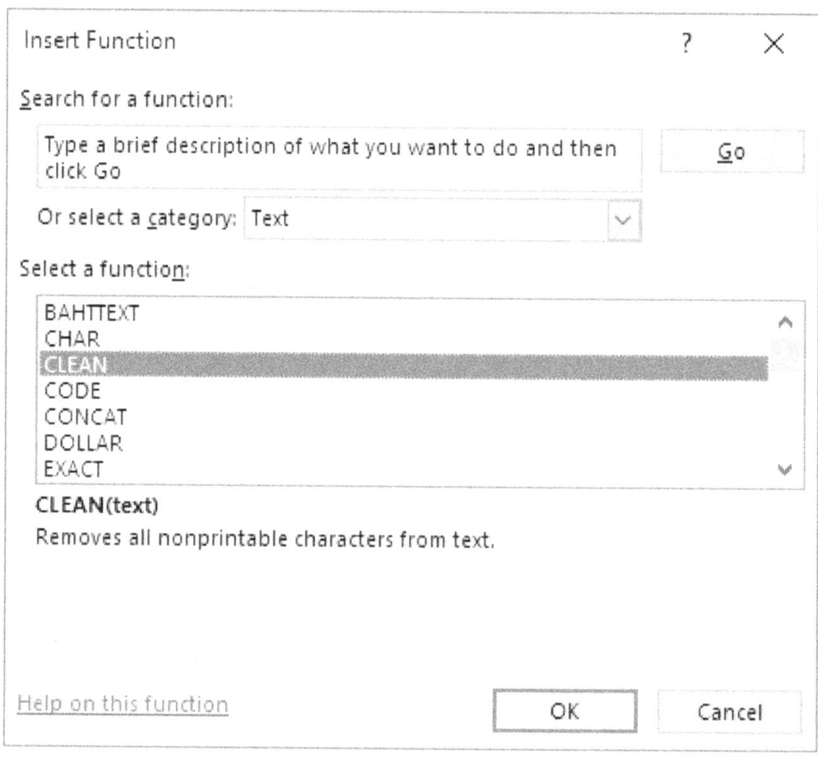

STEP 1: Ensure you have a cell selected and click the Insert Function button depicted as *fx*:

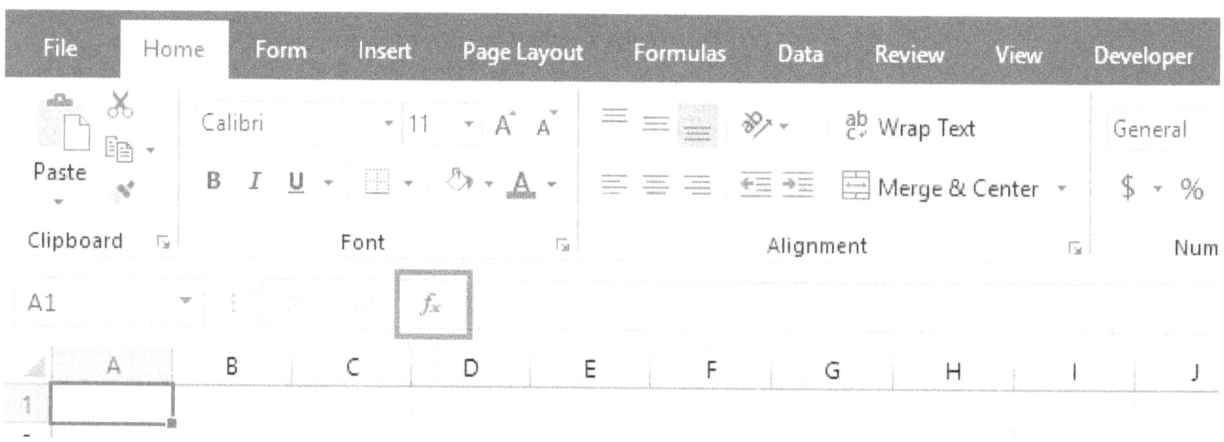

 Inside this window, you can try to search for the function:

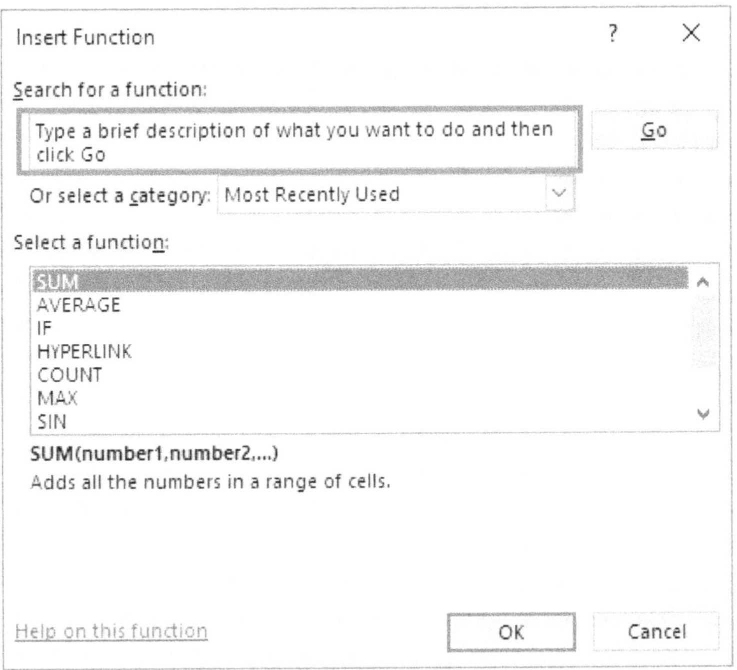

Or filter by category:

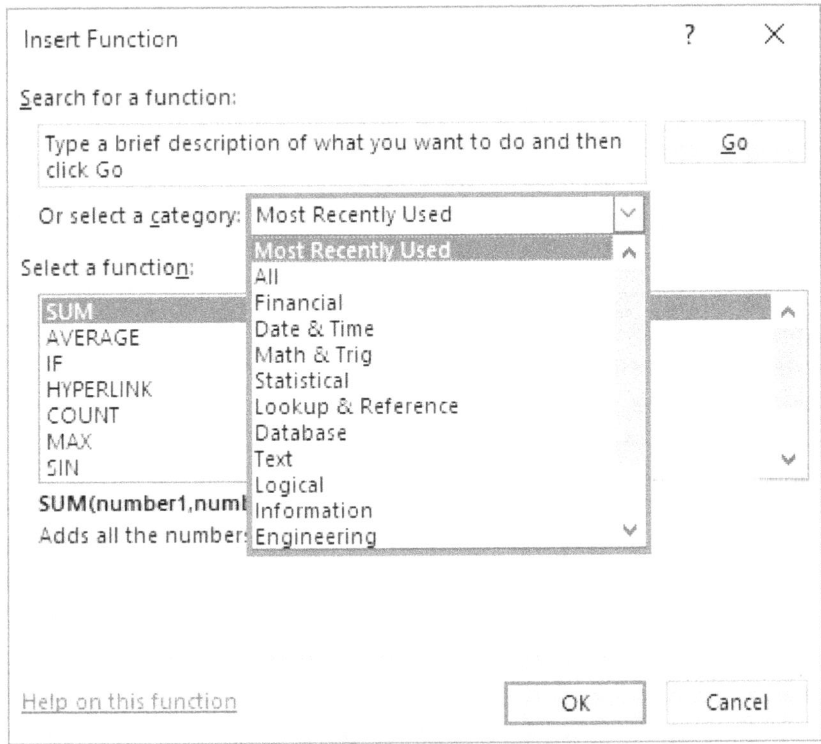

STEP 3: Once you have selected the function you want, click OK.

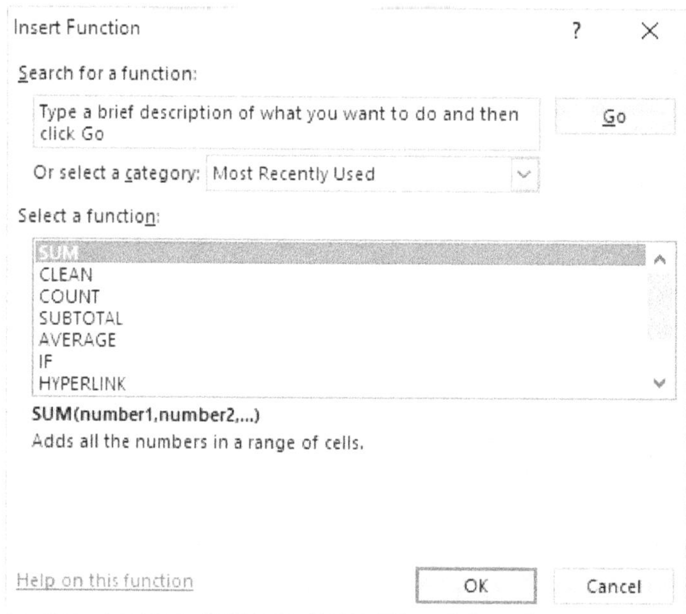

STEP 4: Fill out the arguments of your selected function. Click OK.

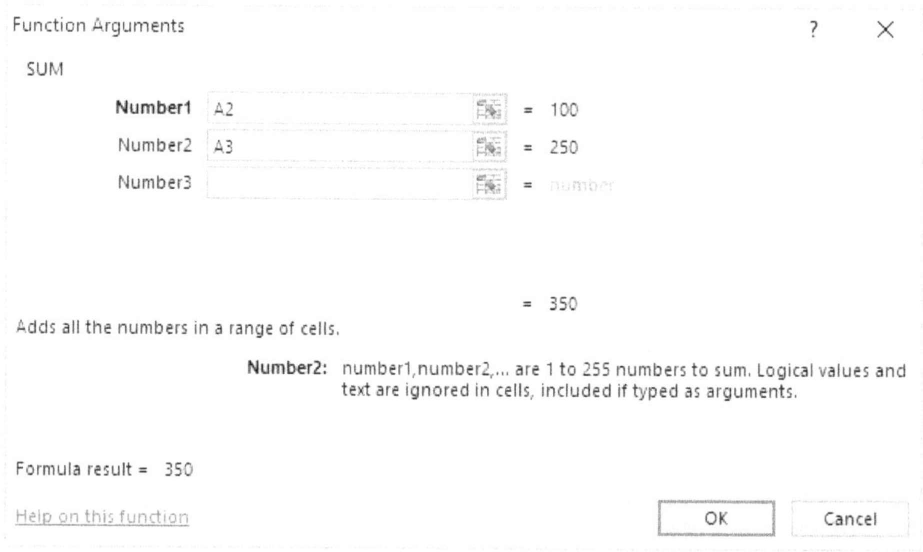

Your Excel Formula is now ready!

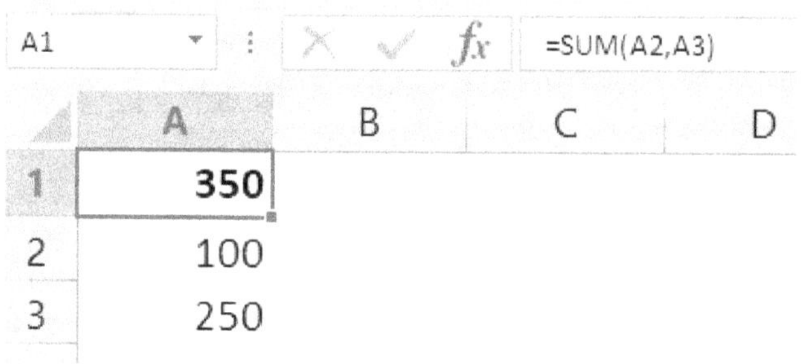

F9 to Evaluate a Formula

What does it do?

Sometimes we need to create complicated formulas, and when that happens it is easy to make mistakes. It becomes hard finding what caused the issue! The fun part is it is easy to evaluate parts of your Formula in Excel by using pressing the **F9** Key!

Our example checks if the date is in the Month of January and has sales greater than 1000. It uses the **AND Function** and we want to understand why it evaluated to **FALSE**.

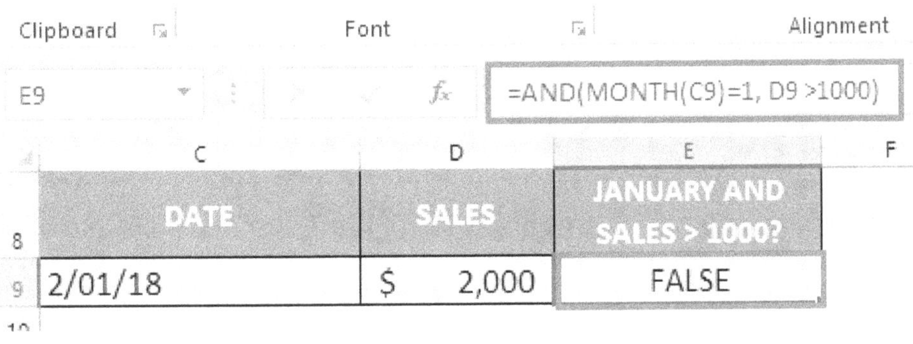

STEP 1: **Double click** or press **F2** on the cell that has the formula

STEP 2: Select the part of the formula that you want to evaluate first. Let us check the first part: **MONTH(C9)=1**

Press **F9** to evaluate this part. It evaluates to FALSE because the month in cell C9 is February and not January or 1

C	D	E
DATE	SALES	JANUARY AND SALES > 1000?
2/01/18	$ 2,000	=AND(FALSE, D9 >1000)
		AND(**logical1**, [logical2], [logical3], ...)

STEP 3: Let us evaluate the second part of the formula. Select the other part: **D9 >1000**

C	D	E
DATE	SALES	JANUARY AND SALES > 1000?
2/01/18	$ 2,000	=AND(FALSE, D9 >1000)
		AND(logical1, [logical2], [logical3], ...)

Press **F9** to evaluate this part. It evaluates to TRUE because D9 is greater than 1000.

C	D	E
DATE	SALES	JANUARY AND SALES > 1000?
2/01/18	$ 2,000	=AND(FALSE, TRUE)
		AND(logical1, [logical2], [logical3], ...)

Press **ESC** to exit the formula editor without making changes.

Now it makes sense why our formula here gave us a value of FALSE!

Clipboard	Font		Alignment

E9 fx =AND(MONTH(C9)=1, D9 >1000)

	C	D	E	F
8	DATE	SALES	JANUARY AND SALES > 1000?	
9	2/01/18	$ 2,000	FALSE	

Named Ranges

What does it do?

A named range in Excel is a cell or range of cells that has a more descriptive name. It goes a long way in using named ranges, because it allows you to create cleaner and easier to understand formulas in Excel!

Our example gets the maximum value with the **MAX Function**. Let us improve this function by replacing the range of cells with a named range.

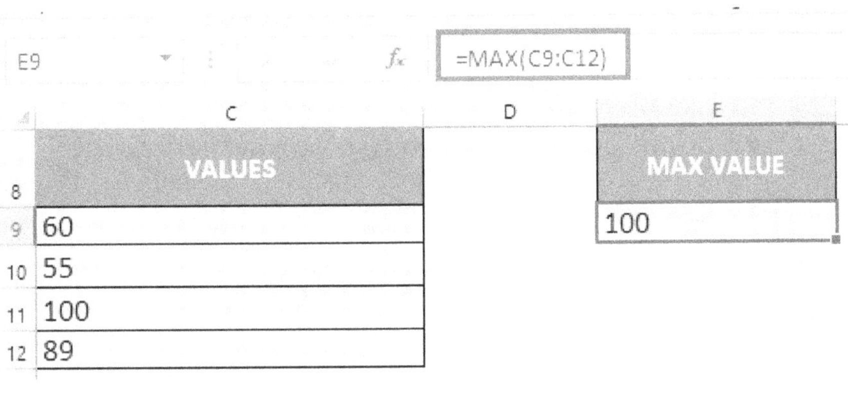

STEP 1: Select the cells that you want to give a named range to.

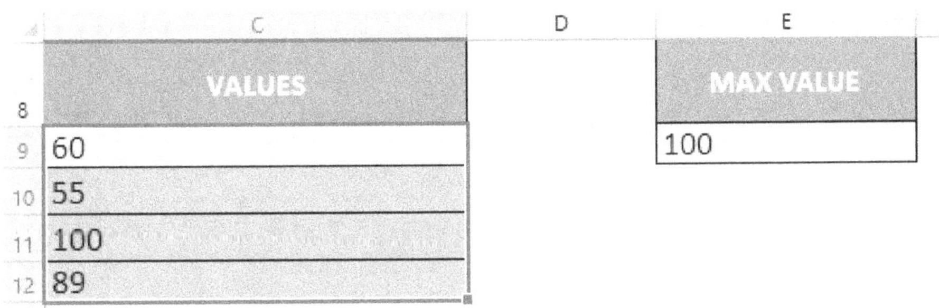

STEP 2: Go to *Formulas > Defined Names > Define Name*

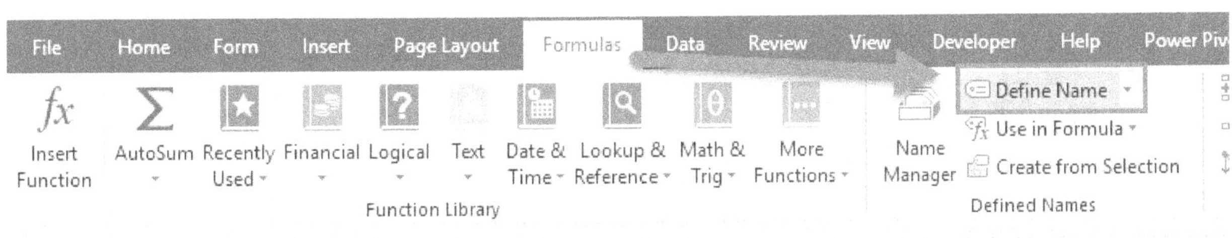

 Give it a meaningful name (it cannot have spaces) and click OK.

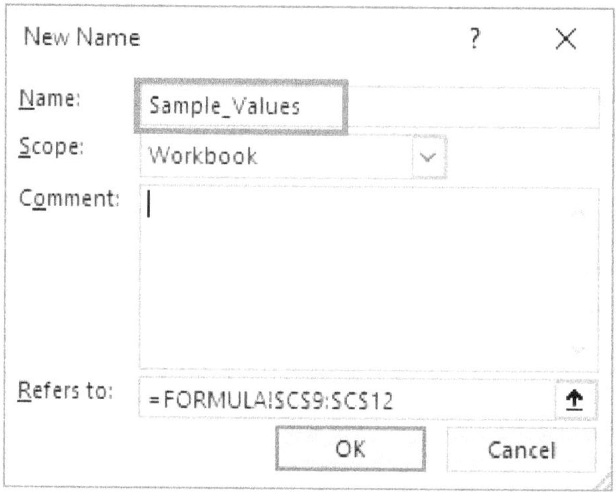

STEP 4: Let us now update our formula to use our named range!

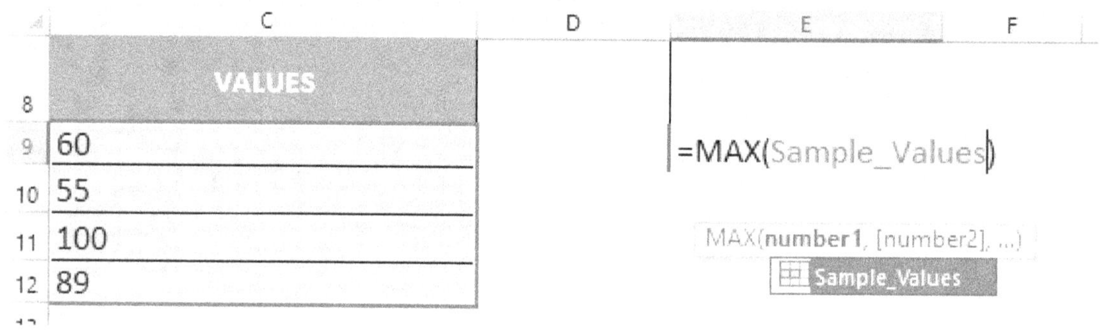

Our formula looks way better now and is still working as expected!

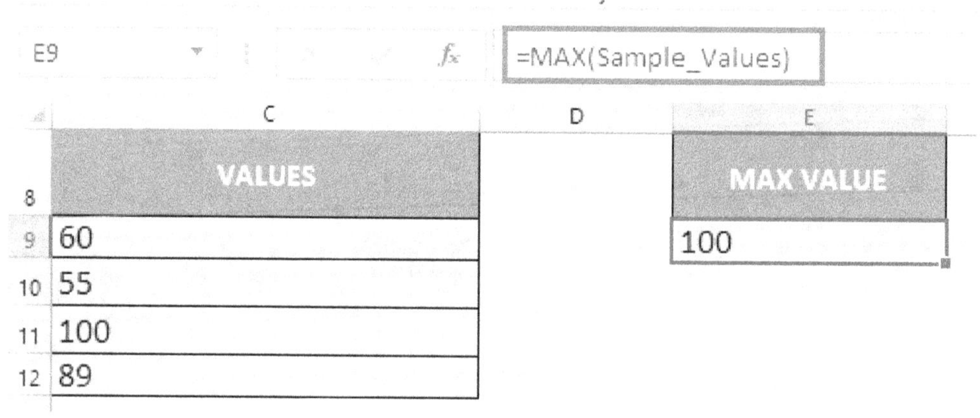

Absolute & Relative References

What does it do?

When creating formulas, it is very important to understand cell references. Let us go over the differences between absolute and relative references.

It will affect how your cell references will appear when you copy an Excel formula from one cell to another.

Excel uses **relative references** by default. A relative reference is useful if you want to use the same pattern across different cells.

For example, we have here a formula that gets the YEAR from cell C9.

	C	D
8	DATE	
9	4/11/85	=YEAR(C9)
10	3/06/62	
11	2/17/50	
12	12/28/90	

STEP 1: If we drag this formula all the way down for it to be copied to other cells:

	C	D
8	DATE	YEAR
9	4/11/85	1985
10	3/06/62	
11	2/17/50	
12	12/28/90	

Notice that the cell references have changed as well:

	DATE	YEAR
8		
9	4/11/85	1985
10	3/06/62	=YEAR(C10)
11	2/17/50	1950
12	12/28/90	1990

	DATE	YEAR
8		
9	4/11/85	1985
10	3/06/62	1962
11	2/17/50	=YEAR(C11)
12	12/28/90	1990

	DATE	YEAR
8		
9	4/11/85	1985
10	3/06/62	1962
11	2/17/50	
12	12/28/90	=YEAR(C12)

You could tell that Excel was smart enough to get the year of the **left cell which contains the date** without us even making a single change.

For **absolute references**, the reference to a cell is always fixed even if we copy our formula to another cell.

We have this example that uses a NETWORKDAYS function. A NETWORKDAYS Function needs a list of holidays to count the correct number of working days.

Since we want to use the NETWORKDAYS function multiple times, it would make sense to have a single list of holidays for it to use. This is where the absolute reference comes in handy.

An absolute reference contains a $ symbol in front of the column letter and the row number. You can see in our example that it has **$A$9:$A$11** pertaining to our Holiday Table. Notice that there are relative cell references in the formula as well (e.g. **C9 and D9**).

	HOLIDAYS		START DATE	END DATE	
9	1/01/18		1/01/18	1/07/18	=NETWORKDAYS(C9,D9,$A$9:$A$11)
10	1/08/18		1/01/18	1/14/18	
11	1/09/18		1/01/18	1/21/18	
12			1/01/18	1/28/18	

STEP 2: The magic happens when we drag our formula downwards.

	HOLIDAYS		START DATE	END DATE	NUMBER OF DAYS
9	1/01/18		1/01/18	1/07/18	4
10	1/08/18		1/01/18	1/14/18	
11	1/09/18		1/01/18	1/21/18	
12			1/01/18	1/28/18	

If we look at the other formulas, the Holiday table is exactly the same and has not changed (**$A$9:$A$11**). While the relative cell references have changed (e.g. **C10 and D10, C11 and D11, C12 and D12**).

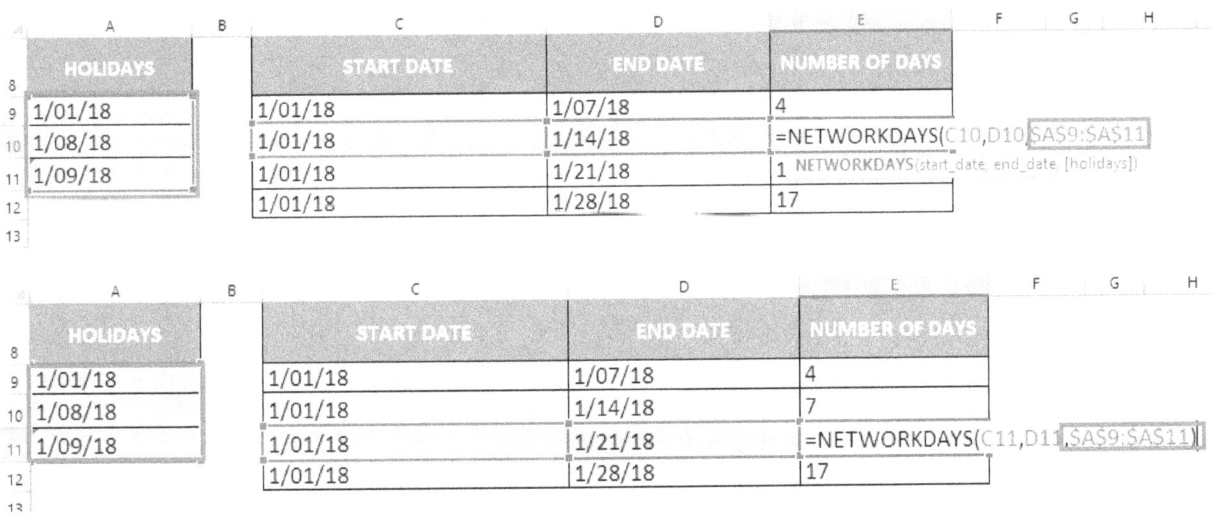

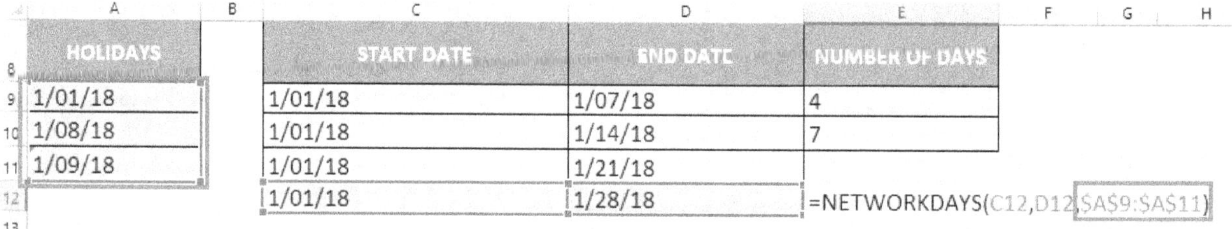

Knowing when to use absolute or relative cell reference will be a crucial skill. It will make your work a lot easier when copying the same formula across multiple cells.

TIP: You can press the F4 key to enter an absolute reference.

Pressing the F4 key multiple times, will change the absolute/relative reference combination to a mixed reference.

Give it a try!

Evaluate Formulas Step By Step

What does it do?

This is one of the coolest tricks I have seen in Excel, as there are countless times where I had a hard time understand formulas. Especially long and complex ones!

Excel provides the way to evaluate your formula, and break it down step by step so that you can understand it!

Let us take the formulas I've created below in the **IS THE VALUE IN BETWEEN** column. We will see how this formula is resolved in a series of steps:

START OF RANGE	END OF RANGE	VALUE TO BE EVALUATED	IS THE VALUE IN BETWEEN?	FORMULA
20	60	50	Yes	=IF(C7=MEDIAN(A7:C7), "Yes", "No")
10	40	50	No	=IF(C8=MEDIAN(A8:C8), "Yes", "No")

STEP 1: You can see our formula uses both the **If formula** and the **Median formula.**

The goal of this formula is to evaluate if a value (**VALUE TO BE EVALUATED**) is in between the range (**START OF RANGE to VALUE TO BE EVALUATED**)

For example: Is 50 the median of the range 20; 60; 50?

$$=IF(C7=MEDIAN(A7:C7), \text{"Yes"}, \text{"No"})$$

To start understanding our formula, highlight the formula, then go to *Formulas > Evaluate Formula*:

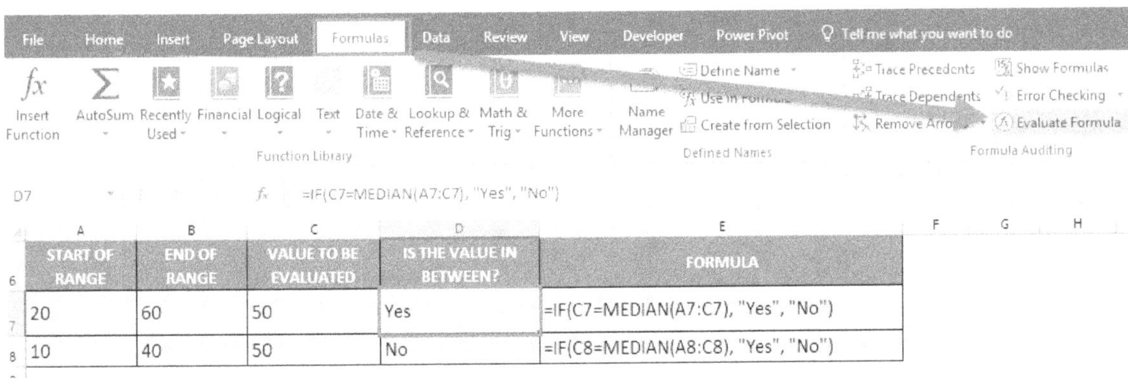

	START OF RANGE	END OF RANGE	VALUE TO BE EVALUATED	IS THE VALUE IN BETWEEN?	FORMULA
6					
7	20	60	50	Yes	=IF(C7=MEDIAN(A7:C7), "Yes", "No")
8	10	40	50	No	=IF(C8=MEDIAN(A8:C8), "Yes", "No")

STEP 2: Our formula is now shown on screen, and the part that is <u>underlined</u> is the one to be evaluated first. Click **Evaluate**.

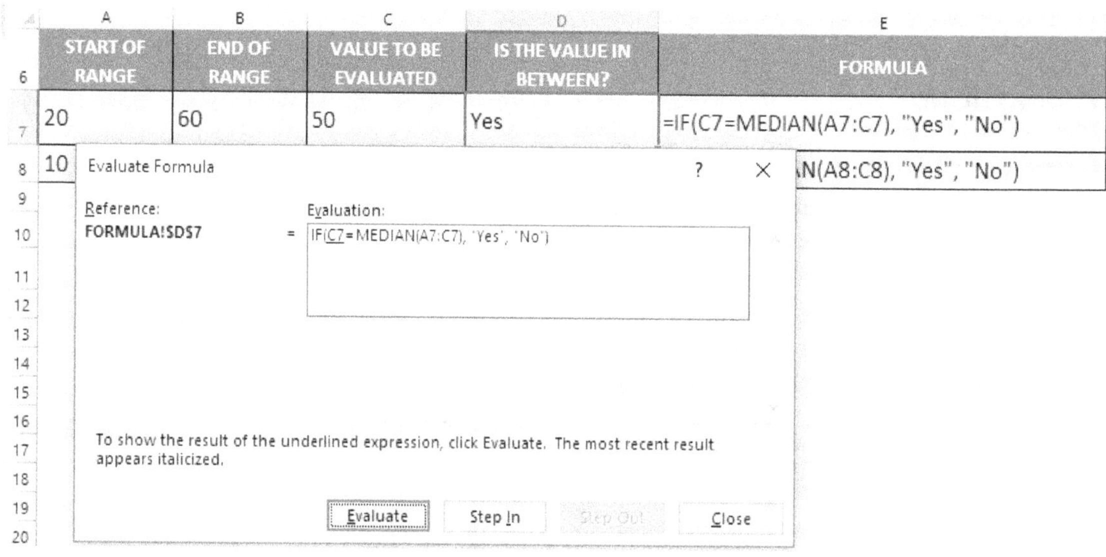

STEP 3: **C7** has been evaluated to **50**. Click **Evaluate**.

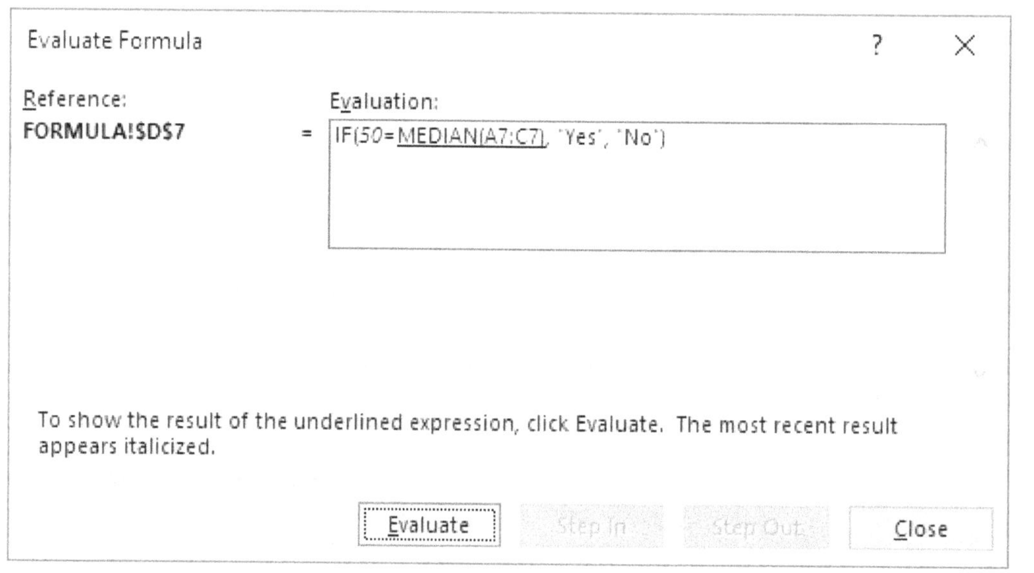

  The median of the values from A7 to C7 (20, 60, 50) is evaluated as **50**. Click **Evaluate**.

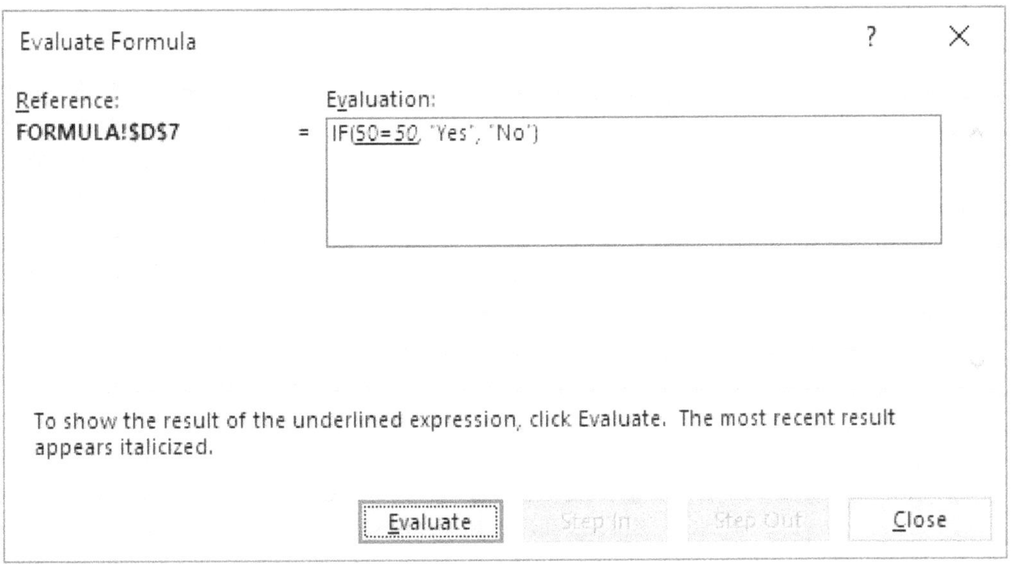

  Is 50 equal to 50?

Excel has evaluated it to *TRUE*. Click **Evaluate**.

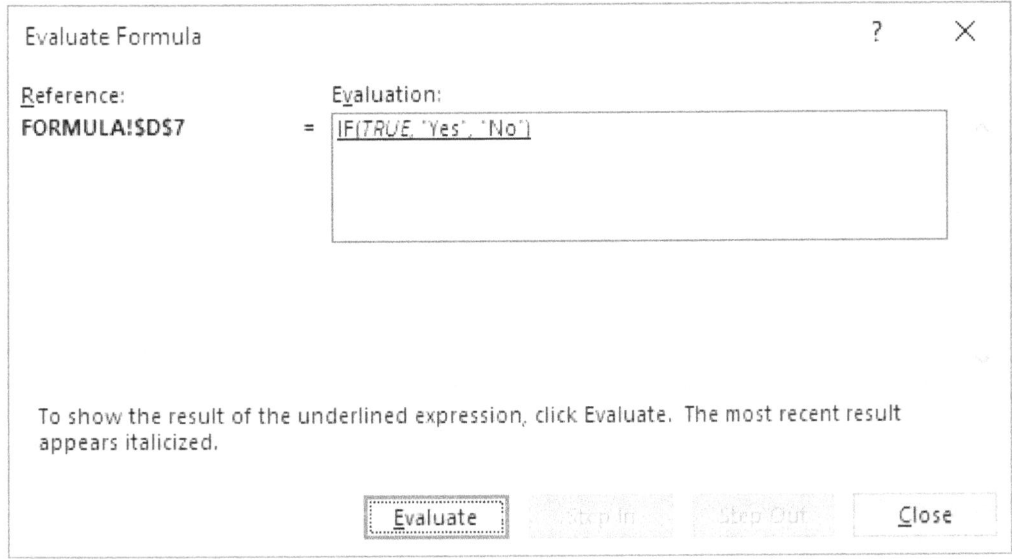

 Since the **If formula** received a *TRUE*, Excel evaluated it as a **Yes** end result. We have seen how the formula gave us the result in a few easy steps!

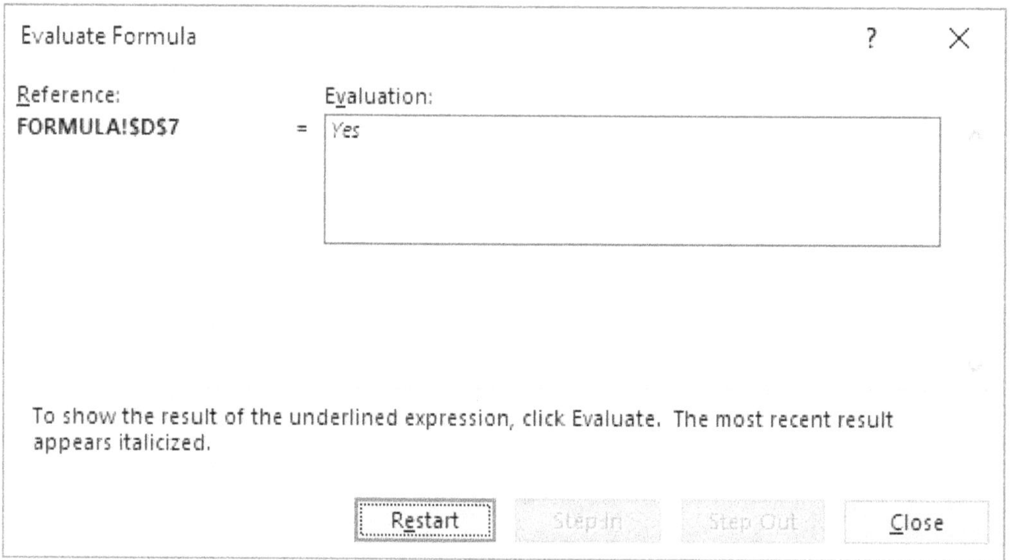

Highlight All Excel Formula Cells

What does it do?

Whenever you are auditing an Excel worksheet and need to know where all the formulas are located, a great way is to highlight the formula cells in a distinctive color.

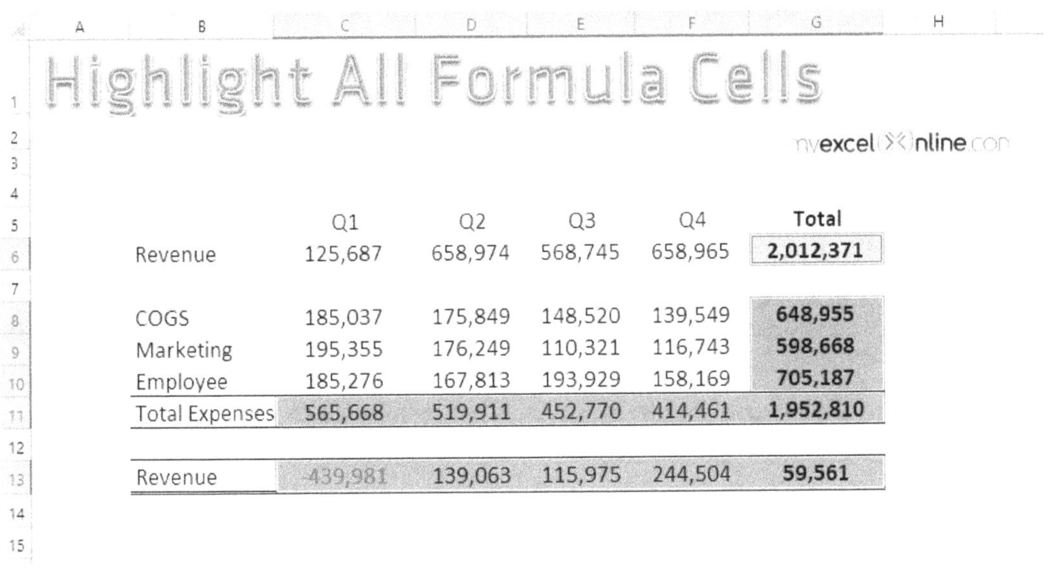

STEP 1: Select all the cells in your Excel worksheet by clicking on the top left hand corner of your worksheet.

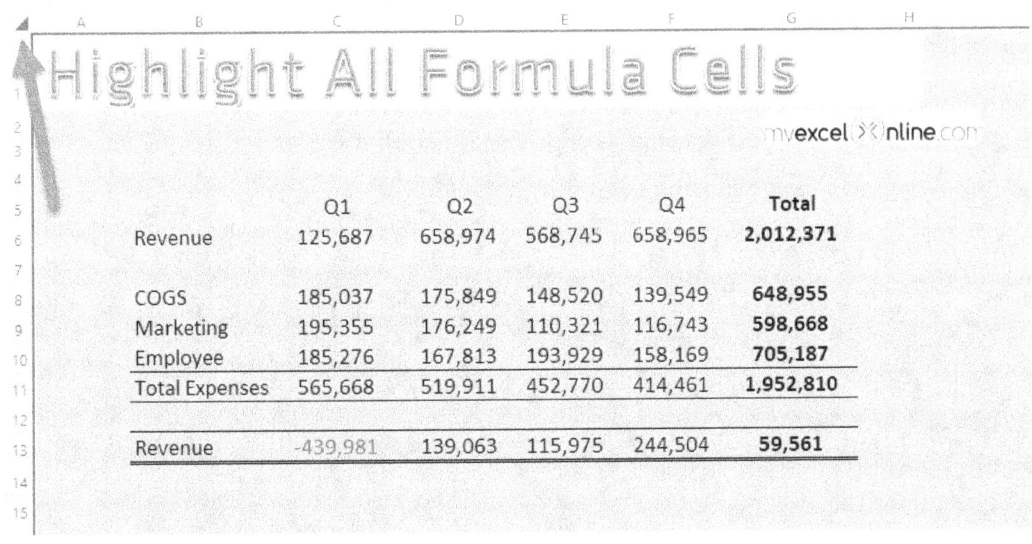

STEP 2: Press the **CTRL+G** shortcut which will open up the **Go To** dialogue box and select the *Special* button.

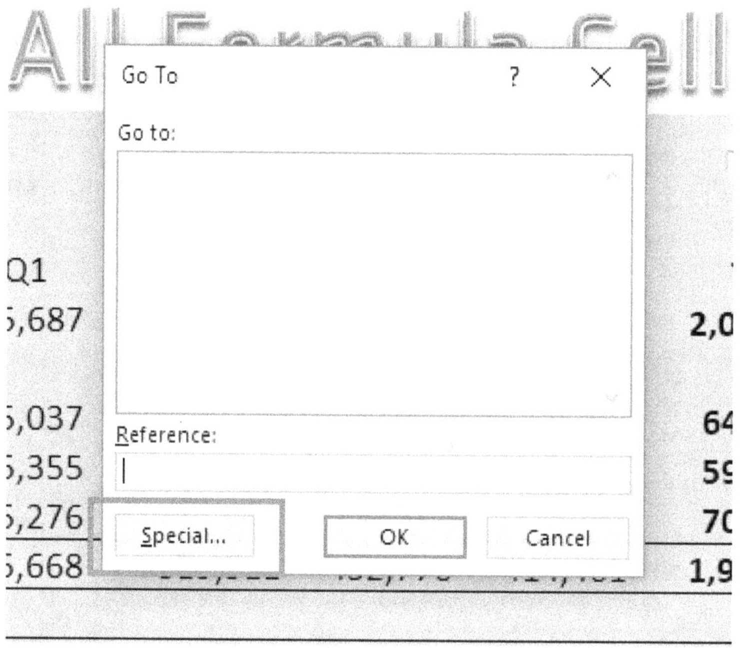

STEP 3: Select the **Formula** radio button and press **OK**.

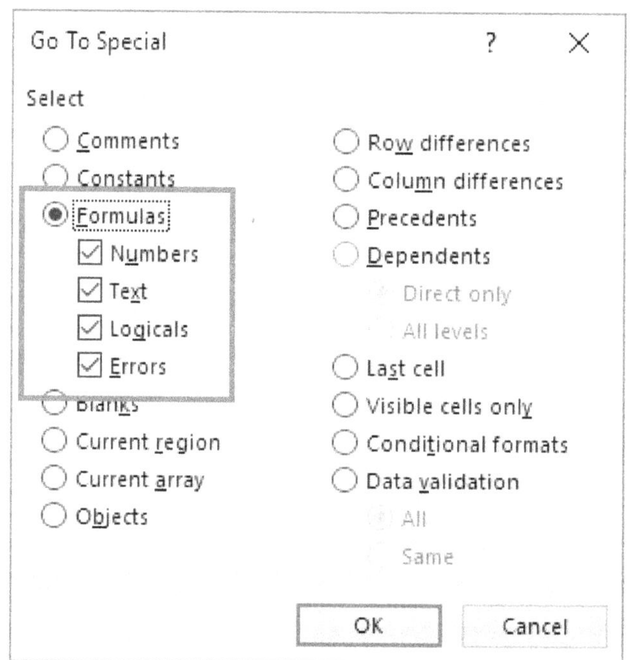

STEP 4: This will highlight all the formulas in your Excel worksheet and you can use the *Fill Color* to color in the formula cells.

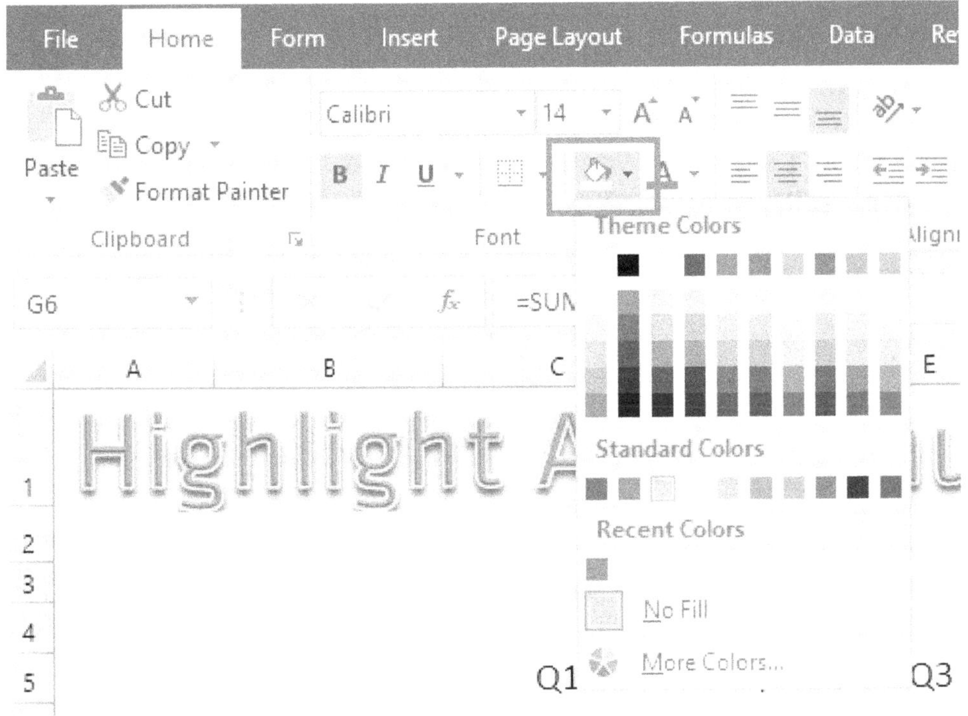

And now all your cells containing formulas are now highlighted!

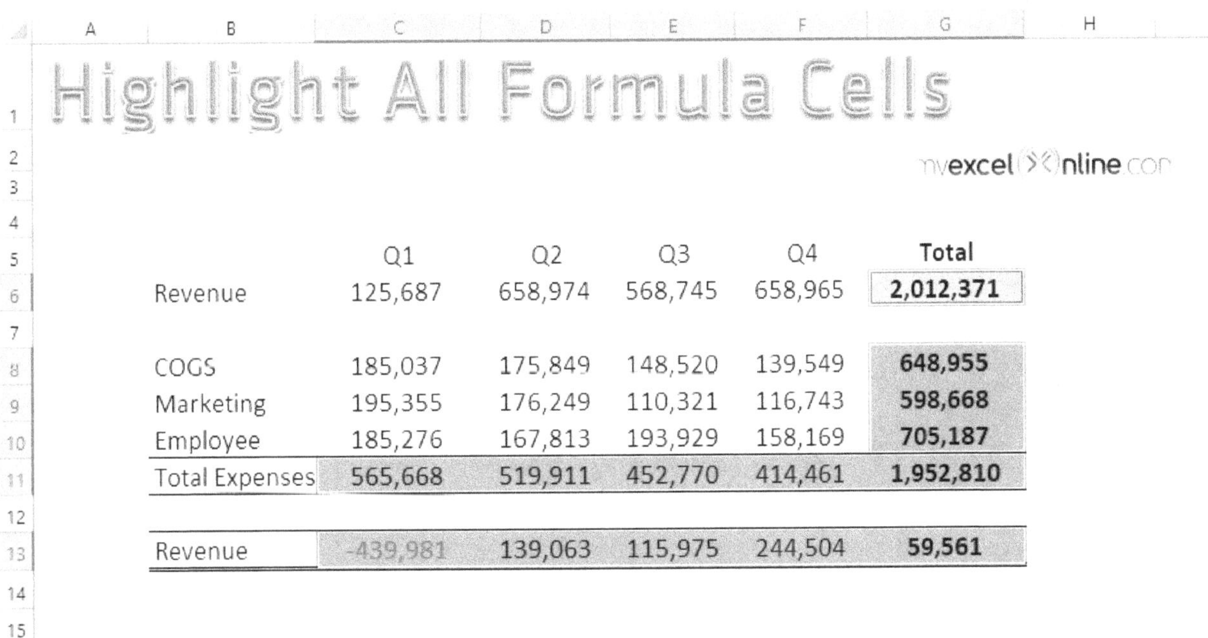

	Q1	Q2	Q3	Q4	Total
Revenue	125,687	658,974	568,745	658,965	2,012,371
COGS	185,037	175,849	148,520	139,549	648,955
Marketing	195,355	176,249	110,321	116,743	598,668
Employee	185,276	167,813	193,929	158,169	705,187
Total Expenses	565,668	519,911	452,770	414,461	1,952,810
Revenue	-439,981	139,063	115,975	244,504	59,561

How to Convert Formulas to Values

What does it do?

Have you ever had a scenario where you write a formula and just want to show the value output only and get rid of the formula?

Here is an example of a formula:

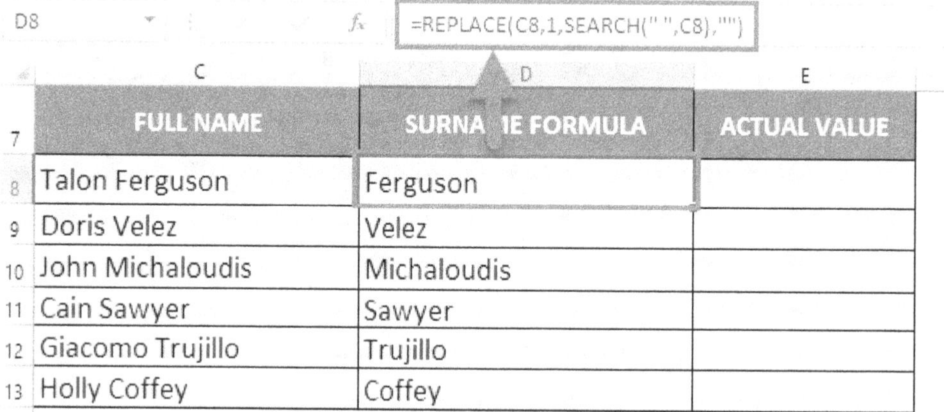

Well I do not need the formula, bit I do want the last names only....hard copied!

Fortunately, I have discovered two ways that you can achieve this...

STEP 1: Select the area that contains the formulas.

Click ***CTRL+C***

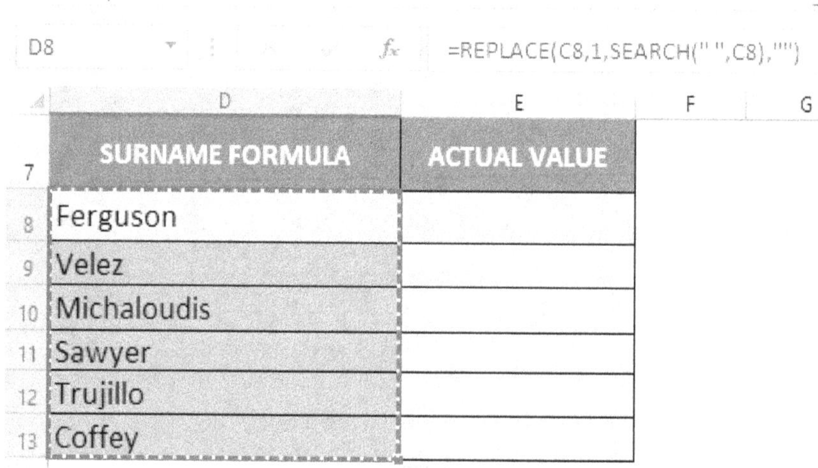

On the column that you want to place the values on, **right-click** and select **Paste Values:**

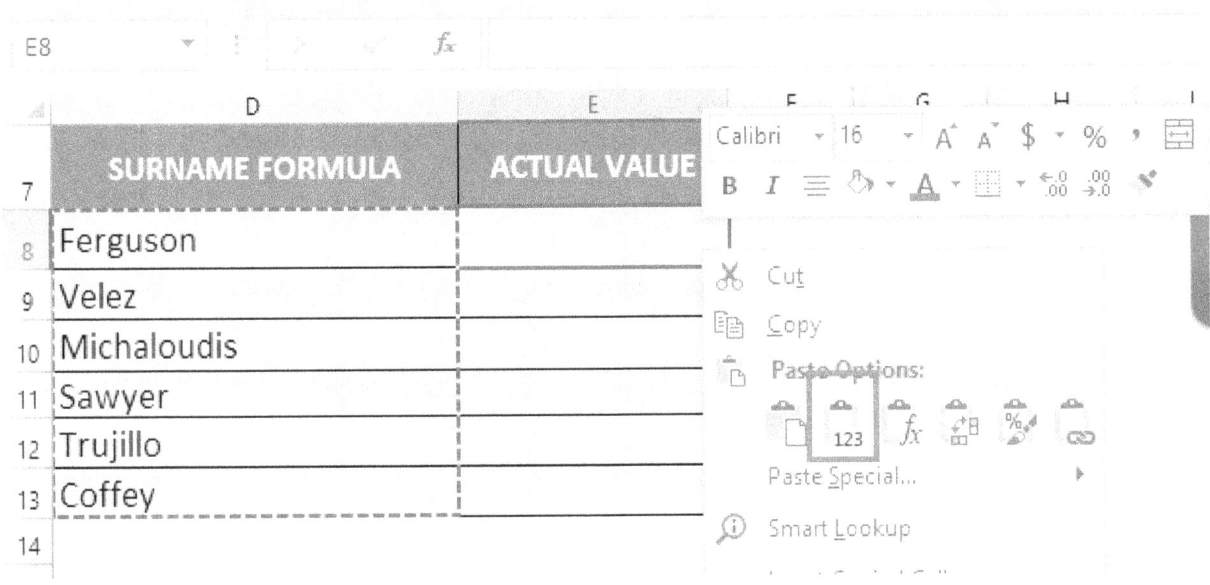

You can see that the actual values are now stored in that column!

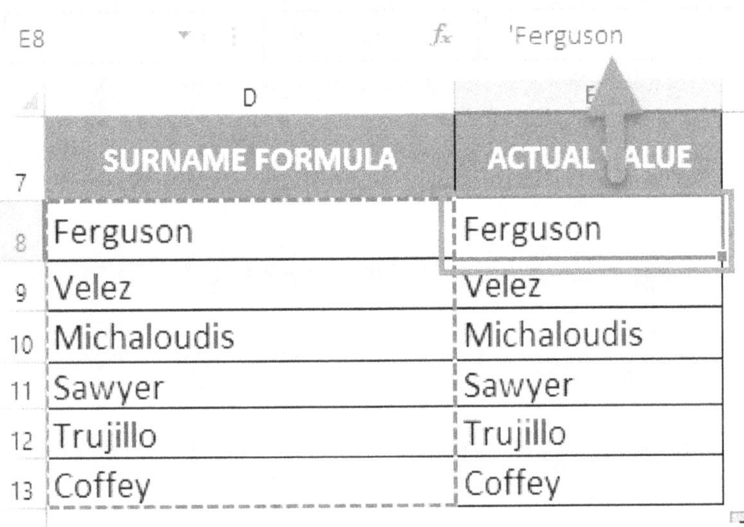

STEP 2: Here's an alternative way. Select the area that contains the formulas.

Right-click and hold on the **right border**.

Drag the border, whilst holding down the right-click on your mouse, to the area you want the values to be placed in.

Select **Copy Here as Values Only.**

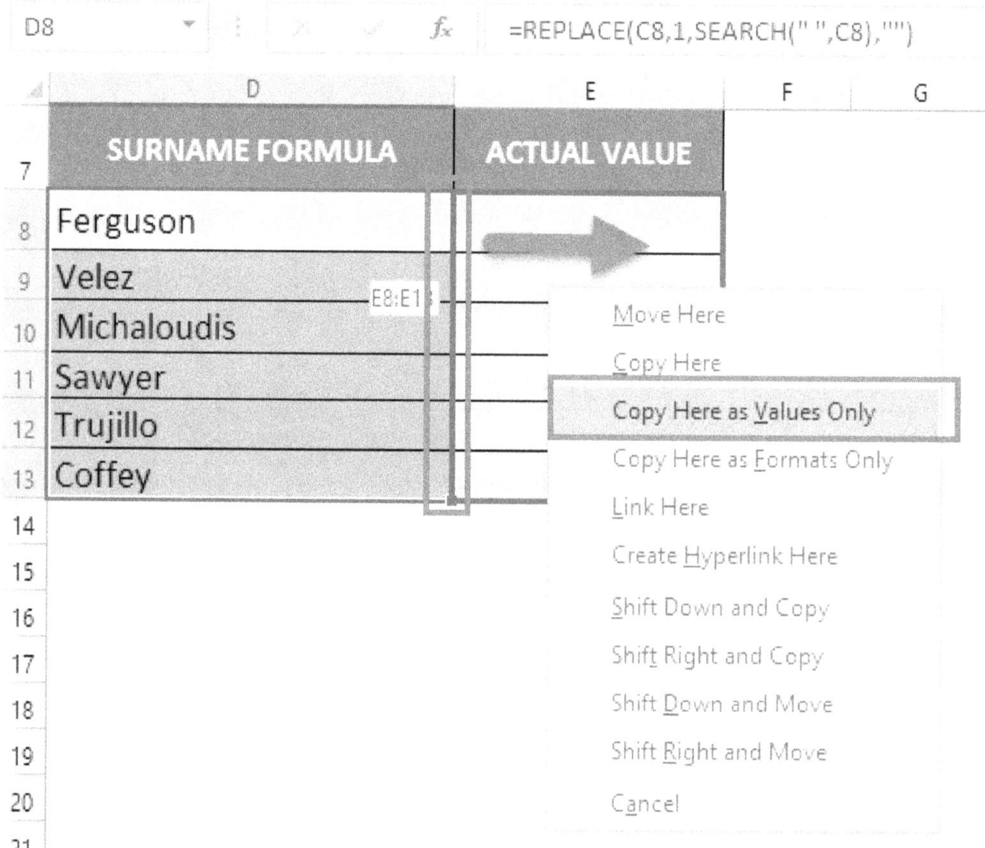

You now have the actual values hardcoded!

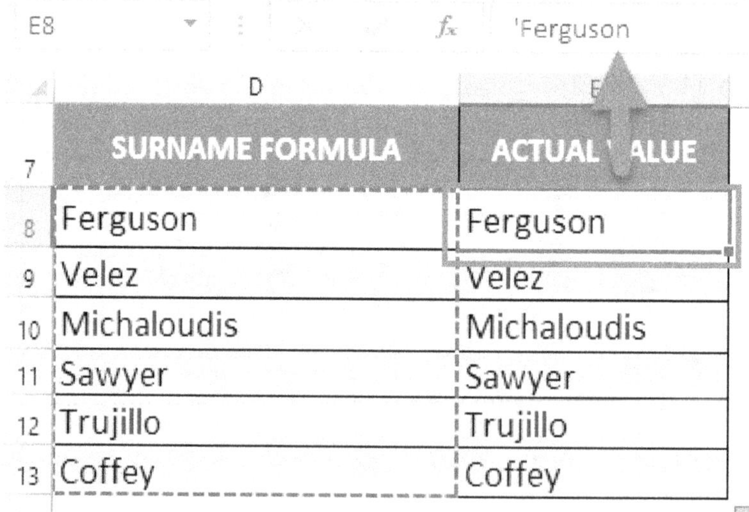

How to Show & Hide Formulas in Excel

What does it do?

When I have a sheet full of Excel formulas, sometimes I want to quickly check how each formula looks like. This is great for spreadsheet auditing.

It is very easy to do so in Excel!

Here is our sample worksheet with formulas:

	D	E	F
	PHONE NUMBER	**NEW PHONE NUMBER**	
9	+1-817-0000000	817-0000000	
10	+1-817-1111111	817-1111111	
11	+1-817-2222222	817-2222222	
12	+1-817-3333333	817-3333333	
13	+1-817-4444444	817-4444444	
14	+1-817-5555555	817-5555555	

E9 f_x =REPLACE(D9, 1, FIND("-",D9), "")

STEP 1: Press on your keyboard the following keys: **Ctrl +** `

The (`) key is usually located on the upper left part of your keyboard. This will show all your Excel formulas in your worksheet!

	D	E
	PHONE NUMBER	**NEW PHONE NUMBER**
9	+1-817-0000000	=REPLACE(D9, 1, FIND("-",D9), "")
10	+1-817-1111111	=REPLACE(D10, 1, FIND("-",D10), "")
11	+1-817-2222222	=REPLACE(D11, 1, FIND("-",D11), "")
12	+1-817-3333333	=REPLACE(D12, 1, FIND("-",D12), "")
13	+1-817-4444444	=REPLACE(D13, 1, FIND("-",D13), "")
14	+1-817-5555555	=REPLACE(D14, 1, FIND("-",D14), "")

Press the **Ctrl +** ` combination again to hide the formulas.

STEP 2: If you prefer to set this via Excel Options, another way is to go to **File > Options**

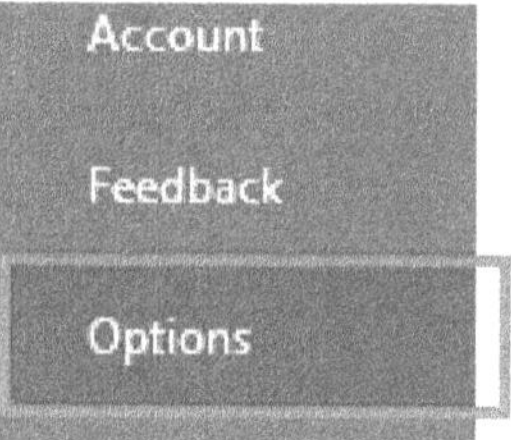

STEP 3: Go to **Advanced> Display Options for this Worksheet > Show formulas in cells instead of their calculated fields**

Ensure this is checked.

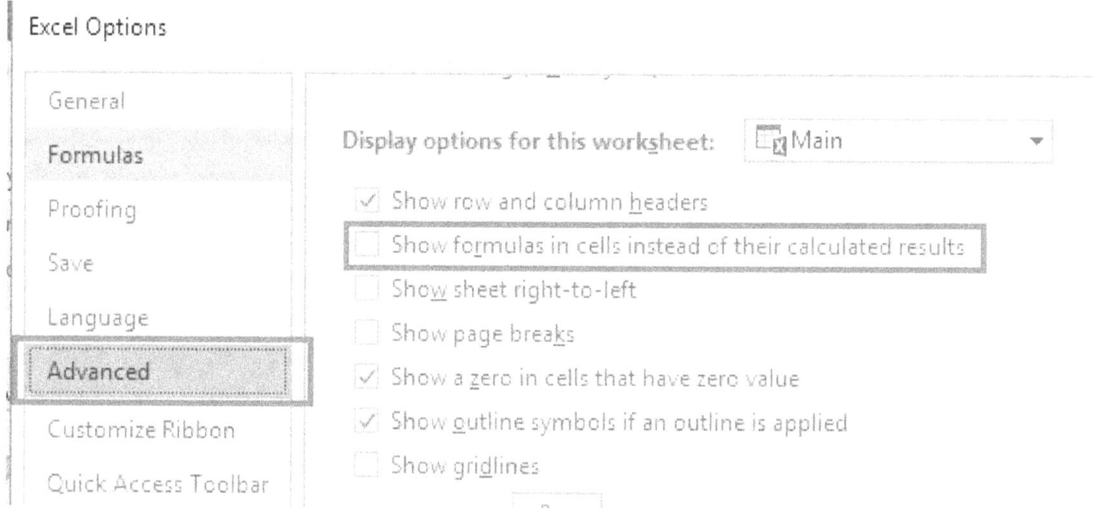

The formulas are all shown now too! You can uncheck it to hide the formulas again.

PHONE NUMBER	NEW PHONE NUMBER
+1-817-0000000	=REPLACE(D9, 1, FIND("-",D9), "")
+1-817-1111111	=REPLACE(D10, 1, FIND("-",D10), "")
+1-817-2222222	=REPLACE(D11, 1, FIND("-",D11), "")
+1-817-3333333	=REPLACE(D12, 1, FIND("-",D12), "")
+1-817-4444444	=REPLACE(D13, 1, FIND("-",D13), "")
+1-817-5555555	=REPLACE(D14, 1, FIND("-",D14), "")

Jump to a Cell Reference in a Formula

What does it do?

When writing, editing or auditing Excel formulas you will come across a scenario where you want to view and access the referenced cells within a formula argument.

This is helpful if you want to check how the formula works or to make any changes to the formula.

There is a cool tip where you can jump to the referenced cell or range within the formula and make your changes.

STEP 1: **Double click** inside your Excel formula

Items	Item id	Supplier

=VLOOKUP($B13,'STOCK LIST'!D9:E23,2,FALSE)

VLOOKUP(lookup_value, table_array, col_index_num, [range_lookup])

STEP 2: **Select the formula argument** that you want to edit with your mouse

Items	Item id	Supplier

=VLOOKUP($B13,'STOCK LIST'!D9:E23,2,FALSE)

VLOOKUP(lookup_value, table_array, col_index_num, [range_lookup])

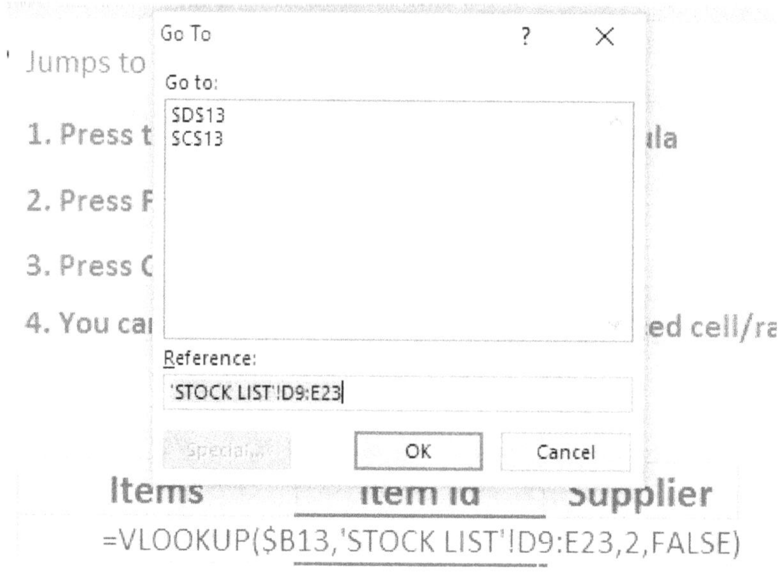

STEP 4: This will take you to the referenced cell/range

Items	Item ID	Supplier
Floppy Disks	610KLO	Acme, inc.
Mic Stand	125FRT	Widget Corp
Laptop	689CDF	123 Warehousing
Tablet	987SDD	Demo Company
Pop filter	658UYG	Smith and Co.
Mouse	125RTY	Foo Bars
iPad	569AER	ABC Telecom
Microphone		Fake Brothers
Pen Drive	589YUI	QWERTY Logistics
Mixer	841MKL	Demo, inc.
Laprop Cover	658UYH	Sample Company
Keyboard	698ADR	Sample, inc
Hard Drives	971UOP	Acme Corp
Television	254CFG	Allied Biscuit
Beers	012KIO	Ankh-Sto Associates

STEP 5: You can **select the new range** with your mouse and also make any changes to the formula bar

fx =VLOOKUP($B13,'STOCK LIST'!D9:F23,3,FALSE)

VLOOKUP(lookup_value, **table_array**, col_index_num, [range_lookup])

Items	Item ID	Supplier
Floppy Disks	610KLO	Acme, inc.
Mic Stand	125FRT	Widget Corp
Laptop	689CDF	123 Warehousing
Tablet	987SDD	Demo Company
Pop filter	658UYG	Smith and Co.
Mouse	125RTY	Foo Bars
iPad	569AER	ABC Telecom
Microphone	569ERT	Fake Brothers
Pen Drive	589YUI	QWERTY Logistics
Mixer	841MKL	Demo, inc.
Laprop Cover	658UYH	Sample Company
Keyboard	698ADR	Sample, inc
Hard Drives	971UOP	Acme Corp
Television	254CFG	Allied Biscuit
Beers	012KIO	Ankh-Sto Associates

STEP 6: Press **Enter** and your formula is updated

Items	Item id	Supplier
Television	=VLOOKUP($B13,'STOCK LIST'!D9:F23,3,FALSE)	
Laptop	689CDF	123 Warehousing
Tablet	987SDD	Demo Company
Keyboard	698ADR	Sample, inc
Mouse	125RTY	Foo Bars
iPad	569AER	ABC Telecom
Microphone	569ERT	Fake Brothers

LOOKUP FUNCTIONS

ADDRESS

What does it do?

Creates a cell reference based on the row and column numbers

Formula breakdown:

=ADDRESS(row_num, column_num, [abs_num], [a1], [sheet_text])

What it means:

=ADDRESS(row number, column number, [absolute or relative], [reference style], [name of the worksheet])

Example:

=ADDRESS(1,1,1) ="$A$1"

Did you know that you can dynamically create cell references in Excel? Yes you can with the **ADDRESS Formula**!

The **ADDRESS Formula** takes this information to create the cell reference:

- row number
- column number
- abs_num - this is reflected if your cell reference is absolute or relative. It has 4 possibilities:
    - 1 - Absolute
    - 2 - Absolute row, Relative column
    - 3 - Relative row, Absolute column
    - 4 - Relative
- a1 - this determines if it's R1C1 or A1 style. For our examples we will not use this, and it will default to A1 Style
    - 0 - R1C1 Style
    - 1 - A1 Style

- sheet_text - this will add the sheet name to your cell reference if populated

STEP 1: We need to **enter the *ADDRESS* function in a blank cell**:

=ADDRESS(

	ROW NUMBER	COLUMN NUMBER	ABSOLUTE NUM	
9	1	1	1	=ADDRESS(
10	1	1	2	
11	1	1	3	ADDRESS(row_num, column_num, [abs_num], [a1], [sheet_text])
12	1	1	4	
13	2	2	1	
14	10	5	1	

STEP 2: The **ADDRESS** arguments:

row_num

What is the row number?

Select the cell containing the row number:

=ADDRESS(C9,

	ROW NUMBER	COLUMN NUMBER	ABSOLUTE NUM	
9	1	1	1	=ADDRESS(C9,
10	1	1	2	
11	1	1	3	ADDRESS(row_num, column_num, [abs_num], [a1], [sheet_text])
12	1	1	4	
13	2	2	1	
14	10	5	1	

column_num

What is the column number?

Select the cell containing the column number:

=ADDRESS(C9, D9,

	ROW NUMBER	COLUMN NUMBER	ABSOLUTE NUM	
9	1	1	1	=ADDRESS(C9, D9,
10	1	1	2	
11	1	1	3	ADDRESS(row_num, column_num, [abs_num], [a1], [sheet_text])
12	1	1	4	
13	2	2	1	
14	10	5	1	

abs_num

Would it be an absolute or relative cell reference?

Select the cell containing the abs_num input. There are 4 modes, so we have included in all of the examples so that you can see it in action.

=ADDRESS(C9, D9, E9)

	ROW NUMBER	COLUMN NUMBER	ABSOLUTE NUM	
9	1	1	1	=ADDRESS(C9, D9, E9)
10	1	1	2	
11	1	1	3	
12	1	1	4	
13	2	2	1	
14	10	5	1	

Apply the same formula to the rest of the cells by dragging the lower right corner downwards.

	ROW NUMBER	COLUMN NUMBER	ABSOLUTE NUM	RESULT
9	1	1	1	$A$1
10	1	1	2	
11	1	1	3	
12	1	1	4	
13	2	2	1	
14	10	5	1	
15				

You have all of your cell references generated now! Notice the differences in the 4 [abs_num] options i.e. AA, A$1, $A1:

	ROW NUMBER	COLUMN NUMBER	ABSOLUTE NUM	RESULT
9	1	1	1	$A$1
10	1	1	2	A$1
11	1	1	3	$A1
12	1	1	4	A1
13	2	2	1	$B$2
14	10	5	1	$E$10

CHOOSE

What does it do?

Selects a specific value from the list of values provided

Formula breakdown:

=CHOOSE(index_num, value1, [value2], ...)

What it means:

=CHOOSE(position to take from the list, first value, [second value and so on], ...)

Example:

=CHOOSE(2, "apple", "orange", "grapes", "lemon") ="orange"

Suppose you have a list, and you want to dynamically retrieve values from your list based on the position, the **CHOOSE formula** in Excel is perfect for this!

STEP 1: We need to **enter the *CHOOSE* function in a blank cell**:

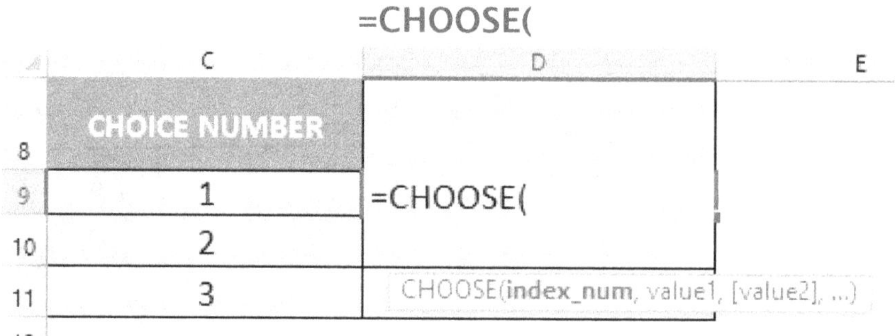

index_num

What is the position to take from the list?

Select the cell containing the choice number. The maximum index you can put in is 254:

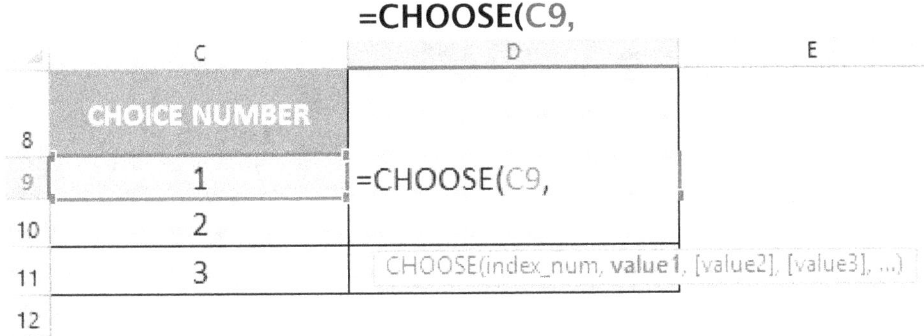

value1, [value2], ...

What are the values in our list?

In our example, let us type in our list that contains names of fruits:

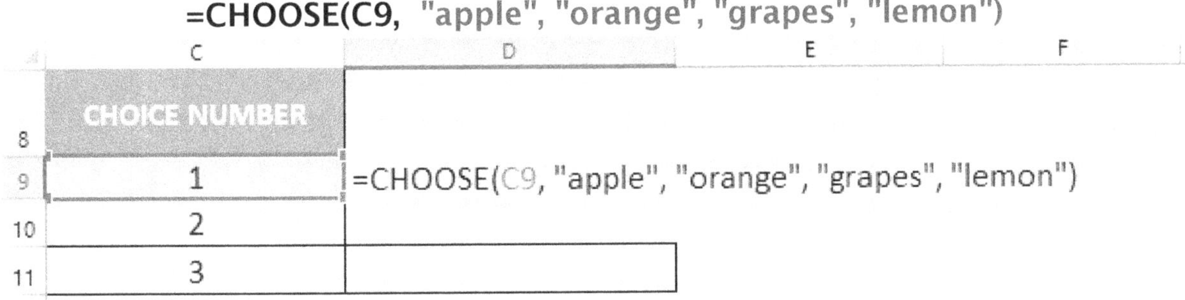

Apply the same formula to the rest of the cells by dragging the lower right corner downwards.

We have now chosen the first, second and third items in our list!

CHOICE NUMBER	RESULT
1	apple
2	orange
3	grapes

HLOOKUP

What does it do?

Searches for a value in the first row of a table array and returns a value in the same column from another row (downwards) in the table array.

Formula breakdown:

=HLOOKUP(lookup_value, table_array, row_index_num, [range_lookup])

What it means:

=HLOOKUP(this value, in this list, and get me value in this row, [Exact Match/FALSE/0])

Example:

=HLOOKUP("Television", A8:D10, 2, FALSE) =$150

Ever had a horizontal table and you want to search for values in the table easily?

I'm sure you do! There is a simple way to do this with Excel's **HLOOKUP function**!

This is very similar to the <u>**VLOOKUP Function**</u>! The only difference is instead of working with vertical tables, you get to do the same thing for horizontal tables!

Let's try it out on this horizontal table!

Stock List	Television	Laptop	Tablet
Price	$ 150.00	$ 185.00	$ 245.00
Cost	$ 85.00	$ 95.00	$ 90.00

Using the **HLOOKUP function** let us get the following values from this table:

- What is the **price** of a **television?**
- What is the **cost** of a **tablet?**

STEP 1: Let us target the first question: ***What is the price of a television?***

We need to **enter the *HLOOKUP* function in a blank cell:**

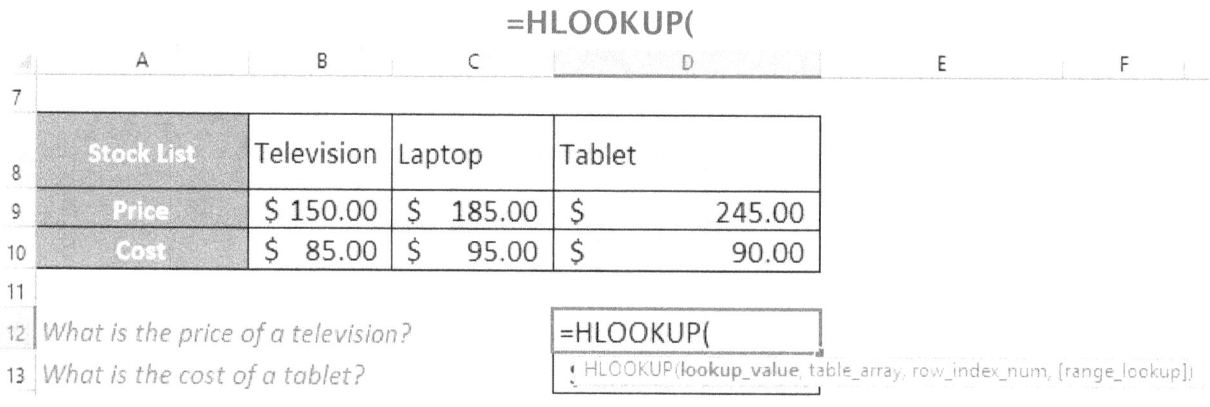

STEP 2: The **HLOOKUP** arguments:

lookup_value

What is the lookup name?

We want to lookup in the "Television" column

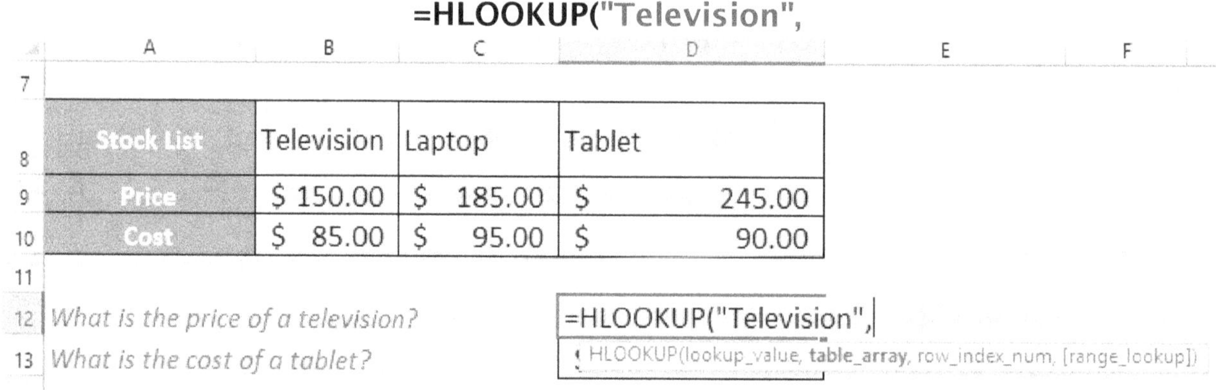

What is our list?

Select the entire table!

=HLOOKUP("Television", A8:D10,

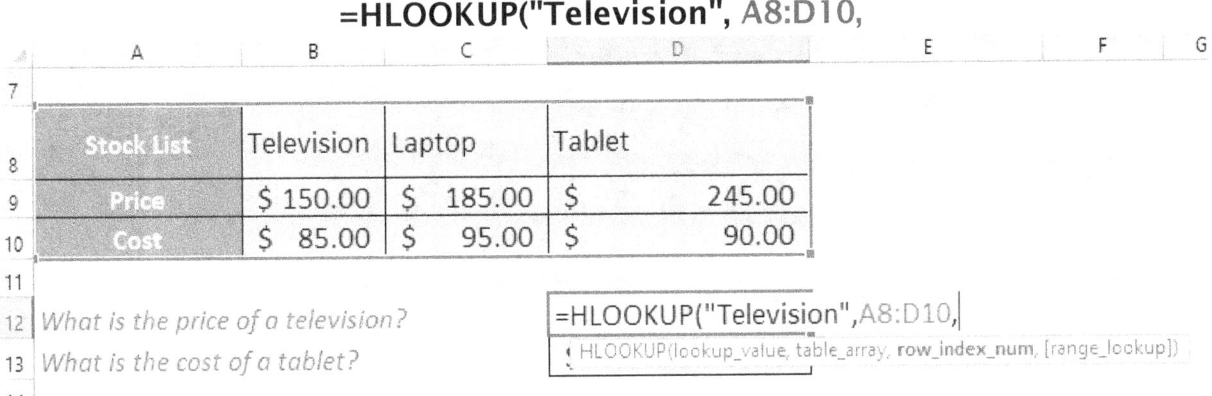

Which row should we get our value from?

We want the price, so it's row #2 in our table!

=HLOOKUP("Television", A8:D10, 2,

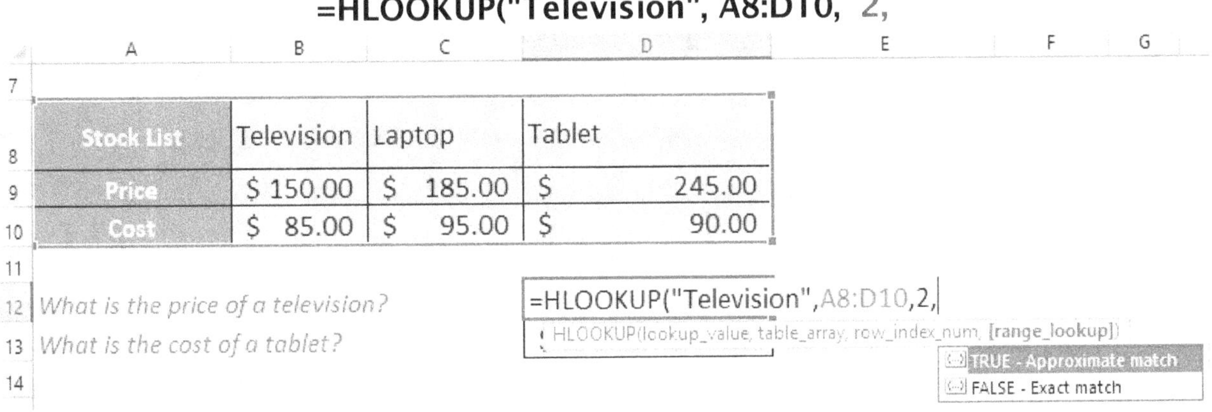

Do we want an appropriate match or exact match?

We want an exact match, so specify FALSE here.

=HLOOKUP("Television", A8:D10, 2, FALSE)

	A	B	C	D	E	F
8	Stock List	Television	Laptop	Tablet		
9	Price	$ 150.00	$ 185.00	$ 245.00		
10	Cost	$ 85.00	$ 95.00	$ 90.00		
11						
12	*What is the price of a television?*		=HLOOKUP("Television", A8:D10, 2, FALSE)		
13	*What is the cost of a tablet?*		HLOOKUP(lookup_value, table_array, row_index_num, [range_lookup])		

You now have your television price!

	A	B	C	D
7				
8	Stock List	Television	Laptop	Tablet
9	Price	$ 150.00	$ 185.00	$ 245.00
10	Cost	$ 85.00	$ 95.00	$ 90.00
11				
12	*What is the price of a television?*			$ 150.00
13	*What is the cost of a tablet?*			

STEP 3: Now let us try doing the same for the cost of the Tablet!

The lookup name is "Tablet", and the cost is on row #3 in our table:

=HLOOKUP("Tablet", A8:D10, 3, FALSE)

	A	B	C	D	E
7					
8	Stock List	Television	Laptop	Tablet	
9	Price	$ 150.00	$ 185.00	$ 245.00	
10	Cost	$ 85.00	$ 95.00	$ 90.00	
11					
12	What is the price of a television?			$ 150.00	
13	What is the cost of a tablet?			=HLOOKUP("Tablet", A8:D10, 3, FALSE)	

You now have your tablet cost!

	A	B	C	D
7				
8	Stock List	Television	Laptop	Tablet
9	Price	$ 150.00	$ 185.00	$ 245.00
10	Cost	$ 85.00	$ 95.00	$ 90.00
11				
12	What is the price of a television?			$ 150.00
13	What is the cost of a tablet?			$ 90.00

HYPERLINK

What does it do?

Creates a shortcut to a webpage, spreadsheet reference, or a file in the hard drive

Formula breakdown:

=HYPERLINK(link_location, [friendly_name])

What it means:

=HYPERLINK(link to a webpage / spreadsheet reference / hard drive file, [display name])

Example:

=HYPERLINK("https://myexcelonline.com", "MyExcelOnline") MyExcelOnline

---

Imagine you can create links in your Excel spreadsheet that either links to: **website urls, other parts in your workbook, or even to a file in your hard drive.**

The **HYPERLINK Formula** in Excel lets you dynamically create these!

STEP 1: We need to **enter the *HYPERLINK* function in a blank cell**:

=HYPERLINK(

	C	D	E	F
8	**LINK LOCATION**	**NAME**		
9	https://myexcelonline.com	MyExcelOnline	=HYPERLINK(	
10	#SHEET1!A1	Jump to Sheet1		
11	C:\Windows\Temp\test.txt	Open Text File	HYPERLINK(link_location, [friendly_name])	
12				

link_location

What is the exact link location?

Select the cell containing the link location:

=HYPERLINK(C9,

	C	D	E	F
8	**LINK LOCATION**	**NAME**		
9	https://myexcelonline.com	MyExcelOnline	=HYPERLINK(C9,	
10	#SHEET1!A1	Jump to Sheet1		
11	C:\Windows\Temp\test.txt	Open Text File	HYPERLINK(link_location, [friendly_name])	

friendly_name

What will be the display name of the link?

Select the cell containing the display name to have a presentable name:

=HYPERLINK(C9, D9)

	C	D	E
8	**LINK LOCATION**	**NAME**	
9	https://myexcelonline.com	MyExcelOnline	=HYPERLINK(C9, D9)
10	#SHEET1!A1	Jump to Sheet1	
11	C:\Windows\Temp\test.txt	Open Text File	
12			

Apply the same formula to the rest by dragging down the lower right corner.

	C	D	E
8	**LINK LOCATION**	**NAME**	**HYPERLINK**
9	https://myexcelonline.com	MyExcelOnline	MyExcelOnline
10	#SHEET1!A1	Jump to Sheet1	
11	C:\Windows\Temp\test.txt	Open Text File	

You now have your **hyperlinks** all ready to go!

	C	D	E
8	**LINK LOCATION**	**NAME**	**HYPERLINK**
9	https://myexcelonline.com	MyExcelOnline	MyExcelOnline
10	#SHEET1!A1	Jump to Sheet1	Jump to Sheet1
11	C:\Windows\Temp\test.txt	Open Text File	Open Text File

INDEX

What does it do?

It returns a cell´s value from within a table/range

Formula breakdown:

=INDEX(array, row_num, [column_num])

What it means:

=INDEX(from this table/range, return me this row number, [and return me this column number])

Example:

=INDEX(C16:E19,2,2) =$652 *i.e. Price of Laptop In Table*

The **INDEX** function in Excel returns a cell´s values from within a table/array.

It works like a map, so you have to select a range (table/array) and tell it to return you the coordinates (Row & Column numbers).

So if you want to return values from a Price List or large data set, then your **INDEX** function is your savior.

We want to get the **price of a laptop in 2014 and 2015** based on price table.

 We need to enter the **INDEX** function in a blank cell:

=INDEX(

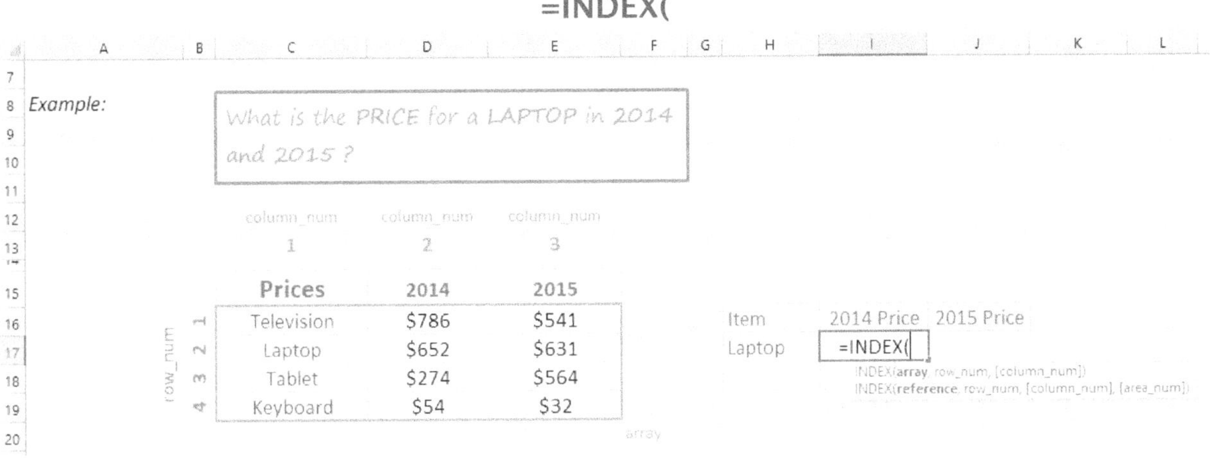

STEP 2: The **INDEX** arguments for the <u>2014 laptop</u> price:

array

What is the table we are searching in?

We need to select the pricing table here.

=INDEX(C16:E19,

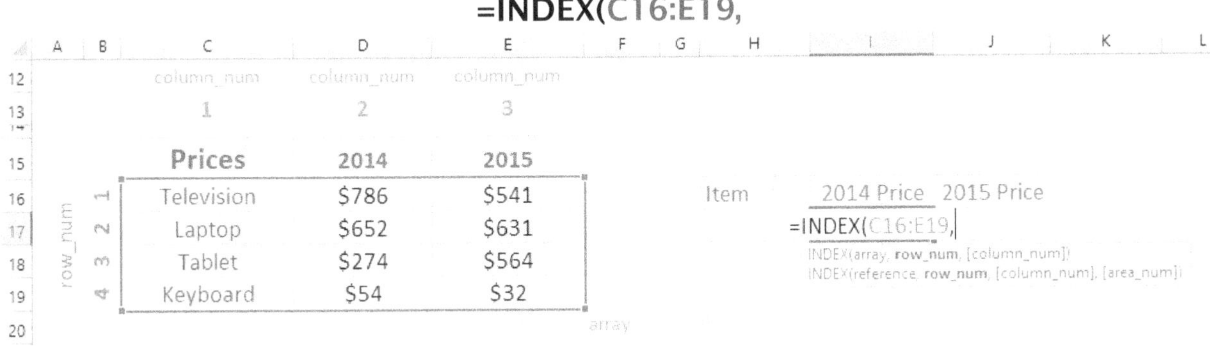

row_num

What row number contains the data?

Since we want the laptop, it's on row #2

=INDEX(C16:E19, 2,

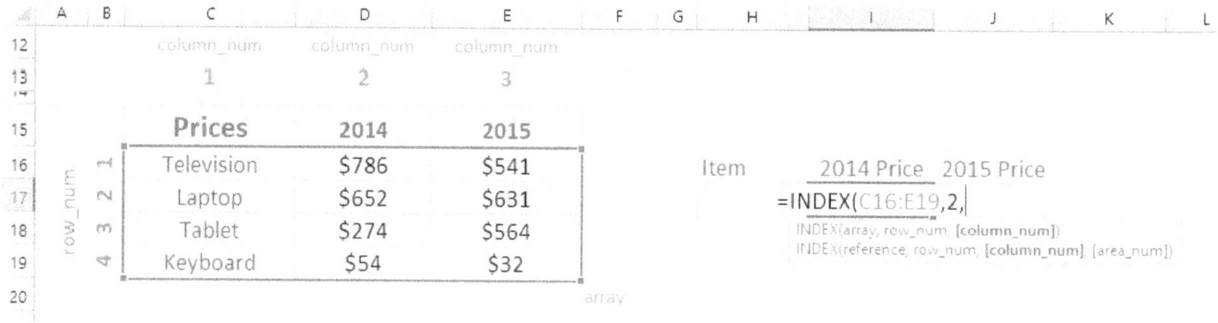

column_num

What column number contains the data?

Since we want the price for the year 2014, it's on column #2

=INDEX(C16:E19, 2, 2)

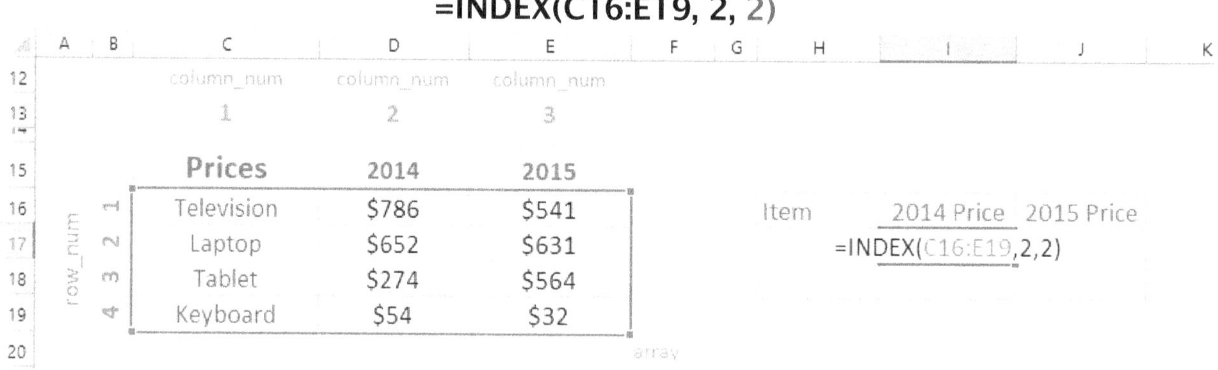

STEP 3: The **INDEX** arguments for the <u>2015 laptop</u> price:

array

What is the table we are searching in?

We need to select the pricing table here.

=INDEX(C16:E19,

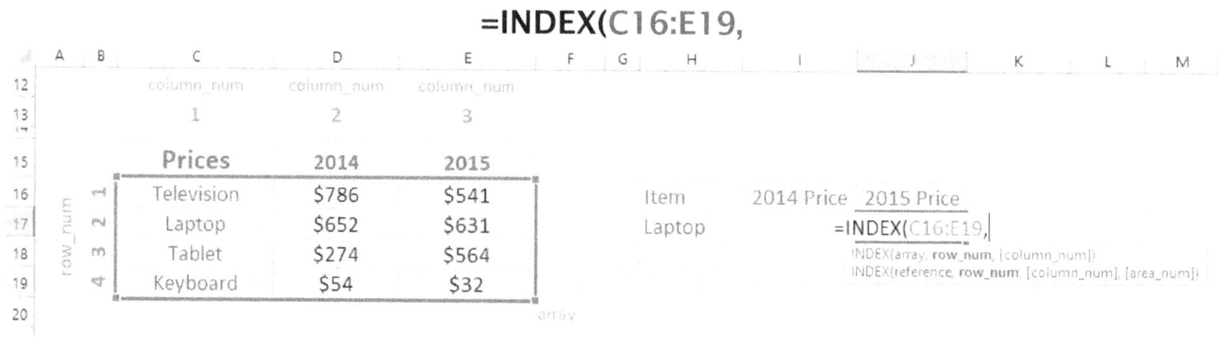

What row number contains the data?

Since we want the laptop, it's on row #2

=INDEX(C16:E19, 2,

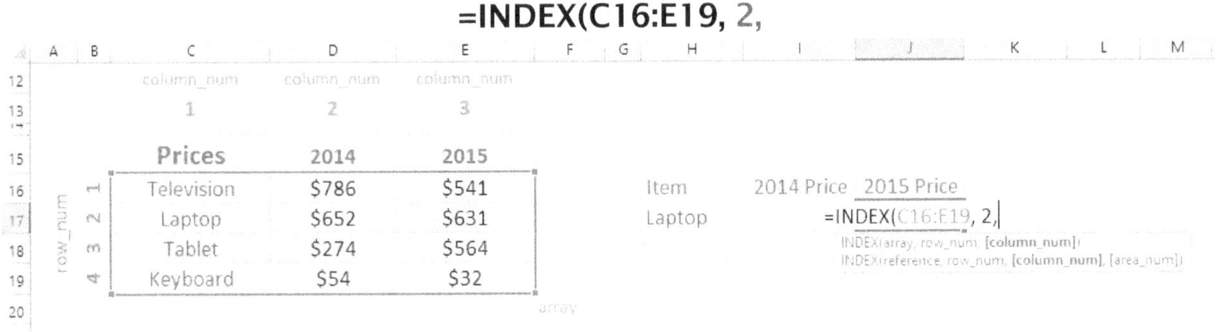

column_num

What column number contains the data?

Since we want the price for the year 2015, it's on column #3

=INDEX(C16:E19, 2, 3)

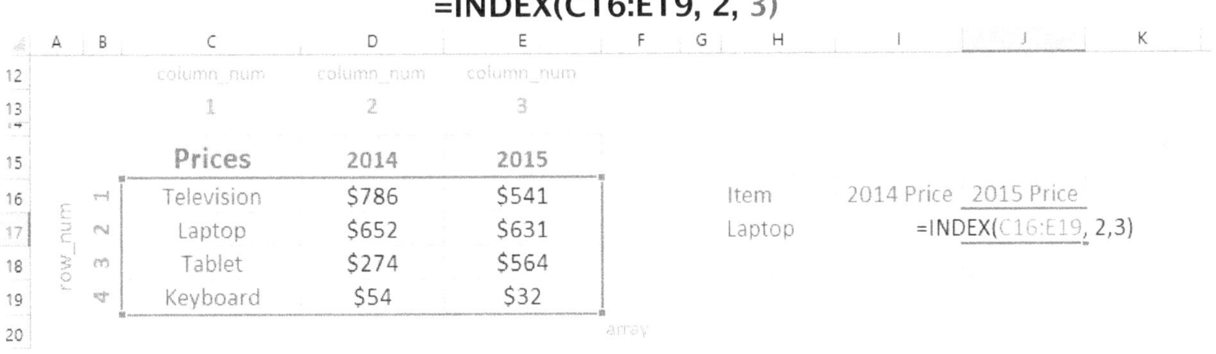

You now have your prices!

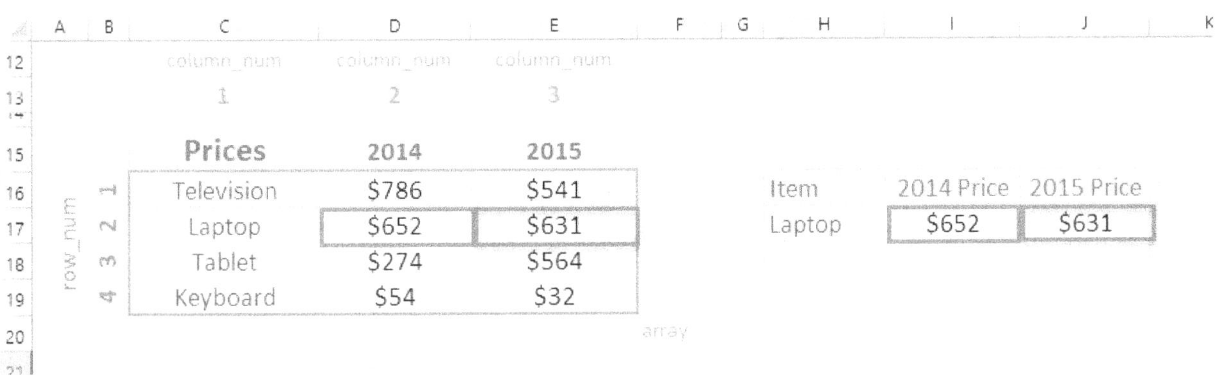

INDEX-MATCH

What does it do?

Searches the row position of a value/text in one column (using the **MATCH** function) and returns the value/text in the same row position from another column to the left or right (using the **INDEX** function)

Formula breakdown:

=INDEX(array, MATCH(lookup_value, lookup_array, [match_type])

What it means:

=INDEX(return the value/text from this range, MATCH(from the row position of this value/text))

Example:

=INDEX(B13:B17,MATCH("Tablet",C13:C17,0)) = TAB698

i.e. Stock Id of a Tablet

The VLOOKUP formula searches for a value in the first column of an array and returns a value to the right of that array.

How about if you wanted to return a value to the left hand side of that array?

Well, this is where the **INDEX-MATCH** formula comes in and gives you a helping hand!

It searches the row position of a value/text in one column (using the **MATCH** function) and returns the value/text in the same row position from another column to the left or right (using the **INDEX** function).

We want to get the **stock id of the tablet**, and we will use a combination of **INDEX** and **MATCH** to get this!

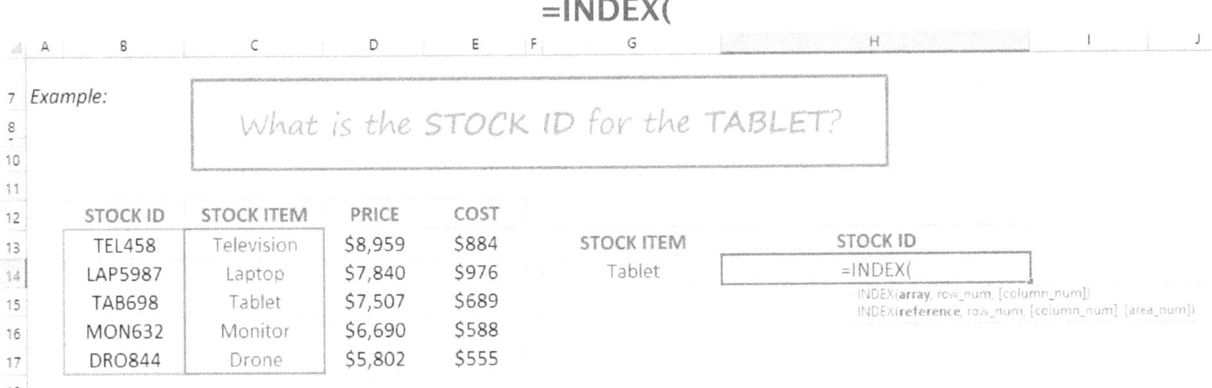

STEP 2: The **INDEX** arguments:

array

Where is the list that contains the stock id that we want to return?

=INDEX(B13:B17,

row_num

What row number contains the data?

Let us use the Match function to get the row number of the stock item.

=INDEX(B13:B17, MATCH(

STEP 3: The **MATCH** arguments:

lookup_value

What is the value that we want to match?

We want to match the Tablet.

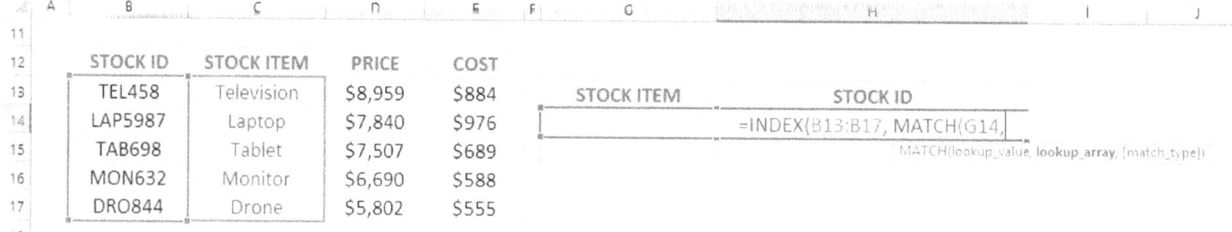

lookup_array

Where is the list that contains the stock items?

match_type

What kind of matching do you want?

Let's put in 0 to get the exact match

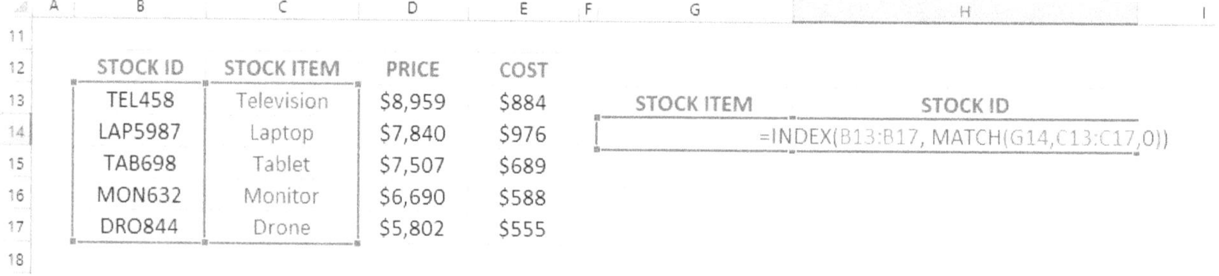

With this, the **MATCH** function will get the row number containing the Tablet, which is row #3. Then with Row #3, we will get the stock id in that same row using the **INDEX** function.

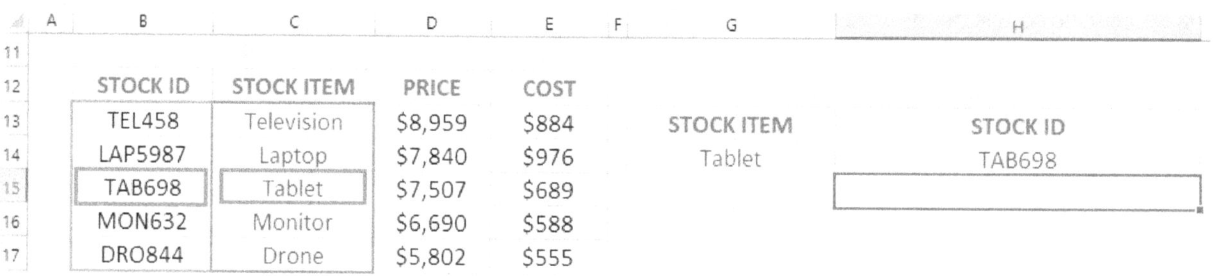

INDIRECT

What does it do?

Returns a reference to a range. The referenced range can be a cell, a range of cells, or a named range.

Formula breakdown:

=INDIRECT(ref_text, [a1])

What it means:

=INDIRECT(Return the contents in this cell, Omit if the reference is an *A1* style or enter FALSE if it is a *R1C1* style)

Example:

=INDIRECT("D10") =Contents of Cell D10

The INDIRECT function mystifies lots of Excel users and one that does not get that much fan fare, but I am about to change that for you!

To be totally honest, I wasn't a big user of the INDIRECT function, but after seeing the various ways that it can be applied in to an Excel workbook, Financial Model or Excel Dashboard, I was hooked!

REFERENCED RANGE IS A CELL

=INDIRECT(G9)

When the referenced range is a cell, the INDIRECT function will go and return the content of the referenced cell.

Say we enter in cell **G9** the following A1 style: *D10*

In another cell we enter **=INDIRECT(G9)**

This will indirectly return the value that resides in cell D10, which is the number **32** in our example below:

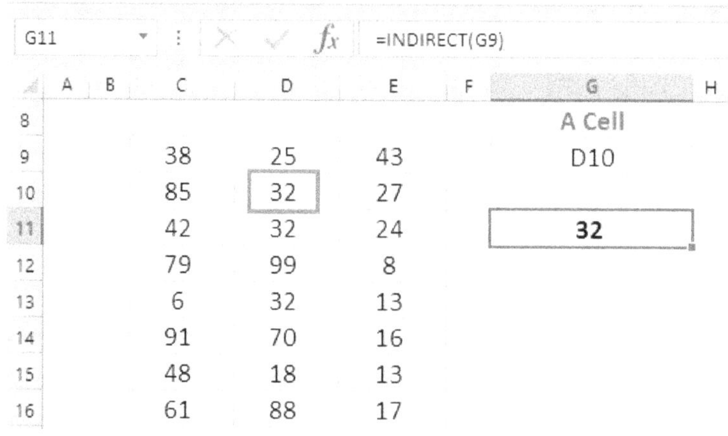

REFERENCE A RANGE OF CELLS

=SUM(INDIRECT(C9:E9))

When the referenced range is a range of cells, the INDIRECT function will go and return the content of the referenced cells.

We can then enter a SUM function which will total the referenced cells.

Say we enter in cell **I9** the following A1 style: *C9:E9*

In another cell we enter **=INDIRECT(I9)**

This will indirectly Sum the values that reside in cells C9:E9, which is **106** in the example below:

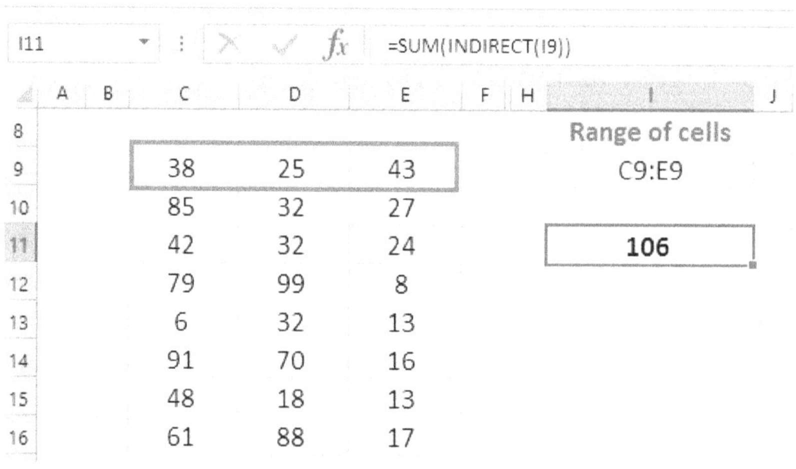

REFERENCE IS A NAMED RANGE

=SUM(INDIRECT(NamedRange))

When the referenced range is Named Range, the INDIRECT function will go and return the content of the Named Range.

We can then enter a SUM function which will total the Named Range.

We need to create a **Named Range** by selecting the data range and entering a name (with no spaces) in the Name Box: *TABLE*

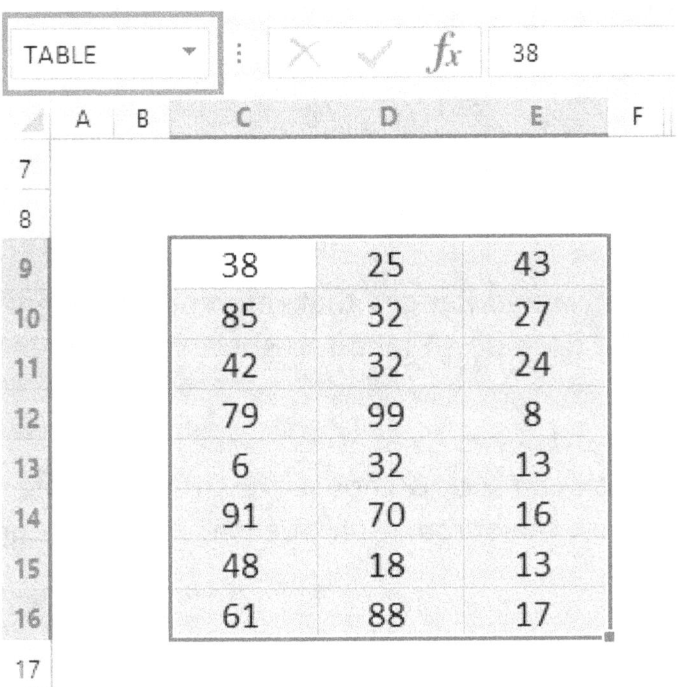

We then enter in cell **K9** the following Named Range: *TABLE*

In another cell we enter **=SUM(INDIRECT(K9))**

This will indirectly Sum the values that reside in the Named Range TABLE, which is **1,007** in our example below:

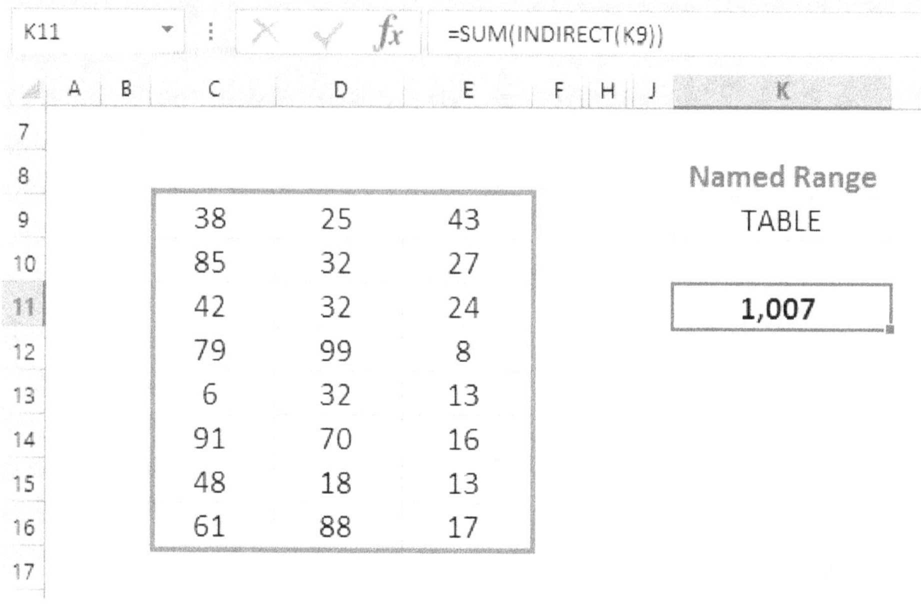

Imagine having several Named Ranges that reference different data sets within a Workbook & adding a drop down menu to show the different Named Ranges.

Using this technique you can pick & choose the different data sets and with the INDIRECT function return the summation of each, thus creating an interactive Dashboard!

LOOKUP

What does it do?

Looks up a value from a table array or one-row / one-column range

Formula breakdown:

=LOOKUP(lookup_value, lookup_vector, [result_vector])

What it means:

=LOOKUP(value to be approximately matched, range of values to be matched against, [the matching value to be displayed])

Example:

=LOOKUP(10000, C9:C14, D9:D14) = 18%

i.e. Approximate match in tax rate

Have you ever tried getting approximate matches in Excel? **Approximate matches** are used when you have an ascending table like *Commission Bonus Rates* or *Income Tax Rates*.

If you have tried out <u>Vlookup Approximate Match in Excel</u>, there is another cool way to do this! You can use the **LOOKUP Formula** to accomplish this as well.

IMPORTANT: *For the LOOKUP Approximate Match to work in Excel, the lookup_vector has to be sorted in ascending order!*

So the way that this formula works is that it looks at the first value in the *lookup_vector* that is greater than the *lookup_value* and then goes back one value. If a *result_vector* is provided, then the **LOOKUP Formula** will get the result from there, otherwise it simply gets it from the *lookup_vector*.

 We need to **enter the *LOOKUP* function in a blank cell**:

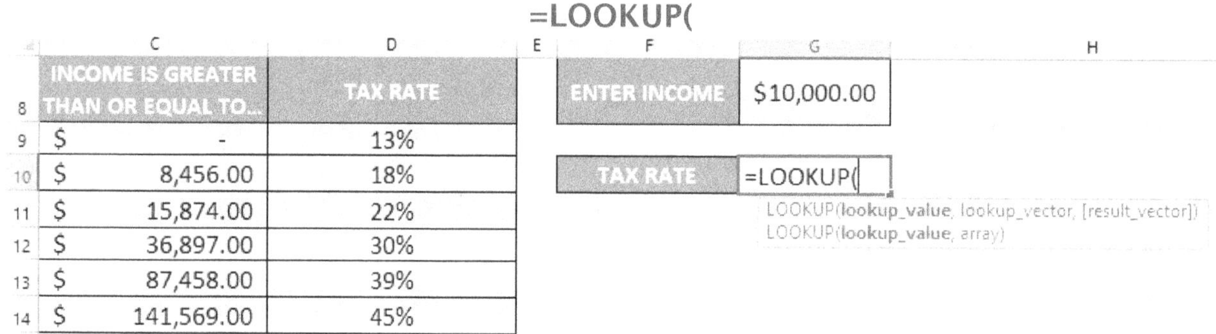

 The **LOOKUP** arguments:

lookup_value

What is the value to be approximately matched?

Select the cell containing the value. In our case, it is the $10,000 income:

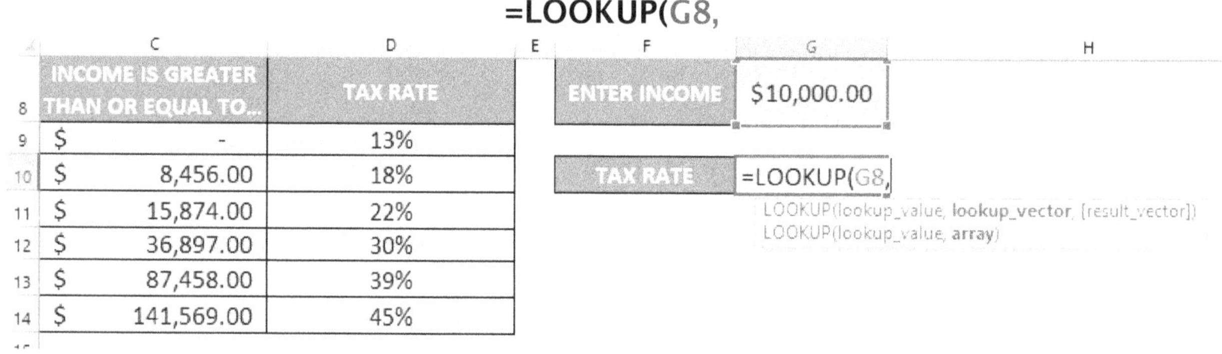

lookup_vector

Where is the range of values to be matched against?

Now we need to select the range that contains the income values. It should be sorted in ascending order for the LOOKUP Formula to work.

=LOOKUP(G8, C9:C14,

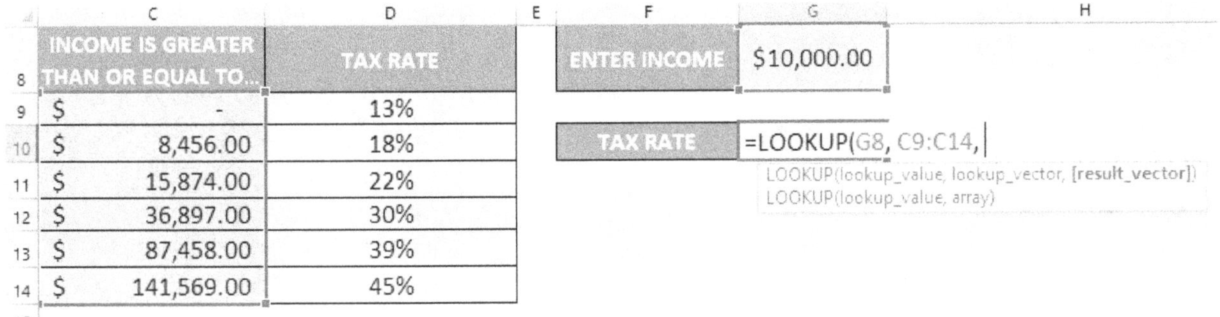

result_vector

Where is the range of values to contains the value to be displayed as the final result?

Now we need to select the range that contains the tax rates. This is what we want to display as our final result of the lookup.

=LOOKUP(G8, C9:C14, D9:D14)

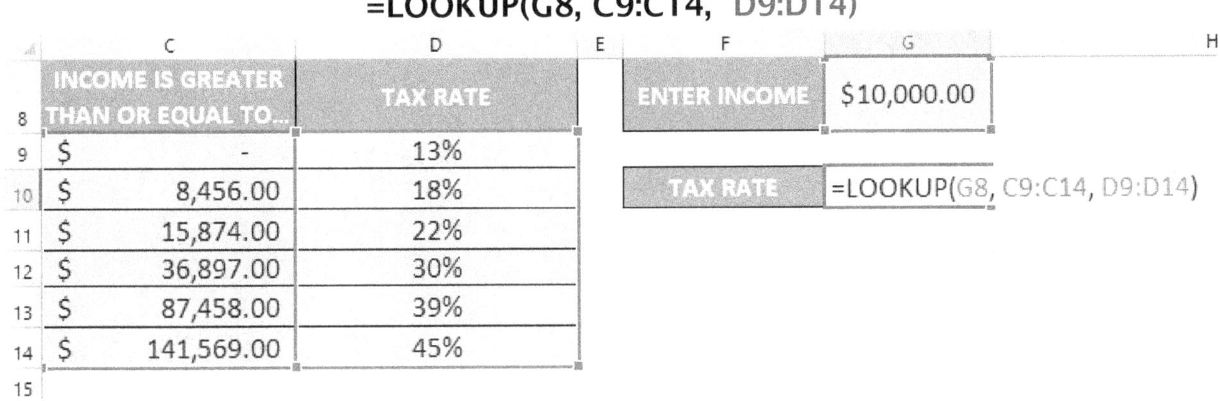

It was able to find out that the tax rate is 18%!

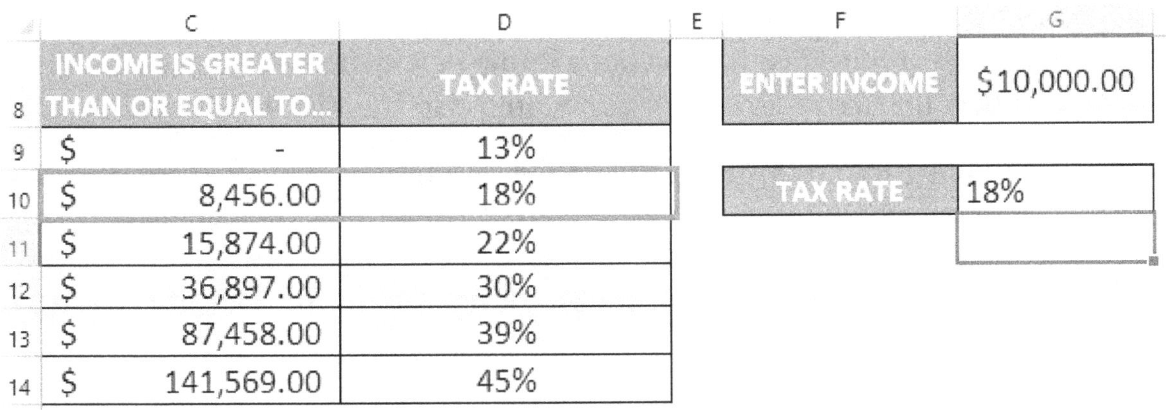

MATCH

What does it do?

It returns the position of a value/text

Formula breakdown:

=MATCH(lookup_value, lookup_array, [match_type])

What it means:

=MATCH(lookup this value, from this list or range of cells, return me the Exact Match)

Example:

=MATCH("Tablet",C12:C16,0) = 3

i.e. Tablet is in the 3rd position in the range

The **MATCH** function in Excel returns the position of a value/text within a list or a range of cells.

Say that you have a Price List and want to know in which position a certain item is located within that Price List, then you would use the **MATCH** function.

NB: The *lookup_value* argument can be a value (number, text, or logical value) or a cell reference to a number, text, or logical value.

We want to get the **position within the Stock list** where the **Tablet** is located.

STEP 1: Enter the following:

We need to enter the **MATCH** function in a blank cell:

=MATCH(

STEP 2: The **MATCH** arguments:

lookup_value

What is the value that we want to match?

We want to match the "Tablet"

=MATCH(G13,

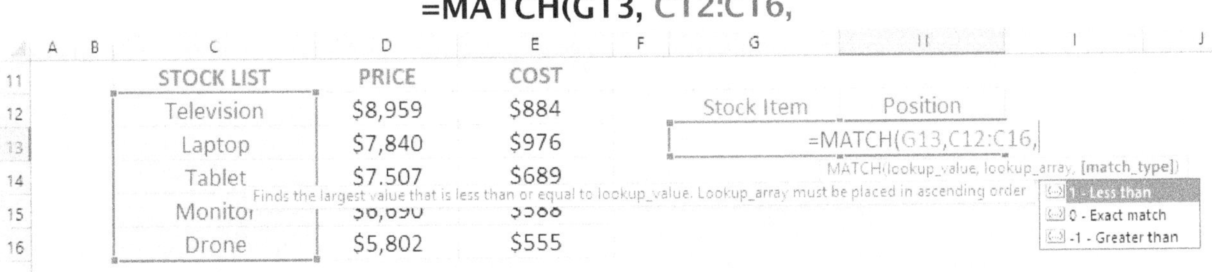

lookup_array

Where is the list that contains the stock items?

=MATCH(G13, C12:C16,

What kind of matching do you want?

Let's put in 0 to get the exact match

=MATCH(G13, C12:C16, 0)

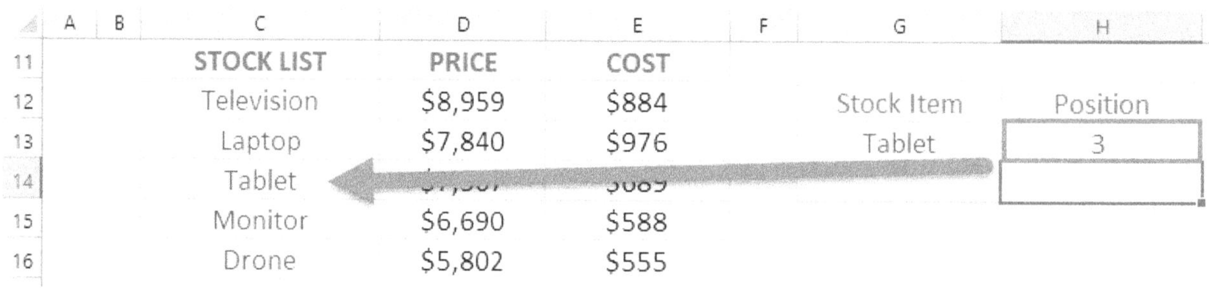

And with that, you will get that tablet is in Row #3!

VLOOKUP

What does it do?

Searches for a value in the first column of a table array and returns a value in the same row from another column (to the right) in the table array.

Formula breakdown:

=VLOOKUP(lookup_value, table_array, col_index_num, [range_lookup])

What it means:

=VLOOKUP(this value, in this list, and get me value in this column, Exact Match/FALSE/0])

Example:

=VLOOKUP("Laptop",B14:D17,2,FALSE) = $185

i.e. The price of the Laptop in the table

Excel's **VLOOKUP** function is arguably the most used function in Excel but can also be the most tricky one to understand. I will show you a **VLOOKUP** example and in a few steps you will be able to extract values from a table and use them to do your custom reports and analysis.

You will be using VLOOKUP with confidence after this!

STEP 1: We need to enter the **VLOOKUP** function in a blank cell:

=VLOOKUP(

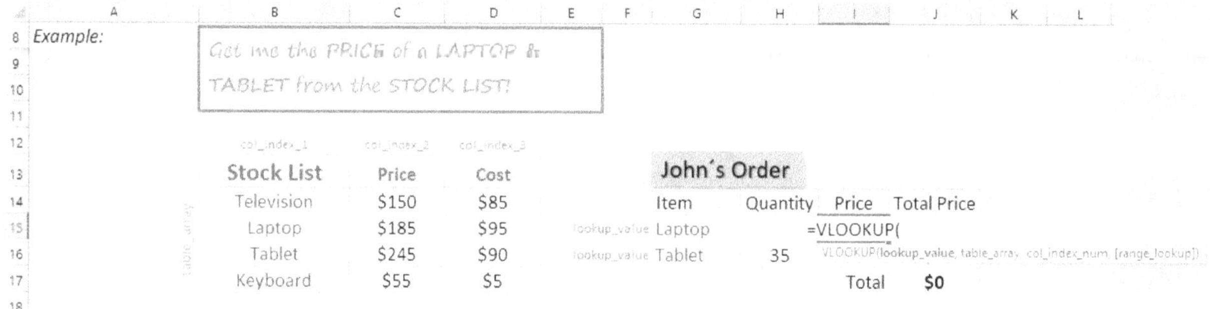

STEP 2: The **VLOOKUP** arguments:

lookup_value

What is the value that you want to look for?

In our first example, it will be "Laptop", so select the Item name

=VLOOKUP(G15,

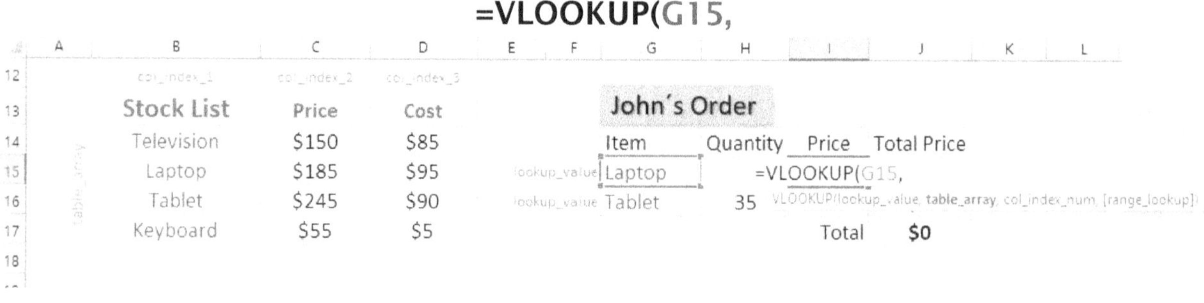

table_array

What is the table or range of cells that contains all your data?

Make sure to select the stock list table so that our VLOOKUP formula will search here

=VLOOKUP(G15, B14:D17,

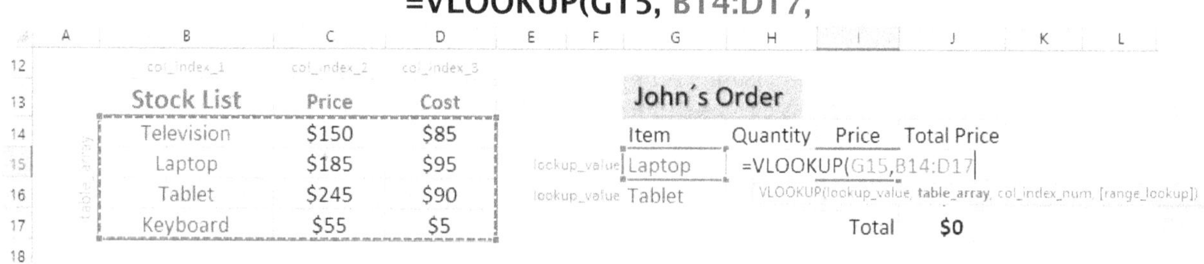

Ensure that you press **F4** so that you can lock the table range.

=VLOOKUP(G15, $B$14:$D$17,

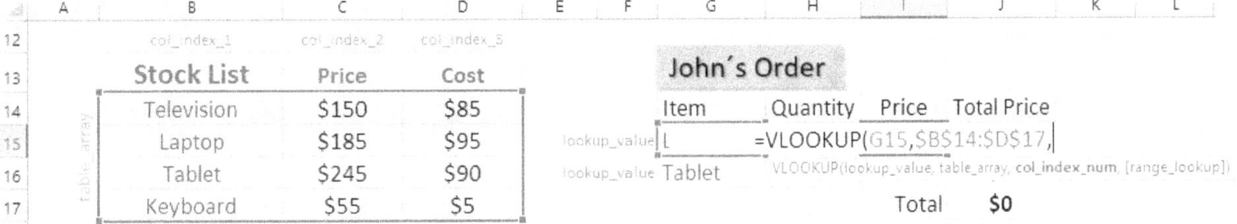

col_index_num

What is the column that you want to retrieve the value from?

*Since we want to get the price, our price is on the **2nd column** of our source data*

=VLOOKUP(G15, $B$14:$D$17, 2,

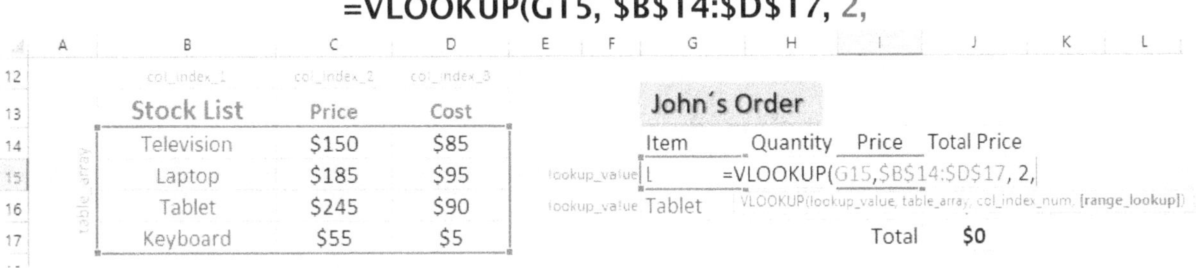

range_lookup

What kind of matching do you need?

*We want an exact match of the Laptop text so make sure **FALSE** is selected (or you can enter 0 instead of FALSE):*

=VLOOKUP(G15, $B$14:$D$17, 2, FALSE)

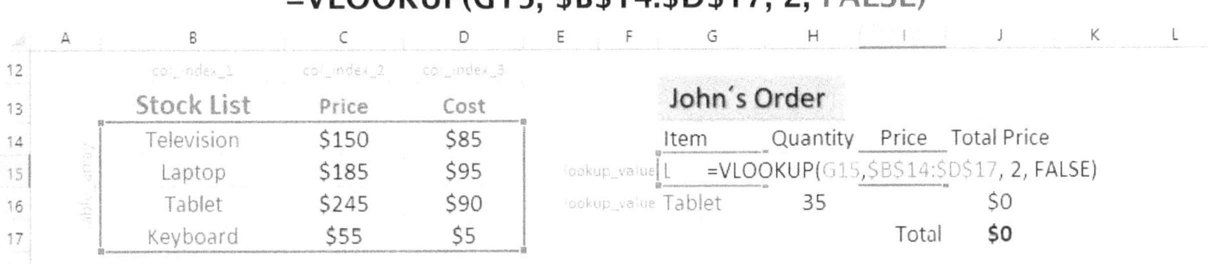

Apply the same formula to the rest of the cells by dragging the lower right corner downwards. And you now have all of the results!

LOGICAL FUNCTIONS

AND

What does it do?

Checks if all of the conditions are satisfied or not

Formula breakdown:

=AND(logical1, [logical2], ...)

What it means:

=AND(first condition, [additional conditions], ...)

Example:

=AND(MONTH("1/01/18")=1, 1500 >1000) =TRUE

Have a couple of conditions that you need to check for and ensure they are met? The **AND Formula** enforces this and will return **TRUE** if all of your required conditions are met!

Let us give this a try in our examples below. We want to **check if the date is in the month of January and the sales amount is greater than $1000.**

I explain how you can do this below:

STEP 1: We need to **enter the *AND* function in a blank cell**:

=AND(

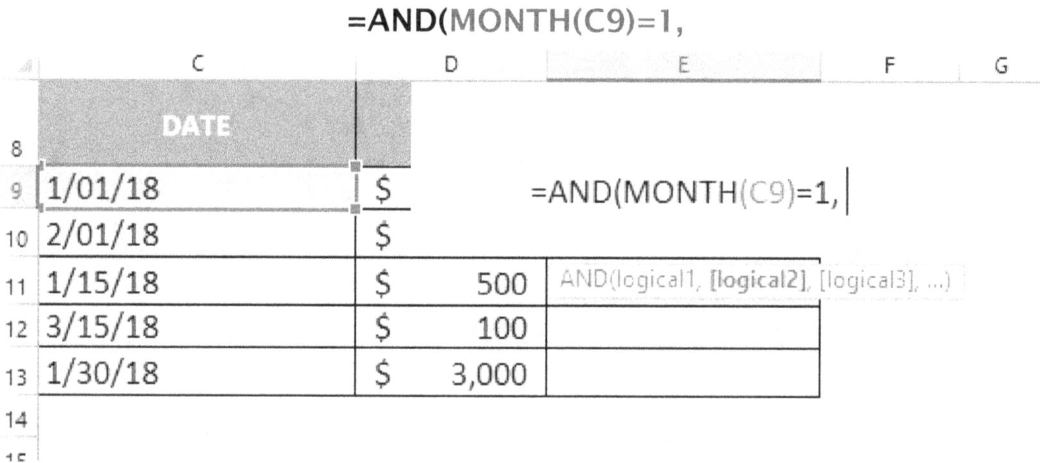

STEP 2: The **AND** arguments:

logical1

What is the first condition?

Let us create the condition to get the month of the date and check if it is January i.e. 1

$$=\textbf{AND}(MONTH(C9)=1,$$

[logical2]

What is the second condition?

Let us create the condition to check if sales is greater than 1000:

$$=\textbf{AND}(MONTH(C9)=1, D9 > 1000)$$

	C	D	E	F
	DATE			
8				
9	1/01/18	$	=AND(MONTH(C9)=1, D9 >1000)	
10	2/01/18	$		
11	1/15/18	$	500	
12	3/15/18	$	100	
13	1/30/18	$	3,000	

Apply the same formula to the rest of the cells by dragging the lower right corner downwards.

	C	D	E
	DATE	**SALES**	**JANUARY AND SALES > 1000?**
8			
9	1/01/18	$ 1,500	TRUE
10	2/01/18	$ 2,000	
11	1/15/18	$ 500	
12	3/15/18	$ 100	
13	1/30/18	$ 3,000	
14			

You now have your results!

	C	D	E
	DATE	**SALES**	**JANUARY AND SALES > 1000?**
8			
9	1/01/18	$ 1,500	TRUE
10	2/01/18	$ 2,000	FALSE
11	1/15/18	$ 500	FALSE
12	3/15/18	$ 100	FALSE
13	1/30/18	$ 3,000	TRUE
14			

IF

What does it do?

It returns a value that you set if a condition is met, and a value if it is not met

Formula breakdown:

=IF(Logical Test,Value if True,Value if False)

What it means:

=IF(The condition to be checked, Value to be shown if the condition is met, Value to be shown if condition is not met)

Example:

=IF(D15>3000,"Bonus","No Bonus") = No Bonus

The **IF function** is probably one of the most used Excel functions because it is easy to understand and very flexible when you apply it to real life situations.

Here I will show you a couple of ways that you can use the **IF function** to get you up and going.

We want to show a **Bonus** value if **sales are bigger than $3000**, and **No Bonus** is shown if this condition is not met. Afterwards let's try computing the **10% bonus**!

STEP 1: We need to enter the **IF function** in a blank cell:

=IF(

Example:

	Sales Rep	Region	Sales	Bonus?	Bonus $
	John	North	$1,092	=IF(	
	Paul	South	$9,951		
	Ringo	East	$2,006		
	George	West	$8,738		
	Ana	North	$3,185		
	Marie	South	$1,661		
	Wayland	East	$5,594		
	Helen	West	$457		
	Paula	North	$4,935		

STEP 2: The **IF** arguments:

logical_test

What is your condition?

Sales Rep has sold more than 3000 dollars.

=IF(D15>3000,

	Sales Rep	Region	Sales	Bonus?	Bonus $
14					
15	John	North	=IF(D15>3000,		
16	Paul	South	$9,951		
17	Ringo	East	$2,006		
18	George	West	$8,738		
19	Ana	North	$3,185		
20	Marie	South	$1,661		
21	Wayland	East	$5,594		
22	Helen	West	$457		
23	Paula	North	$4,935		

What value should be displayed if the condition is true?

*We want "**Bonus**" to be displayed*

=IF(D15>3000, "Bonus",

	B	C	D	E	F
14	**Sales Rep**	Region	Sales	Bonus?	Bonus $
15	John	North	=IF(D15>3000, "Bonus",		
16	Paul	South	$9,951		
17	Ringo	East	$2,006		
18	George	West	$8,738		
19	Ana	North	$3,185		
20	Marie	South	$1,661		
21	Wayland	East	$5,594		
22	Helen	West	$457		
23	Paula	North	$4,935		

What value should be displayed if the condition is false?

*We want "**No Bonus**" to be displayed*

=IF(D15>3000, "Bonus", "No Bonus")

	B	C	D	E	F
14	**Sales Rep**	Region	Sales	Bonus?	Bonus $
15	John		=IF(D15>3000, "Bonus", "No Bonus")		
16	Paul	South	IF(logical_test, [value_if_true], [value_if_false])		
17	Ringo	East	$2,006		
18	George	West	$8,738		
19	Ana	North	$3,185		
20	Marie	South	$1,661		
21	Wayland	East	$5,594		
22	Helen	West	$457		
23	Paula	North	$4,935		

Apply the same formula to the rest of the cells by dragging the lower right corner downwards.

	Sales Rep	Region	Sales	Bonus?	Bonus $
14					
15	John	North	$1,092	No Bonus	
16	Paul	South	$9,951	Bonus	
17	Ringo	East	$2,006	No Bonus	
18	George	West	$8,738	Bonus	
19	Ana	North	$3,185	Bonus	
20	Marie	South	$1,661	No Bonus	
21	Wayland	East	$5,594	Bonus	
22	Helen	West	$457	No Bonus	
23	Paula	North	$4,935	Bonus	
24					

STEP 3: Let us now aim to give the **10% Bonus!**

The **IF** arguments:

logical_test

What is your condition?

Sales Rep has sold more than 3000 dollars.

=IF(D15>3000,

	Sales Rep	Region	Sales	Bonus?	Bonus $	
14						
15	John	North	$1,092		=IF(D15>3000,	
16	Paul	South	$9,951	Bonus		
17	Ringo	East	$2,006	No Bonus		
18	George	West	$8,738	Bonus		
19	Ana	North	$3,185	Bonus		
20	Marie	South	$1,661	No Bonus		
21	Wayland	East	$5,594	Bonus		
22	Helen	West	$457	No Bonus		
23	Paula	North	$4,935	Bonus		

What value should be displayed if the condition is true?

We want give a 10% bonus based on sales

=IF(D15>3000, D15*10%,

	B	C	D	E	F	G
14	**Sales Rep**	Region	Sales	Bonus?	Bonus $	
15	John	North	$1,092	=IF(D15>3000, D15*10%,		
16	Paul	South	$9,951	Bonus		
17	Ringo	East	$2,006	No Bonus		
18	George	West	$8,738	Bonus		
19	Ana	North	$3,185	Bonus		
20	Marie	South	$1,661	No Bonus		
21	Wayland	East	$5,594	Bonus		
22	Helen	West	$457	No Bonus		
23	Paula	North	$4,935	Bonus		

What value should be displayed if the condition is false?

Then no bonus amount should be given, type in 0

=IF(D15>3000, D15*10%, 0)

	B	C	D	E	F	G
14	**Sales Rep**	Region	Sales	Bonus?	Bonus $	
15	John	North	$1,092	=IF(D15>3000, D15*10%, 0)		
16	Paul	South	$9,951	Bonus		
17	Ringo	East	$2,006	No Bonus		
18	George	West	$8,738	Bonus		
19	Ana	North	$3,185	Bonus		
20	Marie	South	$1,661	No Bonus		
21	Wayland	East	$5,594	Bonus		
22	Helen	West	$457	No Bonus		
23	Paula	North	$4,935	Bonus		

Apply the same formula to the rest of the cells by dragging the lower right corner downwards.

	Sales Rep	Region	Sales	Bonus?	Bonus $
14	**Sales Rep**	**Region**	**Sales**	**Bonus?**	**Bonus $**
15	John	North	$1,092	No Bonus	$0
16	Paul	South	$9,951	Bonus	$995
17	Ringo	East	$2,006	No Bonus	$0
18	George	West	$8,738	Bonus	$874
19	Ana	North	$3,185	Bonus	$319
20	Marie	South	$1,661	No Bonus	$0
21	Wayland	East	$5,594	Bonus	$559
22	Helen	West	$457	No Bonus	$0
23	Paula	North	$4,935	Bonus	$494
24					

You now have all of results!

IFERROR

What does it do?

It returns a value that you set if a formula has an error

Formula breakdown:

=IFERROR(Value,Value if Error)

What it means:

=IFERROR(The Formula,What do you want to show if The Formula has an error?)

Example:

=IFERROR(0/0,0) =0

If you have a calculation that results in an error like, #N/A, #VALUE!, #REF!, #DIV/0!, #NUM!, #NAME?, then you can clean it up by using the **IFERROR** function which allows you to replace the error it with a 0, a blank cell "" or whatever value you like.

We want to get the **average sale of each record**. However we need to **handle division by zero errors gracefully**.

STEP 1: We need to enter the **IFERROR** function in a blank cell:

=IFERROR(

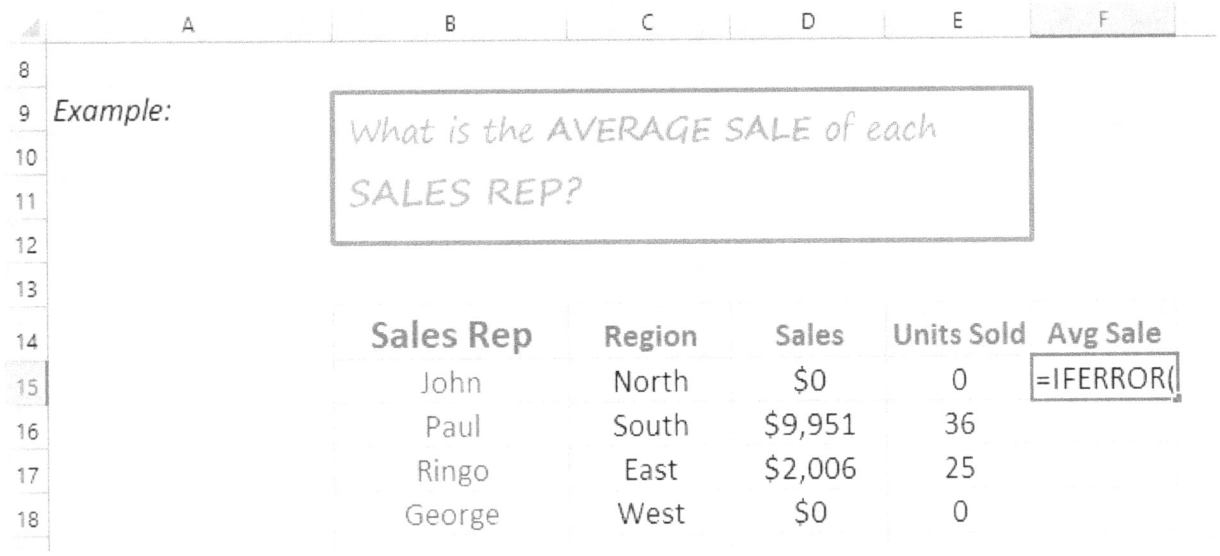

STEP 2: The **IFERROR** arguments:

value

What is the formula?

We need to enter the formula first to calculate the average sale.

=IFERROR(D15/E15,

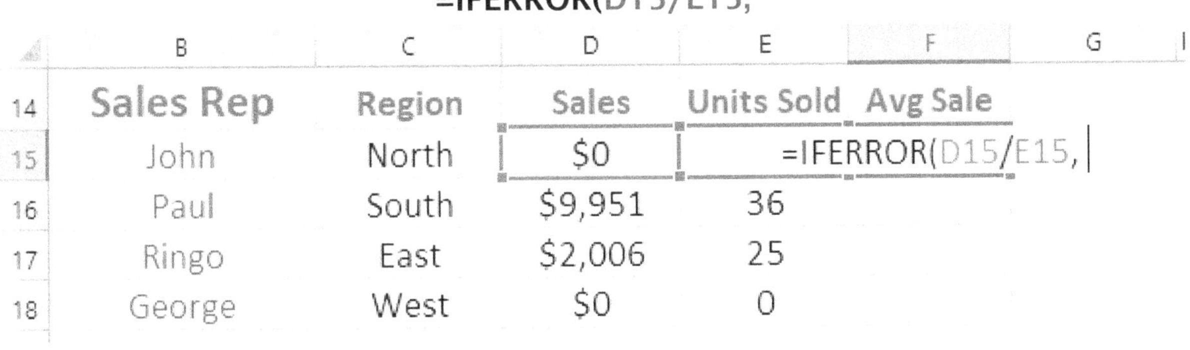

What value should be displayed if there is an error in the formula?

We want "0" to be displayed if there is an error

=IFERROR(D15/E15, 0)

	B	C	D	E	F	G	
14	Sales Rep	Region	Sales	Units Sold	Avg Sale		
15	John	North	$0	=IFERROR(D15/E15, 0)			
16	Paul	South	$9,951	36			
17	Ringo	East	$2,006	25			
18	George	West	$0	0			

Apply the same formula to the rest of the cells by dragging the lower right corner downwards.

	B	C	D	E	F
14	Sales Rep	Region	Sales	Units Sold	Avg Sale
15	John	North	$0	0	$0
16	Paul	South	$9,951	36	$276
17	Ringo	East	$2,006	25	$80
18	George	West	$0	0	$0
19					

You now have all of results!

OR

What does it do?

Checks if any one of the conditions is satisfied or not

Formula breakdown:

=OR(logical1, [logical2], ...)

What it means:

=OR(first condition, [additional conditions], ...)

Example:

=OR(MONTH(C9)=1,1500>1000) =TRUE

Have a couple of conditions that you need to check for and ensure **at least one is met**? The **OR Formula** enforces this and will return TRUE if any one of your required conditions is met!

Let us give this a try in our examples below. We want to **check if the date is in the month of January OR the sales amount is greater than $1000.**

STEP 1: We need to **enter the *OR* function in a blank cell:**

=OR(

	C	D	E	F
	DATE	**SALES**		
8				
9	1/01/18	$ 1,500	=OR(	
10	2/01/18	$ 2,000		
11	1/15/18	$ 500	OR(logical1, [logical2], ...)	
12	3/15/18	$ 100		
13	1/30/18	$ 3,000		

STEP 2: The **OR** arguments:

logical1

What is the first condition?

Let us create the condition to get the month of the date and check if it is January:

=OR(MONTH(C9)=1,

	C		D	E	F	G
8	DATE					
9	1/01/18	$		=OR(MONTH(C9)=1,		
10	2/01/18	$				
11	1/15/18	$	500	OR(logical1, [logical2], [logical3], ...)		
12	3/15/18	$	100			
13	1/30/18	$	3,000			
14						

[logical2]

What is the second condition?

Let us create the condition to check if sales is greater than 1000:

=OR(MONTH(C9)=1, D9 > 1000**)**

	C		D	E	F
8	DATE				
9	1/01/18	$		=OR(MONTH(C9)=1,D9>1000)	
10	2/01/18	$			
11	1/15/18	$	500		
12	3/15/18	$	100		
13	1/30/18	$	3,000		

Apply the same formula to the rest of the cells by dragging the lower right corner downwards.

	DATE	SALES	JANUARY OR SALES > 1000?
9	1/01/18	$ 1,500	TRUE
10	2/01/18	$ 2,000	
11	1/15/18	$ 500	
12	3/15/18	$ 100	
13	1/30/18	$ 3,000	

You now have your results!

	DATE	SALES	JANUARY OR SALES > 1000?
9	1/01/18	$ 1,500	TRUE
10	2/01/18	$ 2,000	TRUE
11	1/15/18	$ 500	TRUE
12	3/15/18	$ 100	FALSE
13	1/30/18	$ 3,000	TRUE

MATH FUNCTIONS

COUNT

What does it do?

Counts the number of cells that contain numbers

Formula breakdown:

=COUNT(value1, [value2]...)

What it means:

=COUNT(range of cells to check, [additional cells to include in the check]...)

Example:

=COUNT(C9:C12) = 2

i.e. There are 2 cells with numbers in them

Ever had a column of data and wanted to check if all of the values contain valid numbers?

It would be cumbersome to count and check them one by one, especially if you had hundreds of entries!

Imagine we have the following data, we see an error, a text and a couple of numbers:

VALUES
#DIV/0!
3
abc
4

Thankfully there is an easy way to count how many of these cells contain valid numbers using the Excel's **COUNT formula.**

 We need to **enter the *COUNT* function in a blank cell**:

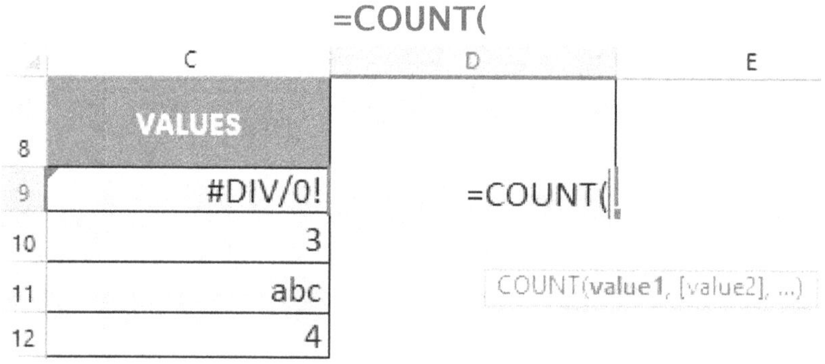

 The **COUNT** arguments:

value

What is the value / range of values that you want to check?

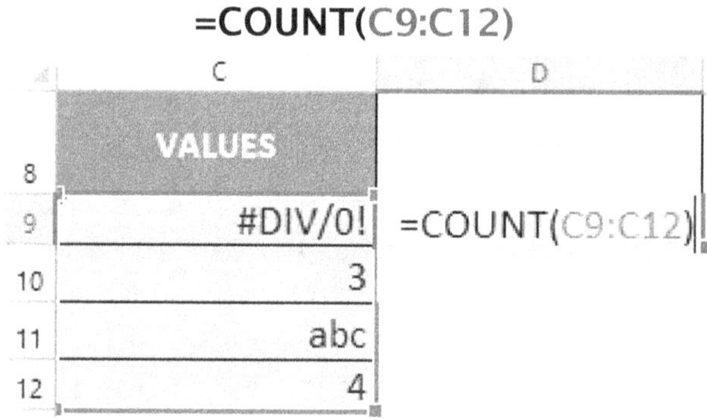

You now have your count of valid numbers!

{ 98 }

COUNTA

What does it do?

Counts the number of cells that are non-blank/non-empty (including empty text "")

Formula breakdown:

=COUNTA(value1, [value2], ...)

What it means:

=COUNTA(value or range of cells to check, [value or range of cells to check], ...)

Example:

=COUNTA(B9:C12) = 6

i.e. There are 6 non-blank cells

Do you have a scenario where you want to count the number of cells that **are non-blank or not empty?**

I'm sure you do! There is a simple way to count this with Excel's **COUNTA formula!**

This formula counts everything: numbers, text, non-empty text "", you name it!

STEP 1: We need to **enter the *COUNTA* function in a blank cell.** Notice there are 6 non-blank cells in here:

=COUNTA(

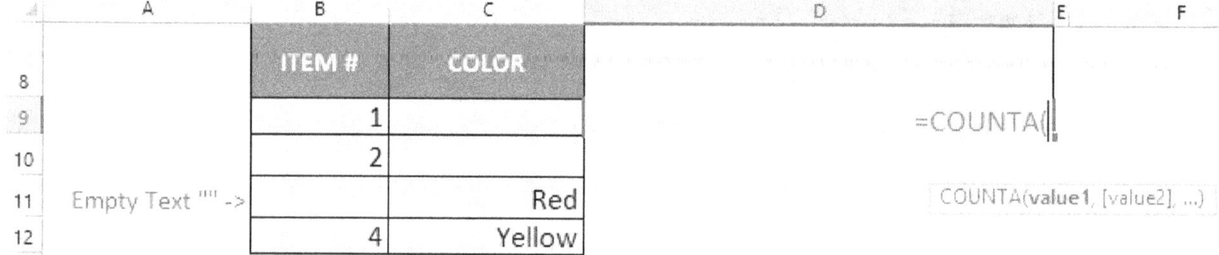

STEP 2: The **COUNTA** arguments:

value

What is the value or range of values that you want to check how many are non-blank?

=COUNTA(B9:C12)

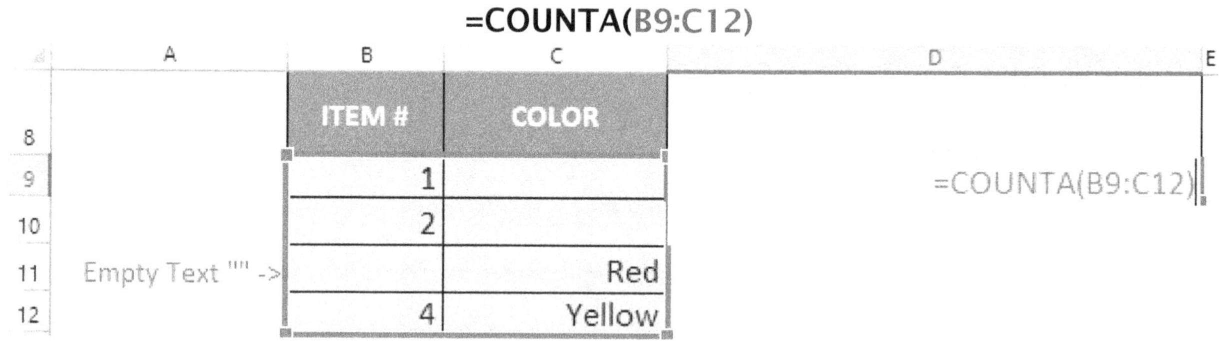

You now have your count of values that are non-blank! There are 6 non-blank values!

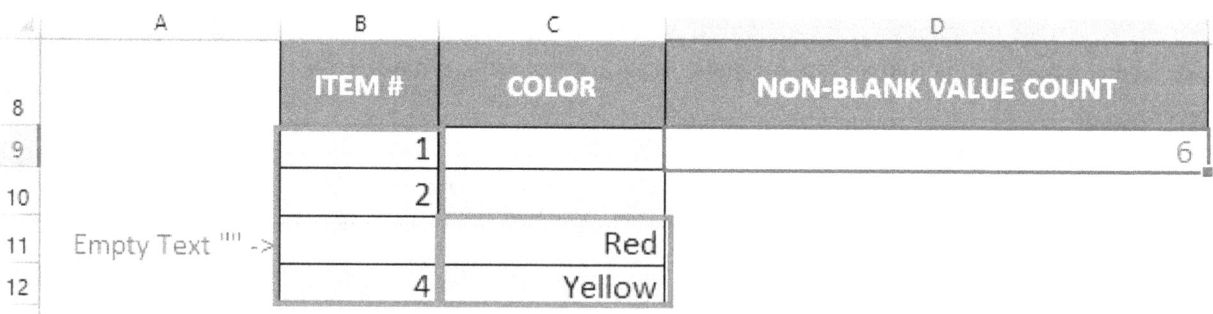

COUNTBLANK

What does it do?

Counts the number of cells that are blank

Formula breakdown:

=COUNTBLANK(range)

What it means:

=COUNTBLANK(range of cells to check)

Example:

=COUNTBLANK(B9:C12) =3

i.e. There are 3 blank cells

Do you have a scenario where you want to count the number of cells that **are blank in your Excel data?**

If you are auditing your data and want to make sure that a blank cell is actually blank (and doesn't contain an invisible character), then this formula is for you.

STEP 1: We need to **enter the *COUNTBLANK* function in a blank cell**:

=COUNTBLANK(

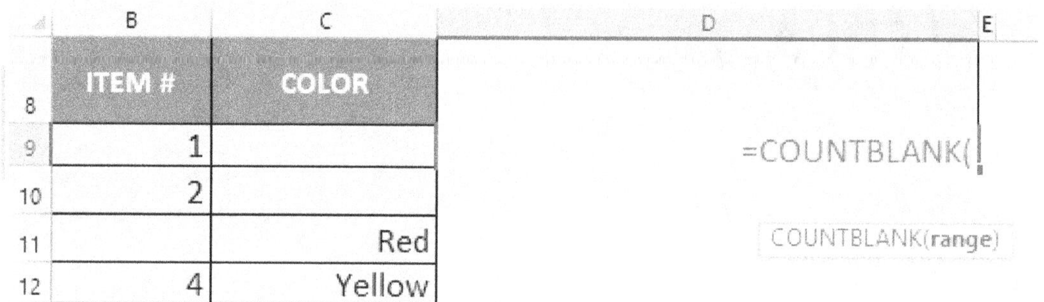

STEP 2: The **COUNTBLANK** arguments:

range

What are the range of values that you want to check to see how many are blank?

=COUNTBLANK(B9:C12)

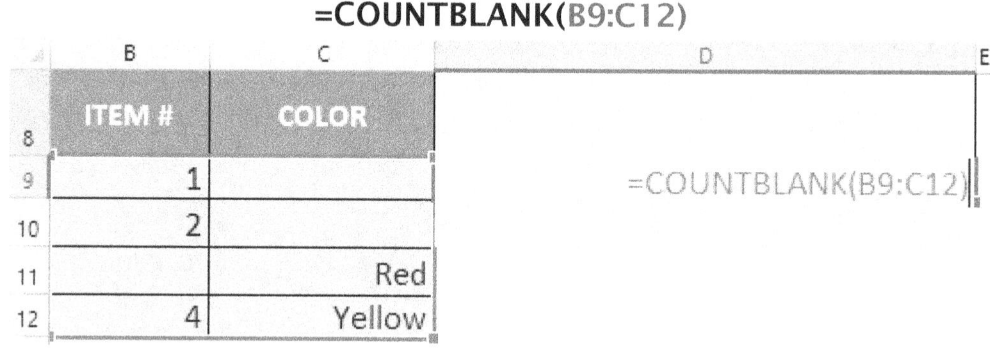

You now have your count of values that are blank! There are 3 blank values!

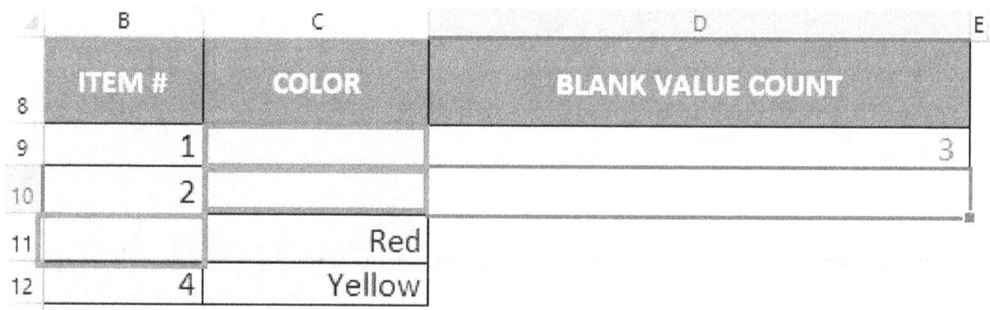

COUNTIF

What does it do?

Counts the number of cells that matches your specified condition

Formula breakdown:

=COUNTIF(range, criteria)

What it means:

=COUNTIF(range of cells to check, condition to check against)

Example:

=COUNTIF(A9:A12, ">2") = 3

i.e. There are 3 cells that are greater than 2

Do you have a scenario where you want to count the number of cells that **match a specific condition?**

I'm sure you do! There is a simple way to count this with Excel's **COUNTIF formula!**

The **COUNTIF formula** is very flexible indeed, so let us try to count the following from our Excel worksheet:

- Number of cells **greater than 2**
- Number of cells that have a **Yellow** value
- Number of cells that **start with the letter "J"**

VALUES	GREATER THAN 2	VALUES	YELLOW VALUES	VALUES	STARTS WITH LETTER J
5		Blue		John	
3		Yellow		Jenny	
abc		Red		Michael	
4		Yellow		Jones	

STEP 1: We need to **enter the *COUNTIF* function in a blank cell**:

=COUNTIF(

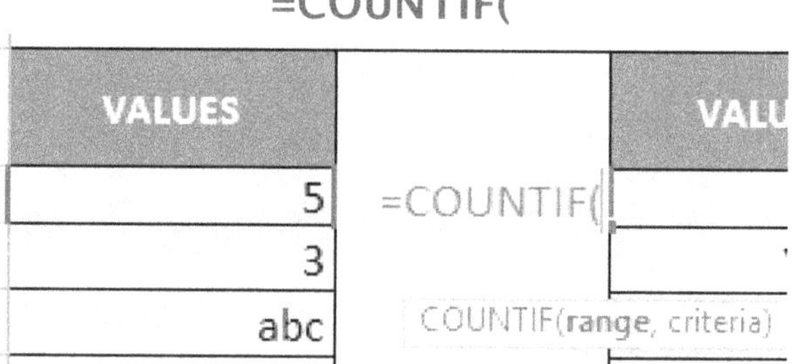

STEP 2: The **COUNTIF** arguments:

range

What are the range of values that you want to check your condition against?

=COUNTIF(A9:A12,

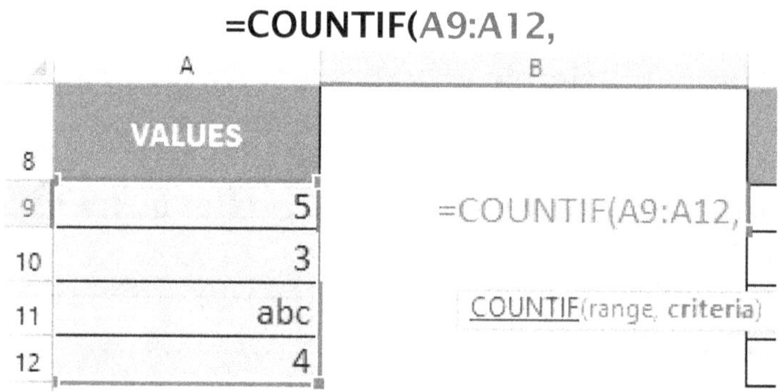

criteria

What is the condition that you want to check against?

For our 1st example, we want to count the number of values greater than 2.

=COUNTIF(A9:A12, ">2")

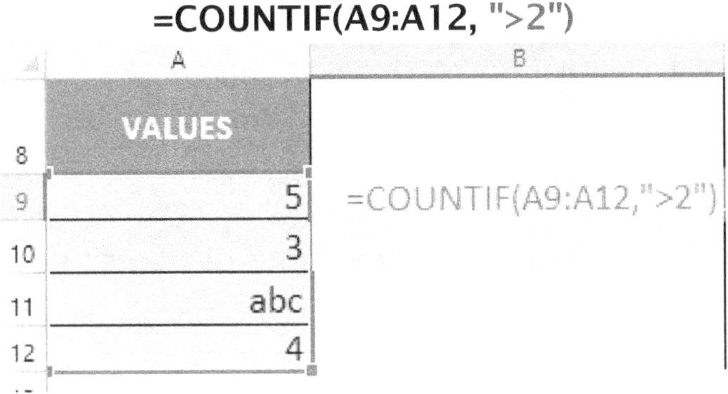

You now have your count of numbers greater than 2!

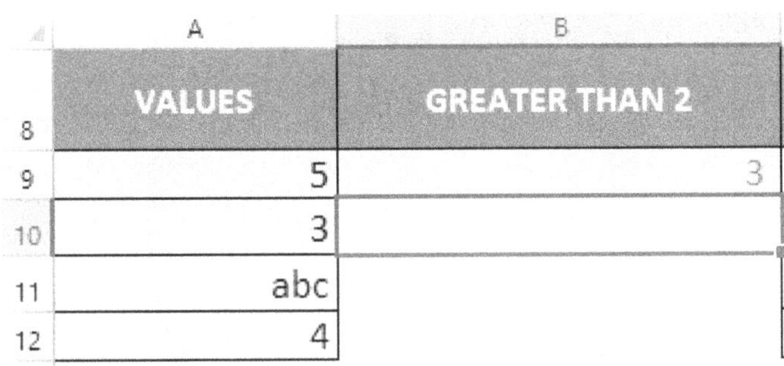

STEP 3: Now let us try for counting the number of **Yellow** values:

=COUNTIF(C9:C12, "Yellow")

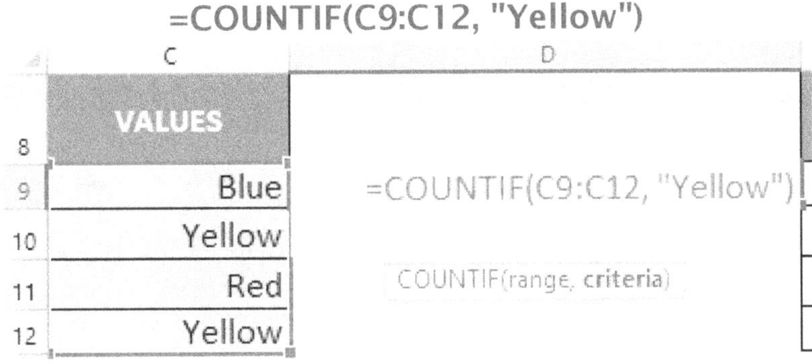

You now have your count of values that have the Yellow text!

	C	D
	VALUES	**YELLOW VALUES**
8		
9	Blue	2
10	Yellow	
11	Red	
12	Yellow	

STEP 4: Now let us try for counting the number of names **starting with the Letter J**:

Let us use the wildcard expression **J***

* signifies a <u>wildcard character</u> i.e. Return any value that **begins with a J**

=COUNTIF(E9:E12, "J*")

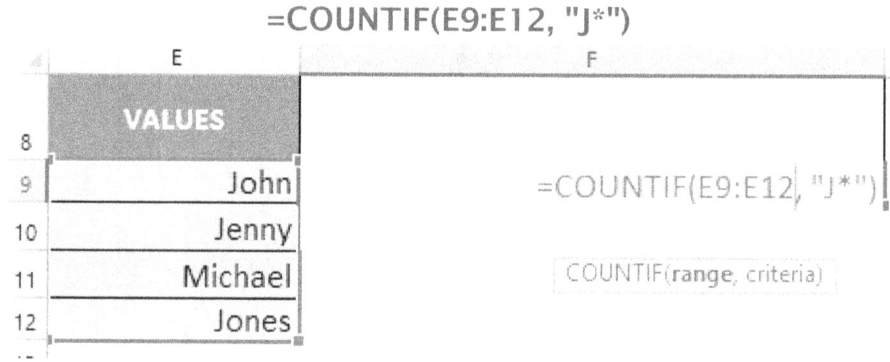

You now have your count of values that have a starting letter of J!

	E	F
	VALUES	**STARTS WITH LETTER J**
8		
9	John	3
10	Jenny	
11	Michael	
12	Jones	

COUNTIFS

What does it do?

Counts the number of cells that matches multiple conditions

Formula breakdown:

=COUNTIFS(range1, criteria1, [range2], [criteria2], ...)

What it means:

=COUNTIFS(range of cells to check1, condition to check against1, [range of cells to check2], [condition to check against2], ...)

Example:

=COUNTIFS(A9:A13, "John", C9:C13, ">10000") = 2

i.e. The number of times John got more than $10,000 in sales

Do you have a scenario where you want to count the number of cells that **match specific conditions?**

I'm sure you do! There is a simple way to count this with Excel's **COUNTIFS formula!**

This is very similar to the <u>CountIf Formula</u>! The only difference is it allows you to add even more conditions as needed...That's POWEFUL!

The **COUNTIFS formula** is very flexible indeed, so let us try to count the following from our Excel worksheet:

- Number of times **John got more than 10,000 sales**
- Number of times **Kim got more than 18,000 sales**

Person	Year	Sales	How many times John got more than 10,000 sales
John	2016	15000	
Kim	2016	20000	
Matt	2016	5000	How many times Kim got more than 18,000 sales
Kim	2017	17000	
John	2017	16000	

STEP 1: Let us target the first question: *How many times John got more than 10,000 sales?*

We need to **enter the *COUNTIFS* function in a blank cell**:

=COUNTIFS(

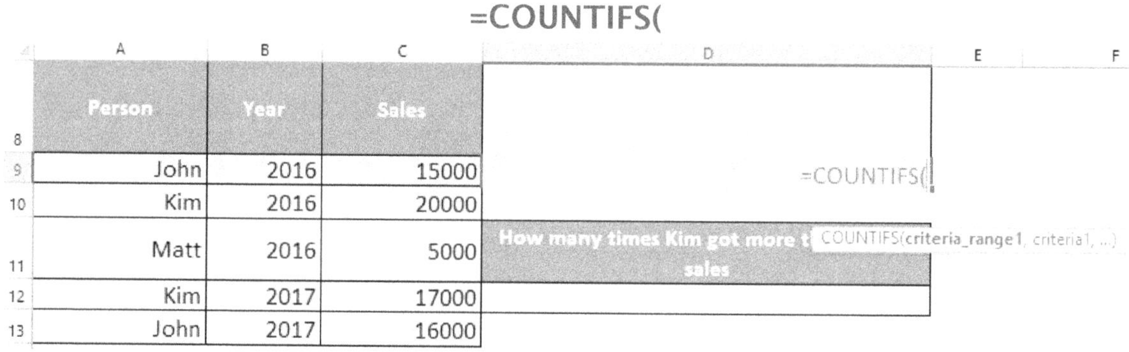

STEP 2: The **COUNTIFS** arguments:

range1, criteria1

What is our first condition?

We want to find the names that match "John"

=COUNTIFS(A9:A13, "John",

What is our second condition?

We want to find sales that are more than 10,000

=COUNTIFS(A9:A13, "John", C9:C13, ">10000")

	A	B	C	D	E	F
	Person	**Year**	**Sales**			
8						
9	John	2016	15000	=COUNTIFS(A9:A13, "John",C9:C13, ">10000")		
10	Kim	2016	20000			
11	Matt	2016	5000	COUNTIFS(criteria_range1, criteria1, [criteria_range2, **criteria2**], [criteria_range3, ...])		
12	Kim	2017	17000			
13	John	2017	16000			

You now have your count of 2!

	A	B	C	D
	Person	**Year**	**Sales**	**How many times John got more than 10,000 sales**
8				
9	John	2016	15000	2
10	Kim	2016	20000	
11	Matt	2016	5000	**How many times Kim got more than 18,000 sales**
12	Kim	2017	17000	
13	John	2017	16000	

STEP 3: Now let us try doing the same for Kim!

range1, criteria1

What is our first condition?

We want to find the names that match "Kim"

=COUNTIFS(A9:A13, "Kim",

	A	B	C	D	E	F
	Person	**Year**	**Sales**	**How many times John got more than 10,000 sales**		
8						
9	John	2016	15000	2		
10	Kim	2016	20000			
11	Matt	2016	5000			
12	Kim	2017	17000	=COUNTIFS(A9:A13, "Kim",		
13	John	2017	16000			
14				COUNTIFS(criteria_range1, criteria1, [criteria_range2, criteria2], ...)		

What is our second condition?

We want to find the sales that are more than 18,000

=COUNTIFS(A9:A13, "Kim", C9:C13, ">18000")

	Person	Year	Sales	How many times John got more than 10,000 sales
8				
9	John	2016	15000	2
10	Kim	2016	20000	
11	Matt	2016	5000	
12	Kim	2017	17000	=COUNTIFS(A9:A13, "Kim", C9:C13, ">18000")
13	John	2017	16000	
14				

You now have your count of 1!

	Person	Year	Sales	How many times John got more than 10,000 sales
8				
9	John	2016	15000	2
10	Kim	2016	20000	
11	Matt	2016	5000	How many times Kim got more than 18,000 sales
12	Kim	2017	17000	1
13	John	2017	16000	

You can have more than 2 conditions in the COUNTIFS formula, so go crazy with the COUNTIFS!

MOD

What does it do?

Gives you the remainder after dividing one number with another

Formula breakdown:

=MOD(number1, number2)

What it means:

=MOD(a number, divided by this number)

Example:

=MOD(15,4) =3

In Excel it is very easy to divide two numbers.

But how about if you need to get the remainder from a division operation?

For example, let's do this the manual way, divide 15 by 4:

- Divide the two numbers (i.e. 15 / 4)
- Get the quotient (which is 3)
- Multiply it back to the divisor (3 * 4)
- Subtract it from the original number (15 - 12)
- And I have the remainder! (3)

So, 4 goes into 13 three times with a remainder of 1.

Thankfully we can do the above complex and manual calculation with ease using Excel's **MOD formula!**

=MOD(

	C	D	E	F
8	**NUMBER**	**DIVIDED BY**		
9	50	10	=MOD(	
10	15	4		
11	21	5	MOD(**number**, divisor)	
12	13	5		

STEP 2: The MOD arguments:

number1

What is the first number that we plan to divide?

Reference the cell that contains the first number:

=**MOD**(C9,

	C	D	E	F
8	**NUMBER**	**DIVIDED BY**		
9	50	10	=MOD(C9,	
10	15	4		
11	21	5	MOD(number, **divisor**)	
12	13	5		

What is the divisor?

Reference the cell that contains the second number:

=MOD(C9, D9)

	NUMBER	DIVIDED BY		
	C	D	E	F
8				
9	50	10	=MOD(C9,D9)	
10	15	4		
11	21	5		
12	13	5		

STEP 3: Do the same for the rest of the cells by dragging the **MOD** formula all the way down using the left mouse button.

Now you are able to get the remainders of all the division operations!

	NUMBER	DIVIDED BY	REMAINDER
	C	D	E
8			
9	50	10	0
10	15	4	3
11	21	5	1
12	13	5	3
13			

PERCENTAGE

What does it do?

In calculating percentages in Excel, there are a lot of ways that you could do this:

- What is the percentage of a number?
- What is the percentage change of value i.e. The percentage increase or decrease
- What is the proportion against a total value?

Calculate Percentage	Formula	Sample	Result
Of a Number	= Number * Percentage	What is 75% of 100?	
Change	= (New - Old) / Old	What is the price change if the price increased from 100 to 150?	
Proportionally	= Portion / Total	What is your percentage if you took 20 shots and 12 went in?	

Example:

=75% * 100 =75

STEP 1: **What is the percentage of a number?**

To calculate the percentage of the number, simply multiply the number and the percentage together:

Percentage x Number

75% * 100

Calculate Percentage	Formula	Sample	Result
Of a Number	= Number * Percentage	What is 75% of 100?	=75%*100
Change	= (New - Old) / Old	What is the price change if the price increased from 100 to 150?	
Proportionally	= Portion / Total	What is your percentage if you took 20 shots and 12 went in?	

 What is the percentage change of value i.e. The percentage increase or decrease

To calculate the change in value as a percentage, get the difference of the new value and the old value, then divide it by the old value:

(New - Old) / Old

(150 - 100) / 100

Calculate Percentage	Formula	Sample	Result
Of a Number	= Number * Percentage	What is 75% of 100?	75
Change	= (New - Old) / Old	What is the price change if the price increased from 100 to 150?	=(150-100)/100
Proportionally	= Portion / Total	What is your percentage if you took 20 shots and 12 went in?	

 What is the proportion against a total value?

To get the proportion as a percentage, divide the portion by the total amount:

Portion / Total

12/20

Calculate Percentage	Formula	Sample	Result
Of a Number	= Number * Percentage	What is 75% of 100?	75
Change	= (New - Old) / Old	What is the price change if the price increased from 100 to 150?	0.5
Proportionally	= Portion / Total	What is your percentage if you took 20 shots and 12 went in?	=12/20

STEP 4: We are almost done! The last two values are not in the percentage format, so let's fix that.

Select the last two values and go to *Home > Number > %*

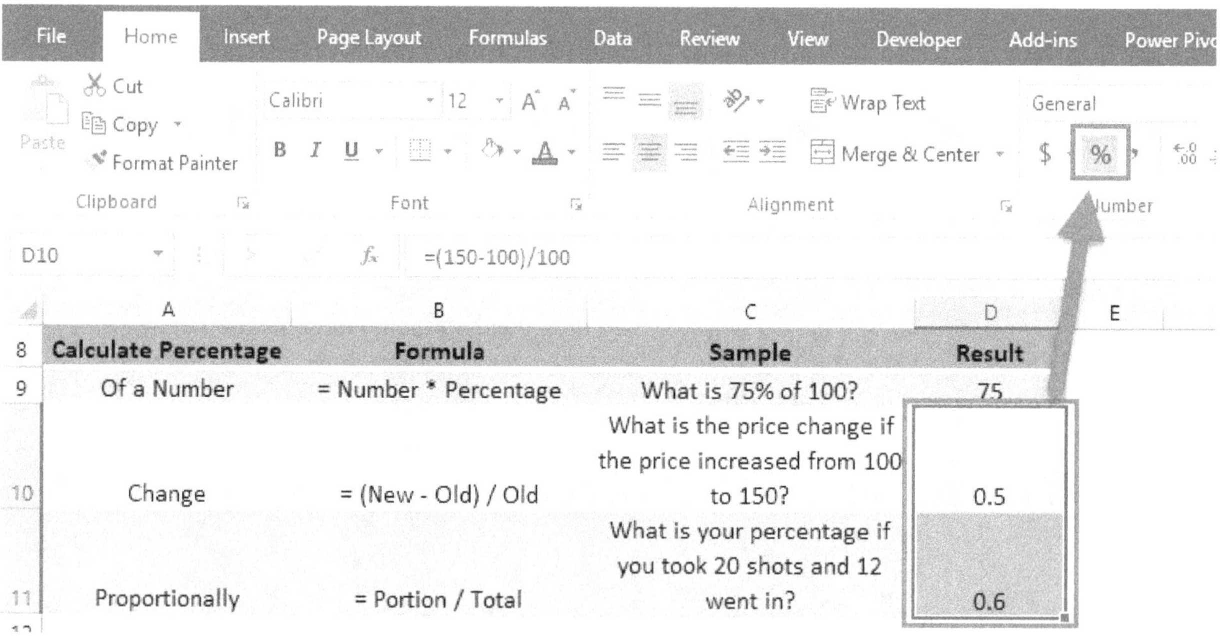

Your percentage values are now all ready!

Calculate Percentage	Formula	Sample	Result
Of a Number	= Number * Percentage	What is 75% of 100?	75
Change	= (New - Old) / Old	What is the price change if the price increased from 100 to 150?	50%
Proportionally	= Portion / Total	What is your percentage if you took 20 shots and 12 went in?	60%

RAND

What does it do?

Gives you a random number between 0 and 1

Formula breakdown:

=RAND()

What it means:

=RAND(Will automatically choose a random number between 0 and 1)

Example:

=RAND() =0.151018728113863

Excel is able to do a lot of things that most users are unaware of! One thing that amazes me & I use almost daily is its ability to create random numbers for me!

But why would I even need random numbers?

Random numbers in Excel are great if you want to fill in a column with random values so you can create quick charts or just do any kind of random Excel analysis.

One of my best uses of the RAND function in Excel is to create random numbers for a raffle draw!

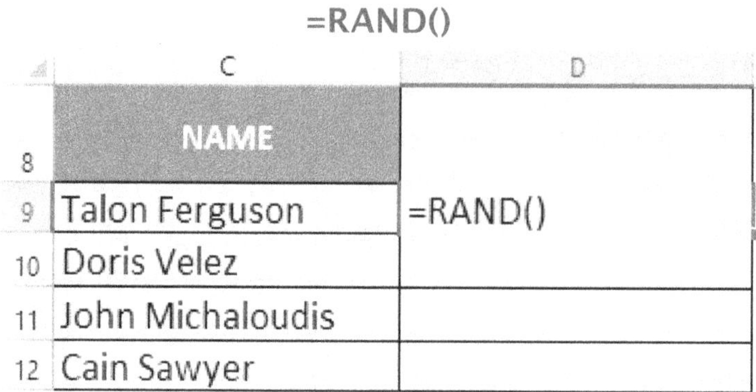

STEP 2: Do the same for the rest of the cells by dragging the **RAND** formula all the way down using the left mouse button.

Now we are able to get random numbers for all the entries without any bias!

I'm actually the winner in this case as I have the lowest value!

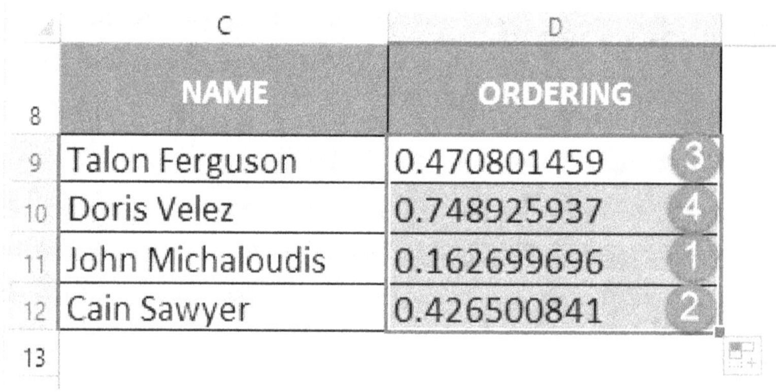

TIP: Press the **F9** button on your keyboard to refresh/update the RAND values until you get your desired result...with bias :)

RANDBETWEEN

What does it do?

Returns a random integer number between the numbers you specify.

Formula breakdown:

=RANDBETWEEN(bottom number, top number)

What it means:

=RANDBETWEEN(bottom number of the range, top number of the range)

Example:

=RANDBETWEEN(10,10000) =2852

I use the **RANDBETWEEN** function all the time whenever I need to create a sample data set.

The cool thing about the **RANDBETWEEN** function is that if you don't like the numbers that it has given you, you can press F9 in a cell and it will give you new numbers.

We want to enter some random numbers from 10 to 10,000.

STEP 1: We need to enter the **RANDBETWEEN** function in a blank cell:

=RANDBETWEEN(

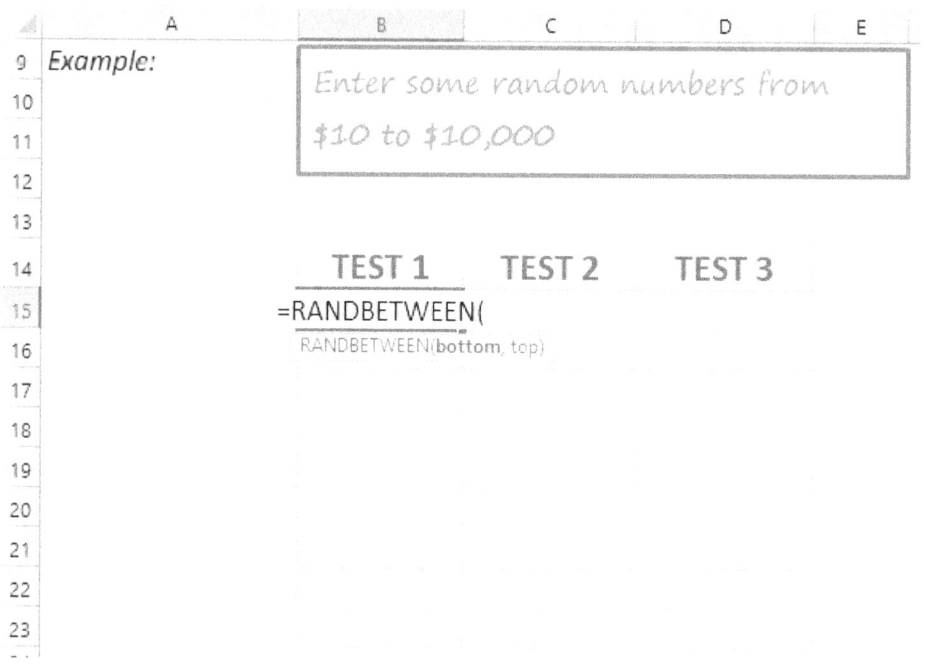

 The **RANDBETWEEN** arguments:

bottom_number

What is your minimum value?

For our example it's 10

=RANDBETWEEN(10,

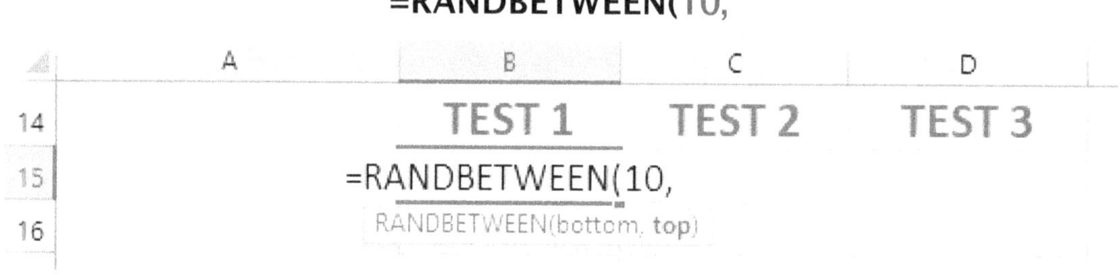

top_number
What is your maximum value?

For our example it's 10,000

=RANDBETWEEN(10, 10000)

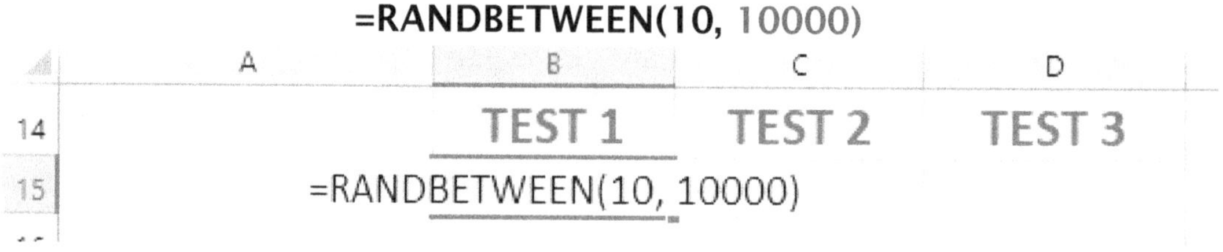

Apply the same formula to the rest of the cells by dragging the lower right corner downwards. Then drag it to the right to populate all the cells.

	A	TEST 1	TEST 2	TEST 3	E
14					
15		1,914			
16		5,139			
17		276			
18		3,503			
19		5,056			
20		9,816			
21		49			
22		9,391			
23		8,062			

	A	TEST 1	TEST 2	TEST 3	
14					
15		7,968	9,746	9,968	
16		9,465	9,983	4,130	
17		1,663	1,425	8,118	
18		4,062	3,325	3,753	
19		5,196	7,736	3,028	
20		5,709	7,081	6,717	
21		5,605	676	4,005	
22		4,382	3,773	2,131	
23		3,347	9,976	1,989	
24					

You now have all of the random numbers!

ROUND

What does it do?

Rounds a number to the nearest decimal based on your specified number of digits

Formula breakdown:

=ROUND(number, num_digits)

What it means:

=ROUND(the number, number of decimal places to round off)

Example:

=ROUND(1.234567, 2) =1.23

Ever had the need to round off numbers?

I do it all the time in my financial calculations. For example, if I need to calculate **percentage discounts** and it gives me a number such as $47.4189349, rounding it off to $47.40 (round off to 1 decimal place) makes it so much more presentable!

STEP 1: We need to **enter the ROUND function**:

=ROUND(

	B	C	D
8	**NUMBER**	**# OF DIGITS**	
9	1.234567	0	=ROUND(
10	1.234567	1	
11	1.234567	2	ROUND(number, num_digits)
12	1.234567	3	

number

What is the number we want to round off?

Reference the cell that contains the number:

=ROUND(B9,

	B	C	D
8	**NUMBER**	**# OF DIGITS**	
9	1.234567	0	=ROUND(B9,
10	1.234567	1	
11	1.234567	2	ROUND(number, num_digits)
12	1.234567	3	

num_digits

Round off to how many digits?

Reference the cell that contains the number of digits:

=ROUND(B9, C9)

	B	C	D
8	**NUMBER**	**# OF DIGITS**	
9	1.234567	0	=ROUND(B9, C9)
10	1.234567	1	
11	1.234567	2	
12	1.234567	3	

STEP 3: Do the same for the rest of the cells by dragging the **ROUND** formula all the way down using the left mouse button.

	B	C	D
8	**NUMBER**	**# OF DIGITS**	**RESULT**
9	1.234567	0	1
10	1.234567	1	1.2
11	1.234567	2	1.23
12	1.234567	3	1.235
13			

SUBTOTAL

What does it do?

It returns a Subtotal in a list or database

Formula breakdown:

=SUBTOTAL(function_num, ref1)

What it means:

=SUBTOTAL(function number 1-11 includes manually-hidden rows & 101-111 excludes them, your list or range of data)

Example:

=SUBTOTAL(9,B2:B9) = $1,945

The SUBTOTAL function in Excel has many great features, like the ability to:

* Return a **SUM, AVERAGE, COUNT, COUNTA, MAX or MIN** from your data;

* **Include hidden values** within your data by entering the first argument *function_num*, as values between 1-11;

* **Ignore hidden values** within your data by entering the first argument *function_num*, as values between 101-111;

* Find the SUBTOTAL of **filtered values**;

* Ignore other SUBTOTALS that are included in your range, **avoiding any double counting!**

This is probably the most useful feature within the SUBTOTAL function!

Let's say you have various SUBTOTALS within your data, one SUBTOTAL to *Sum* the North Region and another SUBTOTAL to *Sum* the South Region.

You can include a third SUBTOTAL for your Grand Total which references all of your data and ignoring the North & South Region SUBTOTALS, meaning that there is **no double counting** in your Grand Total.

See the below images of how this works with the SUBTOTAL function and how it double counts when using the SUM function:

	A	B	C	D	E
1	**REGION**	Q1			
2	North-East	$657			
3	North-West	$550			
4	**Total North**	**$1,207**	=SUBTOTAL(9,B2:B3)		
5					
6	South-East	$295			
7	South-West	$443			
8	**Total South**	**$738**	=SUBTOTAL(9,B6:B7)		
9					
10	TOTAL	**$1,945**	=SUBTOTAL(9,B2:B9)		
11					

	A	B	C	D	E
1	REGION	Q1			
2	North-East	$657			
3	North-West	$550			
4	Total North	$1,207	=SUM(B2:B3)		
5					
6	South-East	$295			
7	South-West	$443			
8	Total South	$738	=SUM(B6:B7)		
9					
10	TOTAL	$3,890	=SUBTOTAL(9,B2:B9)		
11					

Values for the SUBTOTAL *function_num*:

Includes hidden values	Ignores hidden values	Function
1	101	AVERAGE
2	102	COUNT
3	103	COUNTA
4	104	MAX
5	105	MIN
6	106	PRODUCT
7	107	STDEV
8	108	STDEVP
9	109	SUM
10	110	VAR
11	111	VARP

SUMIF

What does it do?

Sums the values in a range that meet a criteria that you specify

Formula breakdown:

=SUMIF(Range or Cells, Criteria, [Sum_Range])

What it means:

=SUMIF(Evaluate this Range/Cells, With this Criteria, [Optional Sum Range])

Example:

=SUMIF(D15:D23,">3000") = $17,435

i.e. Sum of all the values that are above $3,000

The **SUMIF** function is used widely amongst spreadsheet users as it is a simple Excel function. It allows you to Sum the values in a range that meet a criteria that you specify.

So if you want to Sum a range of sales values that are above $3,000 then this is the best Excel function to use, as I explain below.

We want to get the sum of the sales amounts that are above $3000.

STEP 1: We need to enter the **SUMIF** function in a blank cell:

=SUMIF(

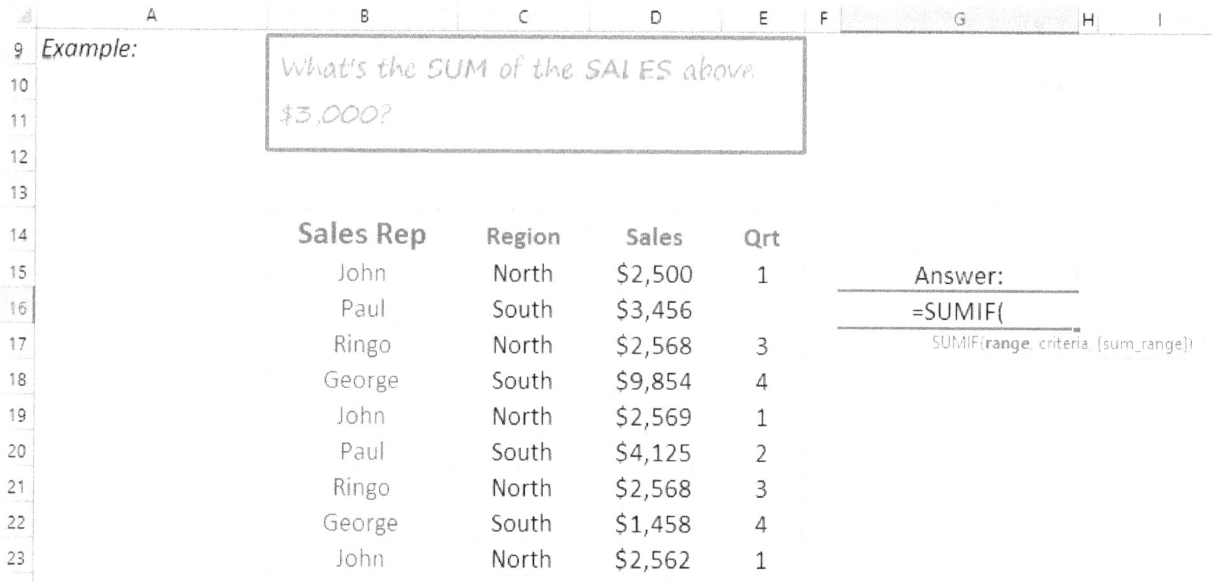

STEP 2: The **SUMIF** arguments:

range

What is your range that contains the source data?

Highlight the column that contains the sales data

=SUMIF(D15:D23,

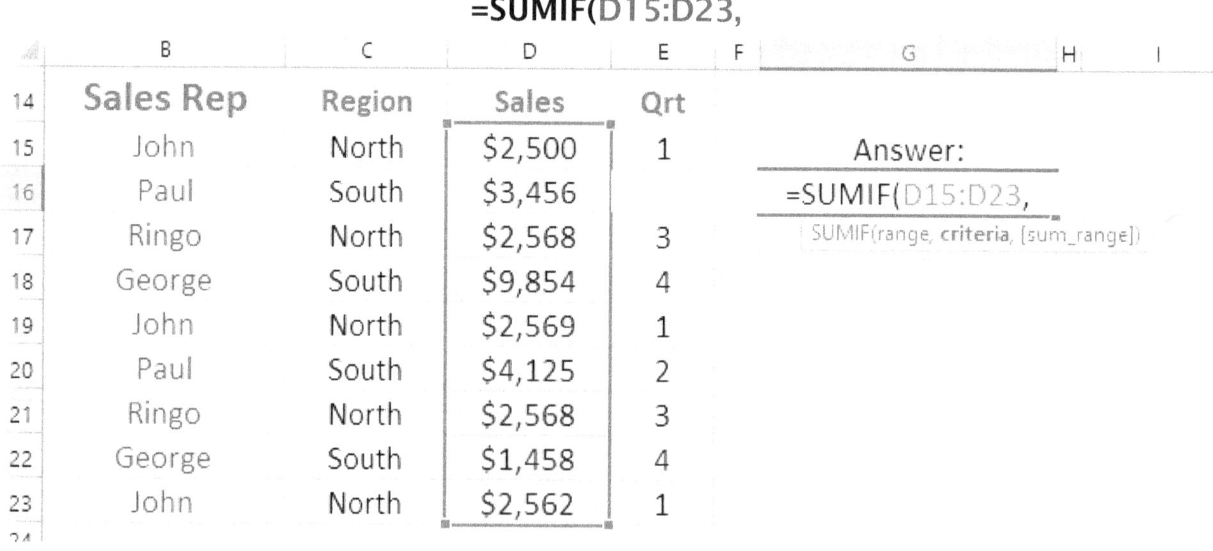

Which records do you want to sum together?

Since we want to sum the amounts greater than 3000, then let's type in >3000

=SUMIF(D15:D23, ">3000")

	B	C	D	E	F	G	H
14	**Sales Rep**	Region	Sales	Qrt			
15	John	North	$2,500	1		Answer:	
16	Paul	South	$3,456			=SUMIF(D15:D23, ">3000")	
17	Ringo	North	$2,568	3			
18	George	South	$9,854	4			
19	John	North	$2,569	1			
20	Paul	South	$4,125	2			
21	Ringo	North	$2,568	3			
22	George	South	$1,458	4			
23	John	North	$2,562	1			

Just like that, Excel has selectively found the values and summed them together!

	B	C	D	E	F	G	H
14	**Sales Rep**	Region	Sales	Qrt			
15	John	North	$2,500	1		Answer:	
16	Paul	South	$3,456	2		$17,435	
17	Ringo	North	$2,568	3			
18	George	South	$9,854	4			
19	John	North	$2,569	1			
20	Paul	South	$4,125	2			
21	Ringo	North	$2,568	3			
22	George	South	$1,458	4			
23	John	North	$2,562	1			

SUMIFS

What does it do?

Sums multiple criteria

Formula breakdown:

=SUMIFS(Sum_Range,Criteria_Range1,Criteria1,Criteria_Range2,Criteria2...)

What it means:

=SUMIFS(Return the Sum from this Range,Evaluate this Range,With this Criteria,Evaluate that Range,With that Criteria...)

Example:

=SUMIFS(D15:D23,B15:B23,"john",C15:C23,"north") = $7,631

i.e. Total sales for John in the North region

The **SUMIFS** function allows you to Sum multiple criteria.

For example, you can select one Sales Rep from a list of Sales Reps and select one Region from a list of Regions and return the Sum of those arguments from a Sales list. See how easy it is...

We want to get the **sum of the sales amounts** for **John** in the **North Region**.

STEP 1: We need to enter the **SUMIFS** function in a blank cell:

=SUMIFS(

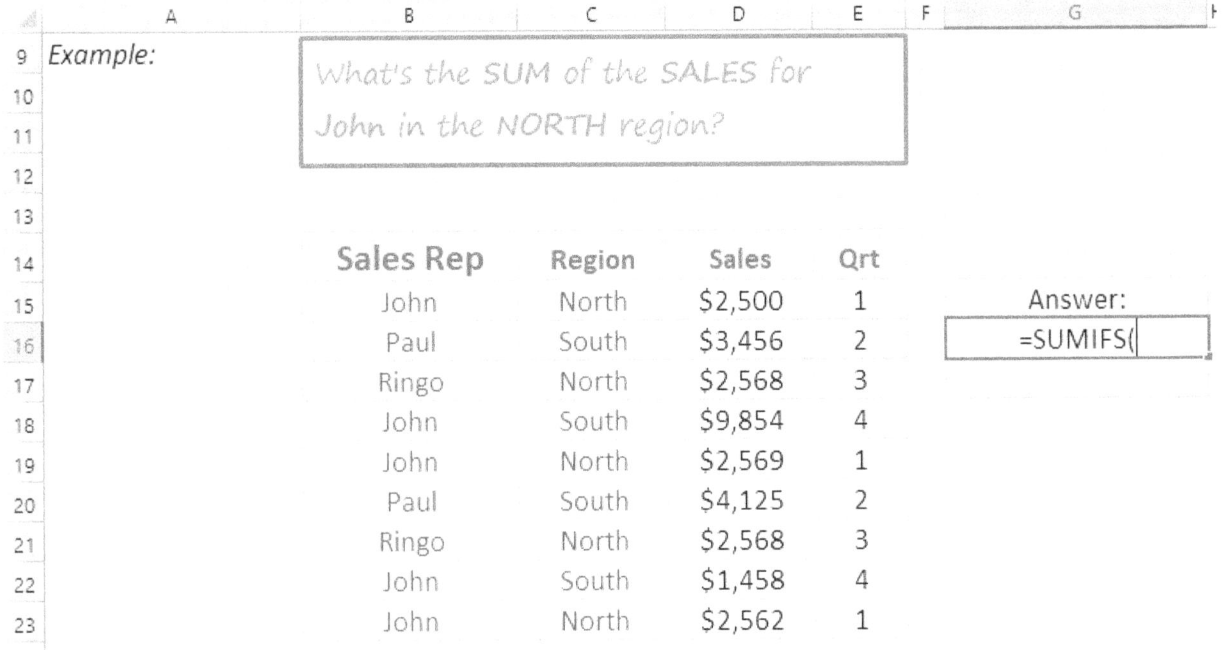

STEP 2: The **SUMIFS** arguments:

range

What is your range that contains the data to add together?

*Highlight the column that contains the **Sales** data*

=SUMIFS(D15:D23,

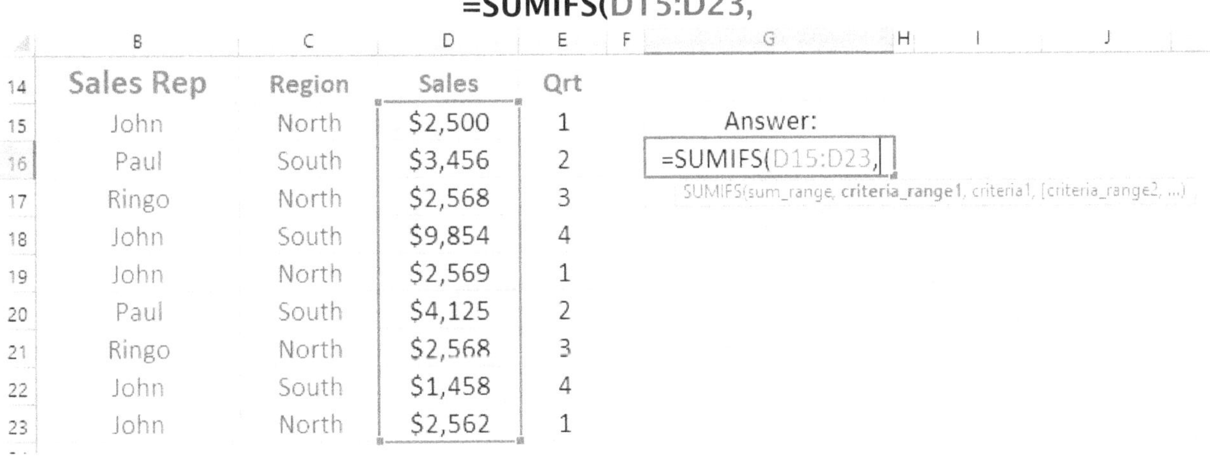

criteria_range1

For the first criteria, which range contains the data?

*Let us target the **Sales Rep** first, so select that column*

=SUMIFS(D15:D23, B15:B23,

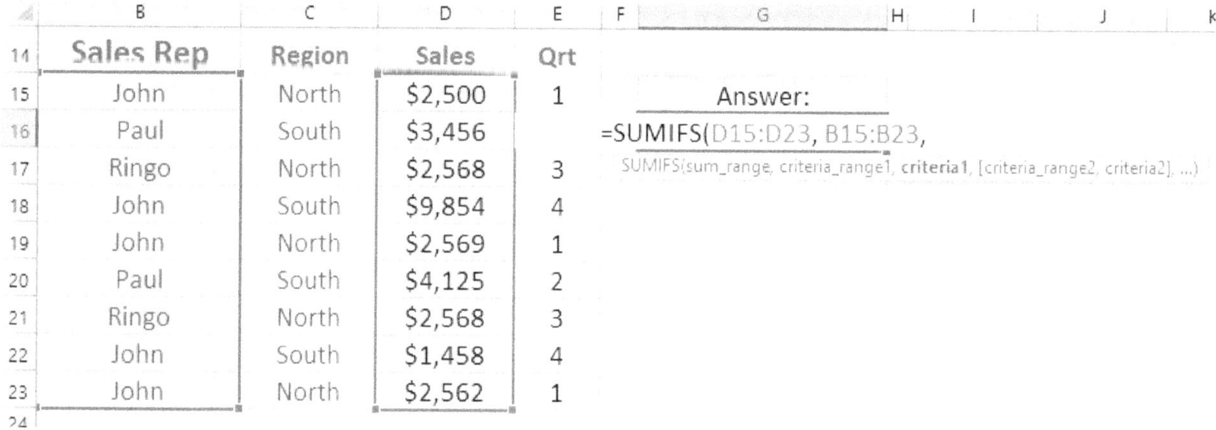

criteria1

What is your filtering criteria?

We want to filter for John, so type in "John"

=SUMIFS(D15:D23, B15:B23, "John",

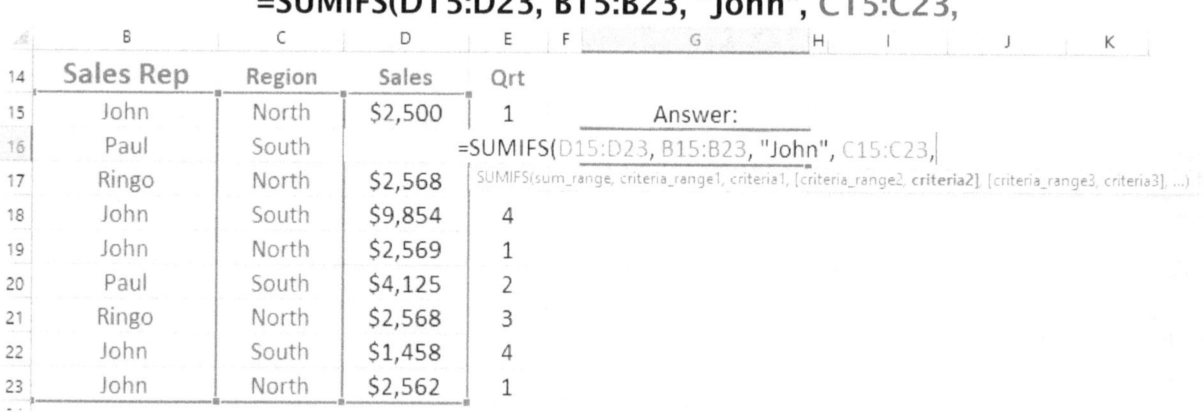

criteria_range2

For the second criteria, which range contains the data?

*Let us now target the **Region**, so select that column*

=SUMIFS(D15:D23, B15:B23, "John", C15:C23,

What is your filtering criteria?

We want to filter for the North Region, so type in "North"

=SUMIFS(D15:D23, B15:B23, "John", C15:C23, "North")

	Sales Rep	Region	Sales	Qrt			
14							
15	John	North	$2,500	1		Answer:	
16	Paul	South			=SUMIFS(D15:D23, B15:B23, "John", C15:C23, "North")		
17	Ringo	North	$2,568	3			
18	John	South	$9,854	4			
19	John	North	$2,569	1			
20	Paul	South	$4,125	2			
21	Ringo	North	$2,568	3			
22	John	South	$1,458	4			
23	John	North	$2,562	1			
24							

Just like that, Excel has selectively found the values and summed them together!

	Sales Rep	Region	Sales	Qrt		
14						
15	John	North	$2,500	1		Answer:
16	Paul	South	$3,456	2		$7,631
17	Ringo	North	$2,568	3		
18	John	South	$9,854	4		
19	John	North	$2,569	1		
20	Paul	South	$4,125	2		
21	Ringo	North	$2,568	3		
22	John	South	$1,458	4		
23	John	North	$2,562	1		

SUMPRODUCT

What does it do?

It returns the sum of the products of corresponding ranges or arrays

Formula breakdown:

=SUMPRODUCT(array1, [array2], [array3]...)

What it means:

=SUMPRODUCT(this array, with that array...)

Example:

=SUMPRODUCT(C14:C17,D14:D17)/SUM(C14:C17) = $455

i.e. The average selling price

A quick way to calculate the weighted average of two lists of data is to use the **SUMPRODUCT** formula. A **weighted average** can be used to determine the average salary of employees, the average grade of an exam or the average selling price of a company´s stock list, as can been seen below.

We want to get the average selling price of our total stock items. This is easily achievable with the **SUMPRODUCT** formula! We will use this to calculate the total value of the items, then **divide this by the total number of units** to get the **average selling price**.

=SUMPRODUCT(

STEP 2: The **SUMPRODUCT** arguments:

array1

What is the first array that contains the data?

*We want to get the **Units Sold** so select those values.*

=SUMPRODUCT(C14:C17,

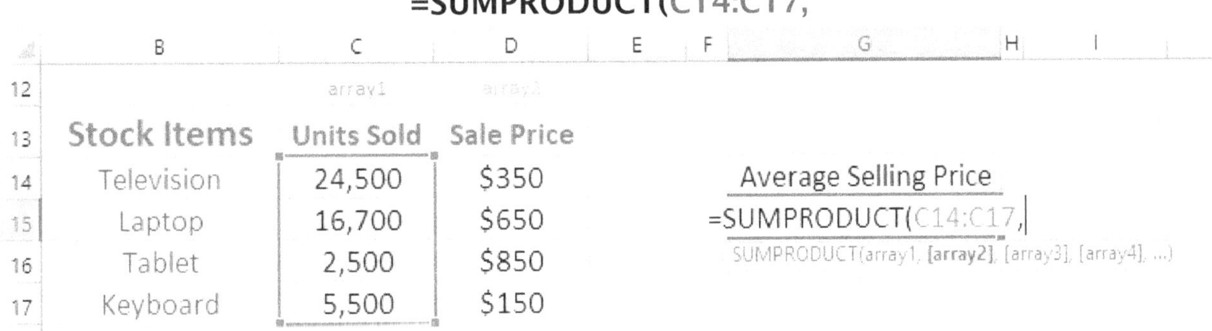

array2

What is the second array that contains the data?

*We want to get the **Sale Price**, so select those values. The values will be
multiplied against the first array that we got.*

=SUMPRODUCT(C14:C17, D14:D17)

	B	C	D	E	F	G	H	I
12		array1	array2					
13	**Stock Items**	Units Sold	Sale Price					
14	Television	24,500	$350			Average Selling Price		
15	Laptop	16,700	$650			=SUMPRODUCT(C14:C17, D14:D17)		
16	Tablet	2,500	$850					
17	Keyboard	5,500	$150					

STEP 3: Now we have the total value, we can easily get the average value by dividing it by the total number of items.

=SUMPRODUCT(C14:C17, D14:D17) / SUM(C14:C17)

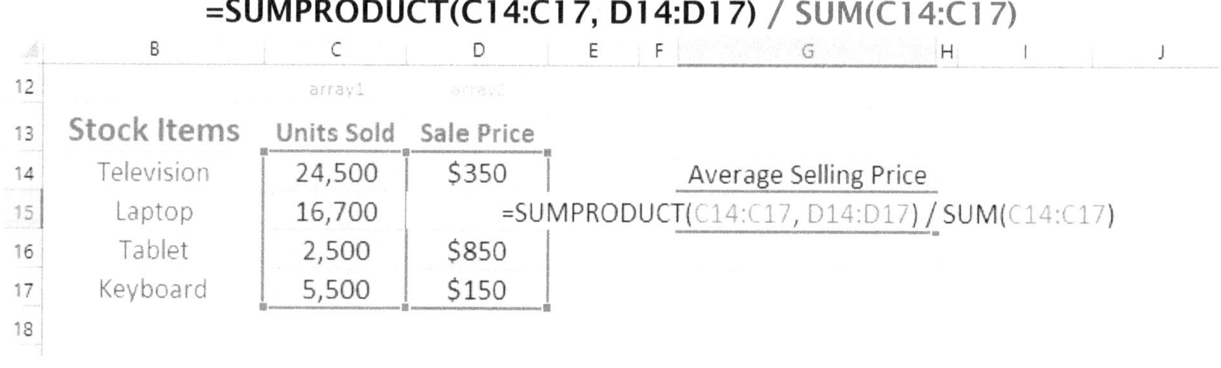

With just this single formula, we are able to get the average selling price without the need of extra helper columns!

	B	C	D	E	F	G	H
12		array1	array2				
13	**Stock Items**	Units Sold	Sale Price				
14	Television	24,500	$350			Average Selling Price	
15	Laptop	16,700	$650			$455	
16	Tablet	2,500	$850				
17	Keyboard	5,500	$150				

STATISTICAL FUNCTIONS

AVERAGE

What does it do?

Gives you the average of a group of values

Formula breakdown:

=AVERAGE(number1, number2...)

What it means:

=AVERAGE(the numbers you want to average)

Example:

=AVERAGE(1,2,3,4) =2.5

There are times when you have to get the average of your values in your Excel worksheet and you would normally have to **SUM** all of the values then divide it by the number of values. And that's the long process!

Thankfully there is a quicker way with Excel's **AVERAGE formula!**

In our example below, we have a table of values that we need to get the average from:

DAY OF THE WEEK	SALES
Monday	$829.41
Tuesday	$894.00
Wednesday	$332.11
Thursday	$1,023.32

STEP 1: We need to **enter the *AVERAGE* function in a blank cell**:

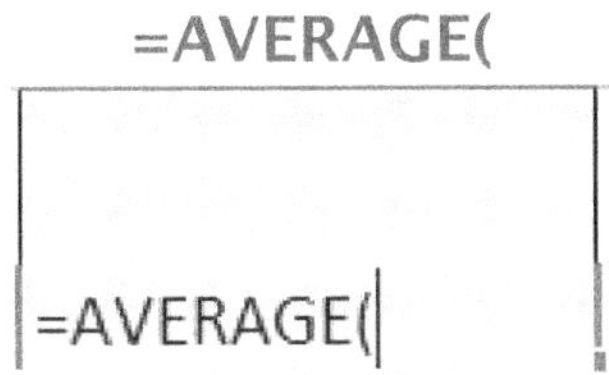

STEP 2: The **AVERAGE** arguments:

text

What numbers do we want to get the average of?

Select the range of values:

=AVERAGE(D9:D12)

	C	D	E	F	G
8	**DAY OF THE WEEK**	**SALES**			
9	Monday	$829.41		=AVERAGE(D9:D12)	
10	Tuesday	$894.00			
11	Wednesday	$332.11			
12	Thursday	$1,023.32			

You have now calculated the average of the Sales numbers!

	C	D	E	F
8	**DAY OF THE WEEK**	**SALES**		**AVERAGE**
9	Monday	$829.41		$769.71
10	Tuesday	$894.00		
11	Wednesday	$332.11		
12	Thursday	$1,023.32		

LARGE

What does it do?

Get the nth largest value from a range of values

Formula breakdown:

=LARGE(array, k)

What it means:

=LARGE(range of values, position of the largest value)

Example:

=LARGE(C9:C12, 3) = 60

i.e. 60 is the 3rd largest value in the range {60;55;100;89}

You have a list of values and you want to get the third (or nth) largest value, no problem! Excel's **LARGE Formula** can easily get that for you!

STEP 1: We need to **enter the *LARGE* function in a blank cell**:

=LARGE(

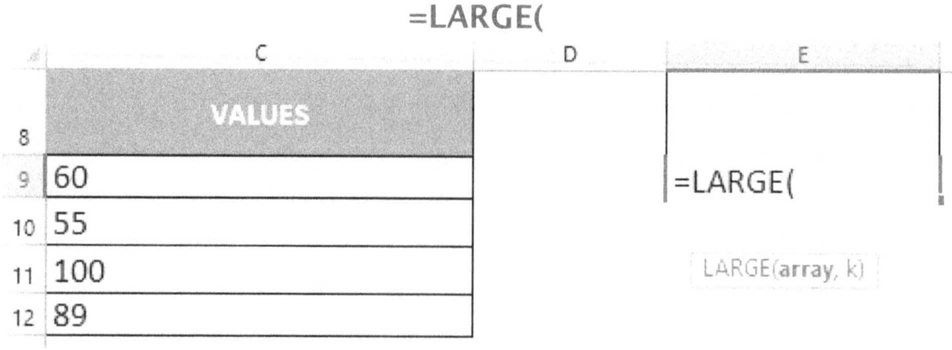

array

What is the range of values?

Select the cells containing your values:

=LARGE(C9:C12,

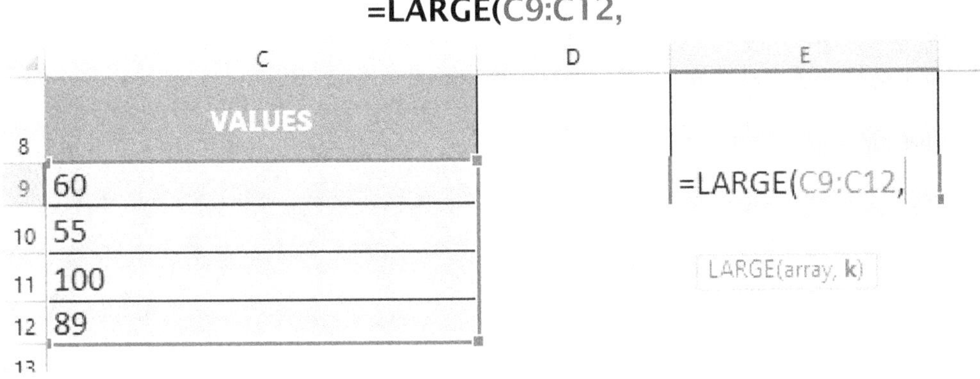

k

What is the nth largest value that you want to get?

We want to get the third largest value so we will place in 3.

=LARGE(C9:C12, 3)

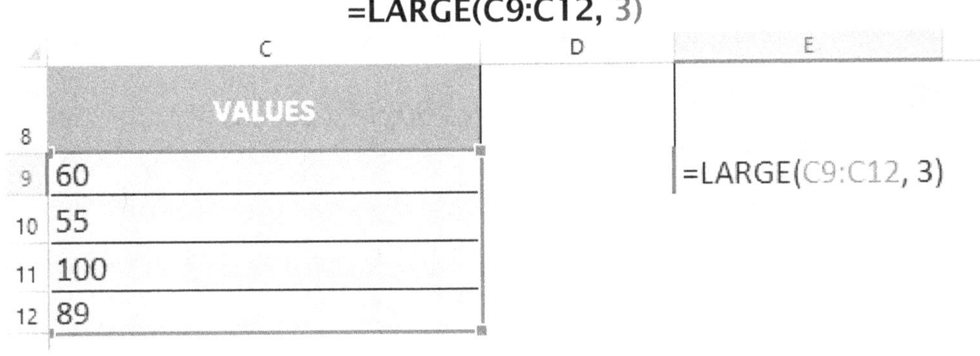

You now have your third largest value!

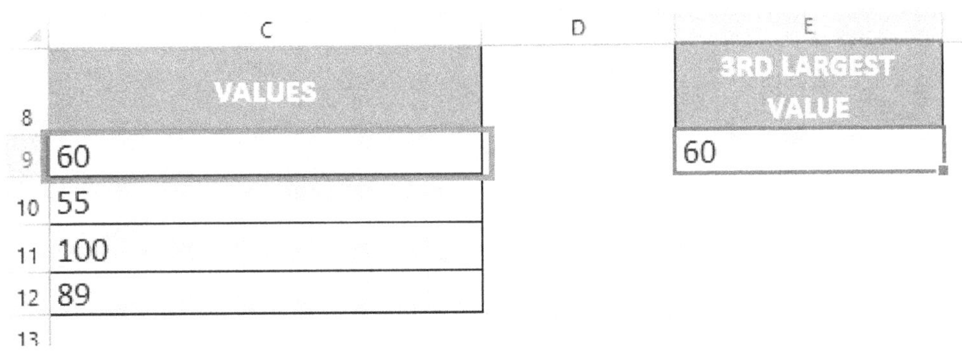

MAX

What does it do?

Get the largest value from a range of values

Formula breakdown:

=MAX(number1, [number2], ...)

What it means:

=MAX(a number or range of values, [additional numbers], ...)

Example:

=MAX(60,55,100,89) = 100

i.e. 100 is the largest number in the range {60;55;100;89}

If you want to get the largest value out of a list of values, just one use of Excel's **MAX Formula** gives you the answer instantly!

STEP 1: We need to **enter the MAX function in a blank cell**:

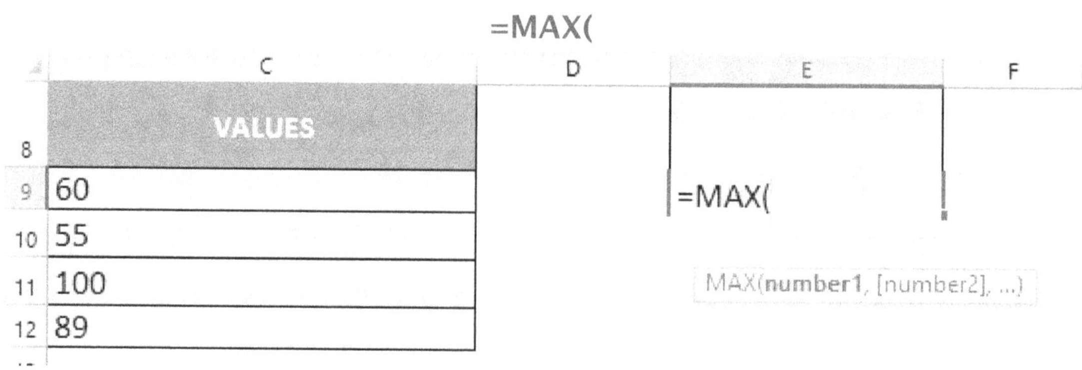

number1, [number2], …

Where is the list of values?

Select the cells containing the values that you want to get the maximum value from.

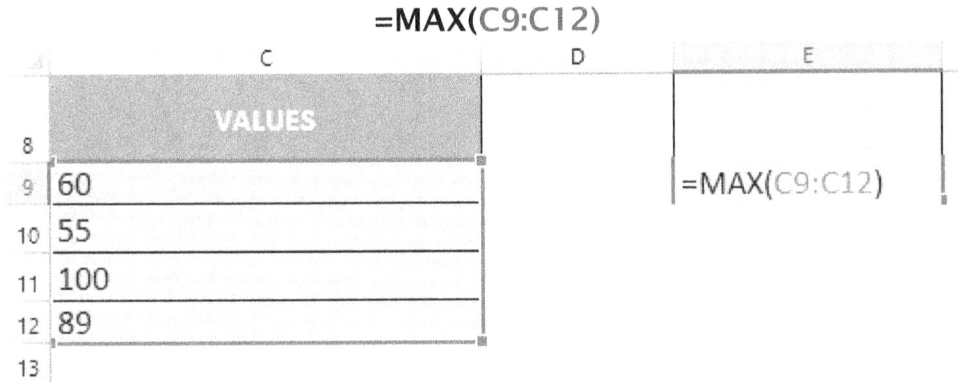

You now have the maximum value of 100 from the list!

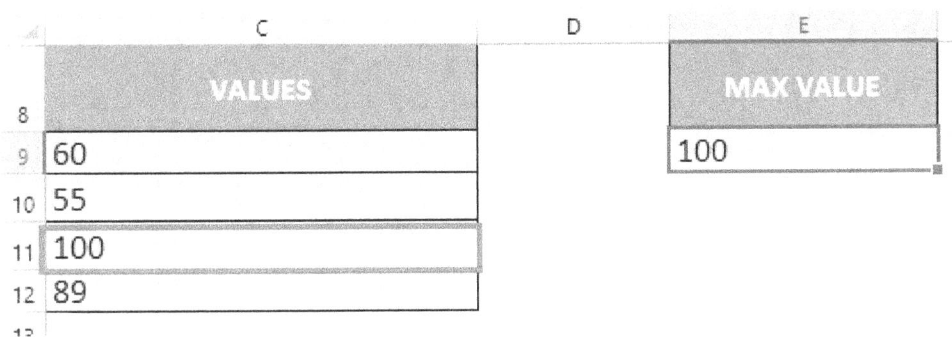

MEDIAN

What does it do?

Gets the middle number in a set of numbers

Formula breakdown:

=MEDIAN(number1, [number2], ...)

What it means:

=MEDIAN(first number, [succeeding numbers in the set], ...)

Example:

=MEDIAN(60,55,100,89) = 74.50

i.e. 74.50 is the middle number (60+89)/2 in the range {60;55;100;89}

You have a list of values and you want to get the median or middle of those values. Excel's **MEDIAN Formula** can easily get that for you!

An important think to note though, if it's an **odd number of values**, it will simply get the middle value. But if it's an **even number of values**, it will get the 2 middle values, then get their average!

STEP 1: We need to **enter the *MEDIAN* function in a blank cell**:

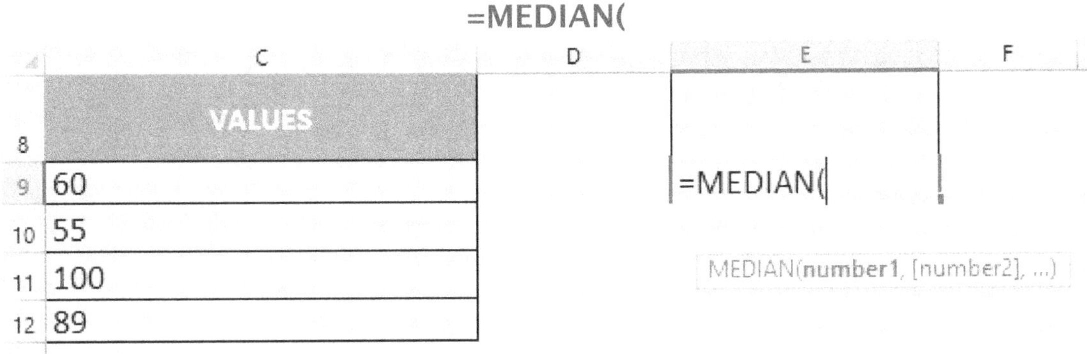

STEP 2: The **MEDIAN** arguments:

number1, [number2], ...

What is the range of values?

Select the cells containing your values:

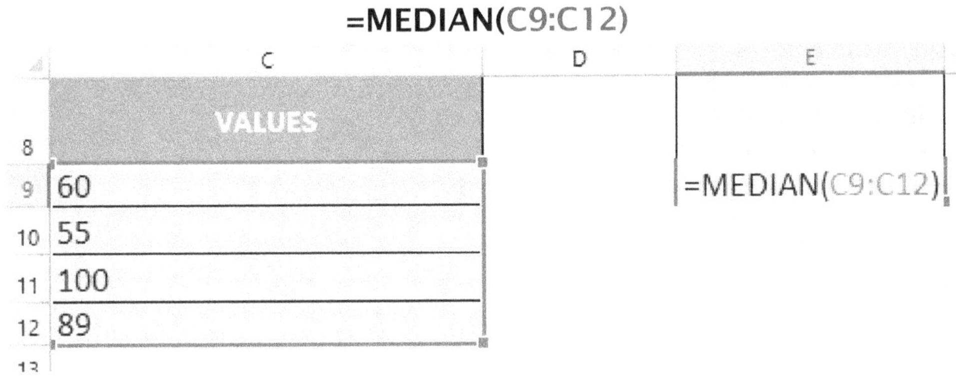

You now have your **median**! It is calculated as the average of the 2 middle values since we have an even number of values: **(60 + 89) / 2 = 74.50**

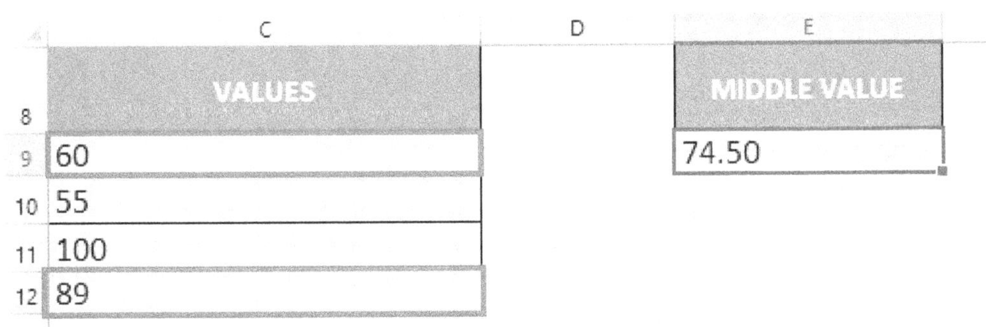

MIN

What does it do?

Get the smallest value from a range of values

Formula breakdown:

=MIN(number1, [number2], ...)

What it means:

=MIN(a number or range of values, [additional numbers], ...)

Example:

=MIN(60,55,100,89) = 55

i.e. 55 is the smallest number in the range {60;55;100;89}

If you want to get the smallest value out of a list of values, just one use of Excel's **MIN Formula** gives you the answer instantly!

STEP 1: We need to **enter the *MIN* function in a blank cell:**

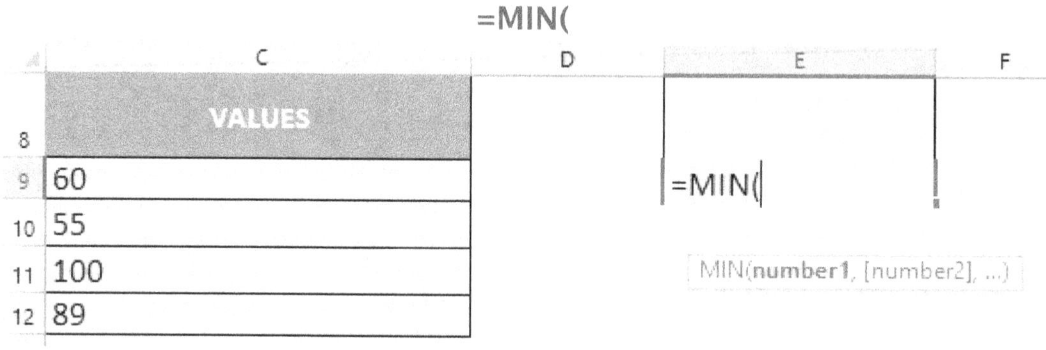

number1, [number2], ...
Where is the list of values?

Select the cells containing the values that you want to get the minimum value from.

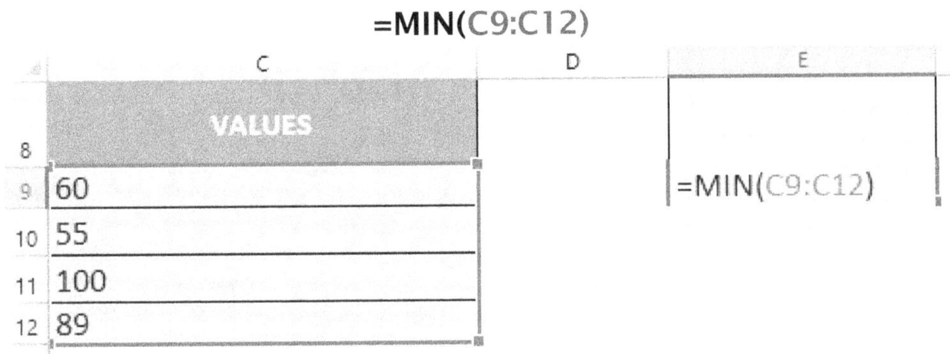

You now have the minimum value of 55 from the list!

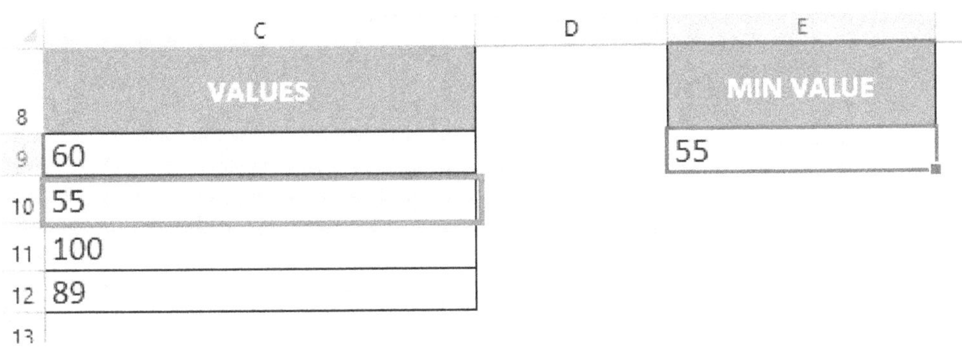

SMALL

What does it do?

Get the nth smallest value from a range of values

Formula breakdown:

=SMALL(array, k)

What it means:

=SMALL(range of values, position of the smallest value)

Example:

=SMALL(C9:C12, 3) = 89

i.e. 89 is the 3rd smallest value in the range {60;55;100;89}

You have a list of values and you want to get the third (or nth) smallest value, no problem! Excel's **SMALL Formula** can easily get that for you!

STEP 1: We need to **enter the *SMALL* function in a blank cell:**

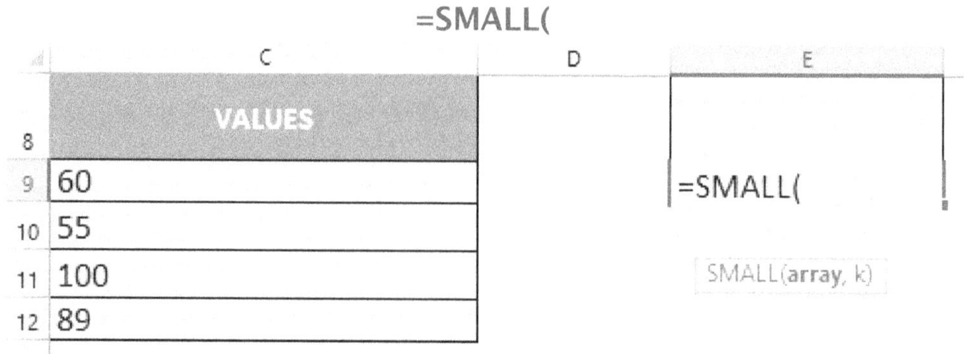

array

What is the range of values?

Select the cells containing your values:

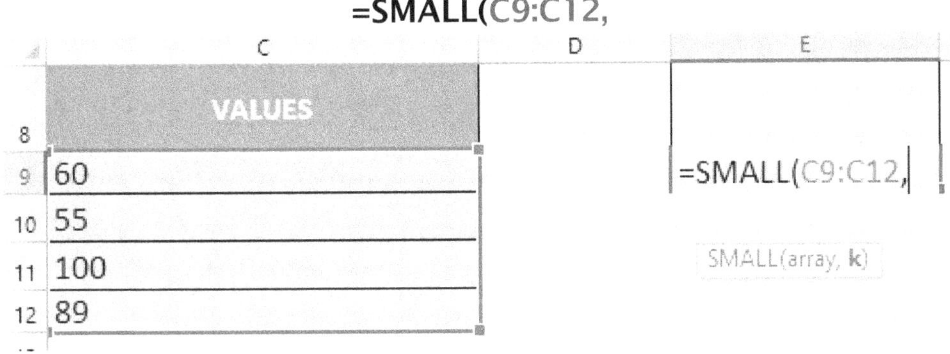

What is the nth smallest value that you want to get?

We want to get the third smallest value so we will place in 3.

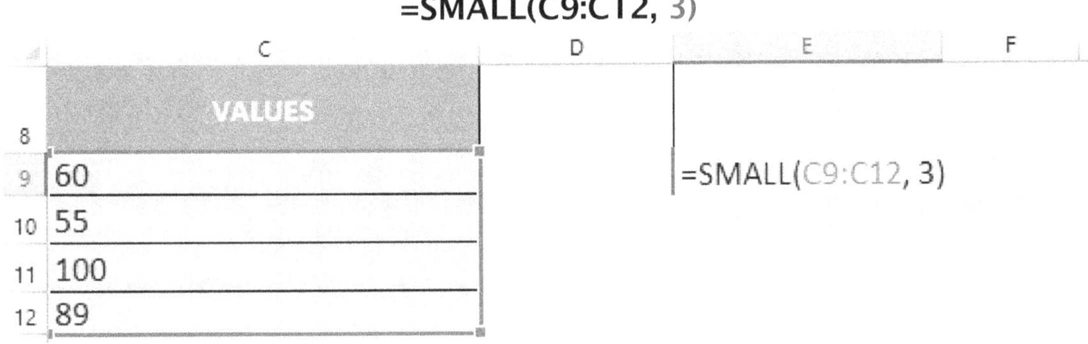

You now have your third smallest value!

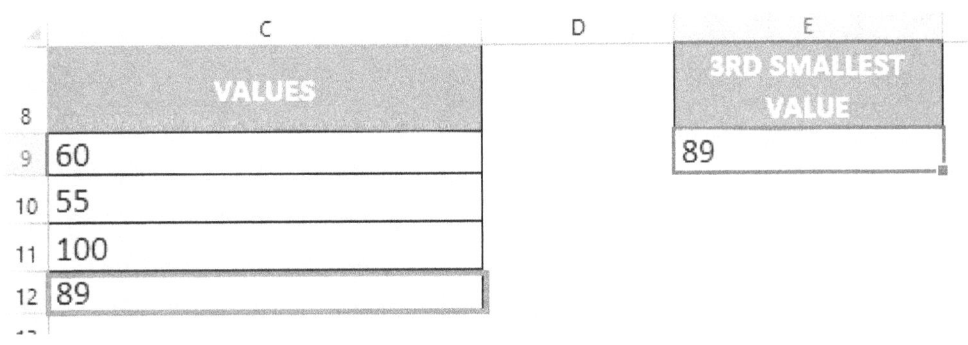

TEXT FUNCTIONS

CLEAN

What does it do?

Removes all nonprintable characters from text

Formula breakdown:

=CLEAN(text)

What it means:

=CLEAN(this dirty text cell)

Example:

=CLEAN(23) =234

There are times when imported text from other applications contain characters that are unprintable. The **CLEAN** formula in Excel can clean up the unprintable characters easily.

STEP 1: We need to **enter the** *Clean* **function**

=CLEAN

 The Clean argument:

Which text do we want to clean the dirty characters from?

This is our data source:

IMPORTED VALUE	CLEANED VALUE
254686698⊠	
25468⊠⌁87	
2⊞4686988	
2546-⊡⊠989	
2546⊙6990	

Reference the cell which has the dirty data:

=CLEAN(C9)

IMPORTED VALUE	
254686698⊠	=CLEAN(C9)
25468⊠⌁87	
2⊞4686988	
2546-⊡⊠989	
2546⊙6990	

STEP 3: Do the same for the rest of the cells by using the **CLEAN** formula, notice all of the unprintable characters (Wingdings) have been cleaned:

IMPORTED VALUE	CLEANED VALUE
254686698⊠	254686986
25468⊠⌁87	254686987
2⊞4686988	254686988
2546-⊡⊠989	254686989
2546⊙6990	254686990

CONCATENATE

What does it do?

Joins two or more text strings into one string. The item can be a text value, number, or cell reference.

Formula breakdown:

=CONCATENATE(text1, [text2], [text3], ...)

What it means:

=CONCATENATE(the first text, the second text, and so on...)

Example:

=CONCATENATE("Hello", " ", "World") = "Hello World"

Excel's **CONCATENATE** functions joins two or more text strings into one string. The item can be a text value, number, or cell reference.

If you add a double quotation with a space in between " " then this will add a space between the texts selected on either side.

You can also add a line break in between each text string. This is done by entering the **CHAR(10)** function in between each text string/argument. You will then need to select WRAP TEXT in order to see each text on a separate line.

See how easy this is to implement this by using employee data on the example below.

=CONCATENATE(

	A	B	C	D	E
11	**SALES REPRESENTATIVE**	**EMAIL**	**DEPARTMENT**	**PHONE EXTENSION**	**CONCATENATE**
12	Homer Simpson	hs@email.com	MARKETING	3456	=CONCATENATE(
13	Ian Wright	iw@email.com	SALES	2566	
14	John Michaloudis	jm@email.com	FINANCE	2642	
15	Michael Jackson	mj@email.com	SHIPPING	3455	
16					
17					
18					
19					

STEP 2: The **CONCATENATE** arguments:

text1, [text2], [text3], ...

Which text do you want to join together?

Let us select all the columns:

=CONCATENATE(A12, B12, C12, D12)

	A	B	C	D	E
11	**SALES REPRESENTATIVE**	**EMAIL**	**DEPARTMENT**	**PHONE EXTENSION**	**CONCATENATE**
12	Homer Simpson	hs@email.com	MARKETING	3456	=CONCATENATE(A12,B12,C12,D12)
13	Ian Wright	iw@email.com	SALES	2566	
14	John Michaloudis	jm@email.com	FINANCE	2642	
15	Michael Jackson	mj@email.com	SHIPPING	3455	
16					
17					
18					

Now let's add the function CHAR(10) to add a line break between each text

=CONCATENATE(A12, CHAR(10), B12, CHAR(10), C12, CHAR(10), D12)

	A	B	C	D	E	F	G
11	**SALES REPRESENTATIVE**	**EMAIL**	**DEPARTMENT**	**PHONE EXTENSION**	**CONCATENATE**		
12	Homer Simpson	hs@email.com	MARKETING		=CONCATENATE(A12, CHAR(10), B12, CHAR(10), C12, CHAR(10), D12)		
13	Ian Wright	iw@email.com	SALES	2566			
14	John Michaloudis	jm@email.com	FINANCE	2642			
15	Michael Jackson	mj@email.com	SHIPPING	3455			

Apply the same formula to the rest of the cells by dragging the lower right corner downwards.

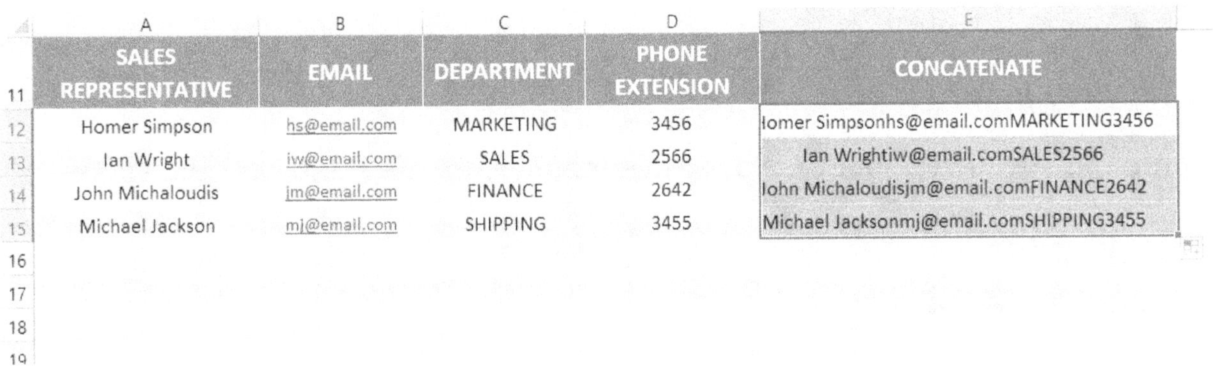

STEP 3: Go to *Home > Alignment > Wrap Text* to show the text in multiple lines and you now have all of results!

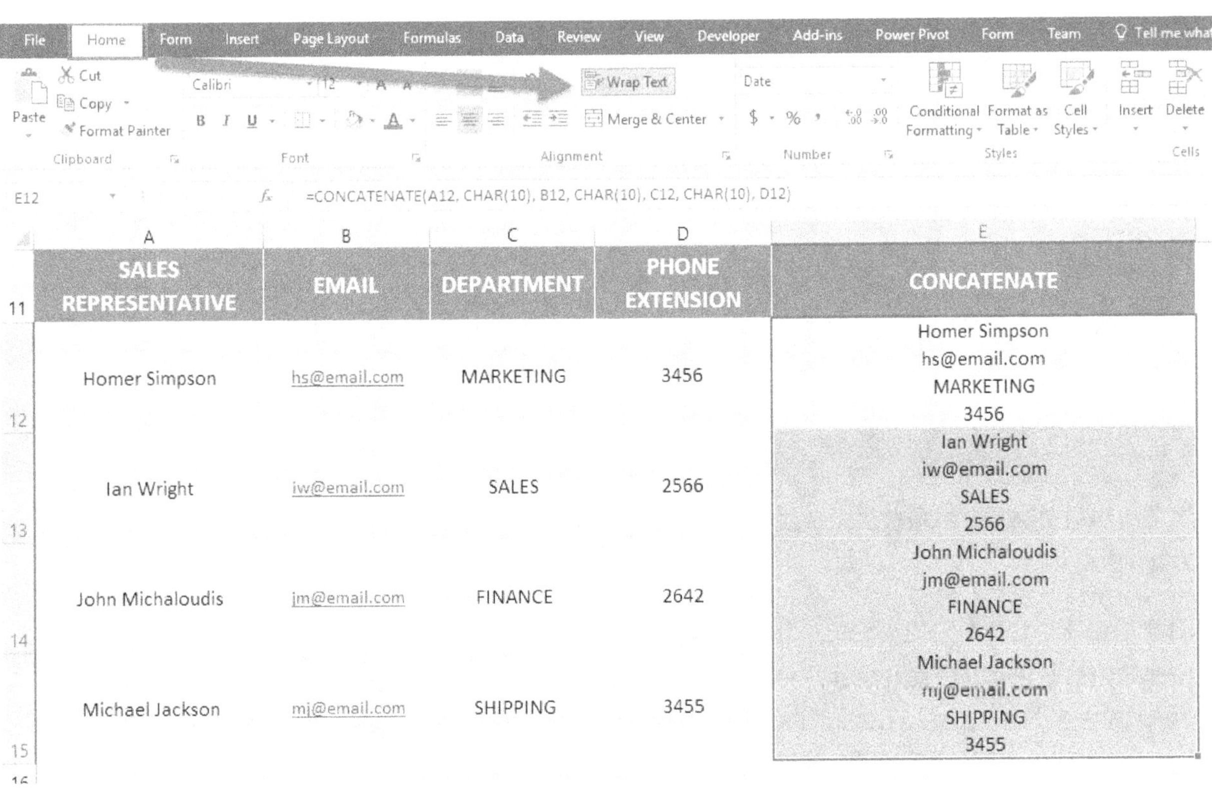

EXACT

What does it do?

Compares two texts, in a case-sensitive manner, to see if they are the same

Formula breakdown:

=EXACT(text1, text2)

What it means:

=EXACT(first text to be compared, second text to be compared)

Example:

=EXACT("EXCEL","ExCEL") =FALSE

We can easily compare two texts if they are equal or not with the **EXACT formula.**

But I can hear you say now, hold on, I can easily do that with the equal (sign) operator! The difference is, equal compares text and does not consider case sensitivity. However the **EXACT formula** compares text in a **case-sensitive manner.**

=EXACT(

	C	D	E
8	**TEXT #1**	**TEXT #2**	
9	Excel	Excel	=EXACT(
10	EXCEL	ExCEL	
11	excel	excel	EXACT(text1, text2)
12	Excel	excel	

STEP 2: The **EXACT** arguments:

text1

What is the first text to be compared?

Select the cell containing leftmost text that you want to compare:

=EXACT(C9,

	C	D	E
8	**TEXT #1**	**TEXT #2**	
9	Excel	Excel	=EXACT(C9,
10	EXCEL	ExCEL	
11	excel	excel	EXACT(text1, text2)
12	Excel	excel	

What is the second text to be compared?

Select the cell containing rightmost text that you want to compare:

=EXACT(C9, D9)

	TEXT #1	TEXT #2	
8			
9	Excel	Excel	=EXACT(C9,D9)
10	EXCEL	ExCEL	
11	excel	excel	
12	Excel	excel	

Apply the same formula to the rest of the cells by dragging the lower right corner downwards.

You can see that the Excel values that have different capital letters have a **FALSE** result! (e.g. EXCEL vs. ExCEL)

	TEXT #1	TEXT #2	ARE THEY THE SAME?
8			
9	Excel	Excel	TRUE
10	EXCEL	ExCEL	FALSE
11	excel	excel	TRUE
12	Excel	excel	FALSE
13			

FIND

What does it do?

Gets the position of a specific text within another text

Formula breakdown:

=FIND(find_text, within_text, [start_num])

What it means:

=FIND(text to be searched, the source text, [starting position of the source text])

Example:

=FIND("x","Excel",1) =2

If you want to check where a specific text is located in the source text, it is very easy to search for the position using the **FIND Formula**!

You need to take note that the **FIND Formula** is **case-sensitive** when searching for your text! And it always matches the **first occurrence**. We will see in our examples below!

 We need to **enter the _FIND_ function in a blank cell**:

=FIND(

	C	D	E	F	G
	SOURCE TEXT	**SEARCH TEXT**			
8					
9	Excel	x	=FIND(		
10	Excel with excel 2019	excel			
11	How are you?	o	FIND(find_text, within_text, [start_num])		
12	Can you find this?	excel			

STEP 2: The **FIND** arguments:

_find_text_

What is the text to be searched for?

Select the cell containing the text to be searched for. In our first example, we want to search for 'x' in the word 'Excel':

=FIND(D9,

	C	D	E	F	G
	SOURCE TEXT	**SEARCH TEXT**			
8					
9	Excel	x	=FIND(D9,		
10	Excel with excel 2019	excel			
11	How are you?	o	FIND(find_text, within_text, [start_num])		
12	Can you find this?	excel			

_within_text_

What is your source text?

Select the cell source text. So let's select 'Excel' as our source text:

=FIND(D9, C9,

	C	D	E	F	G
	SOURCE TEXT	**SEARCH TEXT**			
8					
9	Excel	x	=FIND(D9,C9,		
10	Excel with excel 2019	excel			
11	How are you?	o	FIND(find_text, within_text, [start_num])		
12	Can you find this?	excel			

Where do you want to start searching in your source text?

You can leave this blank, it will default to 1 which means it will start looking from the first character of your source text. In our case, let us put in 1 to start searching from there:

=FIND(D9, C9, 1)

	SOURCE TEXT	SEARCH TEXT	
8			
9	Excel	x	=FIND(D9,C9,1)
10	Excel with excel 2019	excel	
11	How are you?	o	
12	Can you find this?	excel	

Apply the same formula to the rest of the cells by dragging the lower right corner downwards.

	SOURCE TEXT	SEARCH TEXT	POSITION
8			
9	Excel	x	2
10	Excel with excel 2019	excel	
11	How are you?	o	
12	Can you find this?	excel	
13			

You can see that the matching is **case sensitive**! And if it's unable to find your text, it will return **#VALUE.**

	SOURCE TEXT	SEARCH TEXT	POSITION
8			
9	Excel	x	2
10	Excel with excel 2019	excel	12
11	How are you?	o	2
12	Can you find this?	excel	#VALUE!
13			

LEFT

What does it do?

It returns the first character or characters in a text string, based on the number of characters you specify.

Formula breakdown:

=LEFT(text, [num_chars])

What it means:

=LEFT(look in this cell, extract X characters)

Example:

=LEFT("19281013-2",8) = 19281013

There are times when you will need to extract the first few characters of text within a cell, e.g. From a serial number, part number, name, phone number etc.

The **LEFT** formula in Excel can help you parse and extract the needed text easily.

In our example below, we have a Part # which has 10 characters and we want to extract all the characters before the hyphen "-".

STEP 1: We need to **enter the *LEFT* function** next to the cell that we want to extract the data from:

$$=LEFT($$

STEP 2: The **LEFT** arguments:

text

Which text do we want to extract the first X characters from?

Reference the cell that contains the text or value:

$$=LEFT(C9$$

C	D
PART #	**NEW PART #**
19281013-2	=LEFT(C9
20767748-5	LEFT(text, [num_chars])
46612687-k	
10017191-0	
34793800-9	
46677751-k	

[num_chars]

How many characters do we want to extract from cell C9?

Enter a positive number only:

$$=LEFT(C9, 8)$$

	PART #	NEW PART #
8		
9	19281013-2	=LEFT(C9,8)
10	20767748-5	
11	46612687-k	
12	10017191-0	
13	34793800-9	
14	46677751-k	

STEP 3: Do the same for the rest of the cells by dragging the **LEFT** formula all the way down using the left mouse button.

Notice all of the first 8 characters in each text are now extracted:

PART #	NEW PART #
19281013-2	19281013
20767748-5	20767748
46612687-k	46612687
10017191-0	10017191
34793800-9	34793800
46677751-k	46677751

LEN

What does it do?

Gives you the number of characters in a text string

Formula breakdown:

=LEN(text)

What it means:

=LEN(text that you want to get the number of characters from)

Example:

=LEN("John Michaloudis") =16

There are times when you need to get the number of characters within a cell in Excel. Thankfully this is very easy to do with Excel's **LEN (Length) formula!**

You can use the LEN function in Excel to **count all characters** in a cell, including letters, numbers, special characters, and all spaces.

The LEN function can be used as a data cleansing technique to find leading or trailing spaces or can be nested with other TEXT functions.

STEP 1: We need to **enter the LEN function** next to the cell that we want to get the number of characters from:

=LEN(

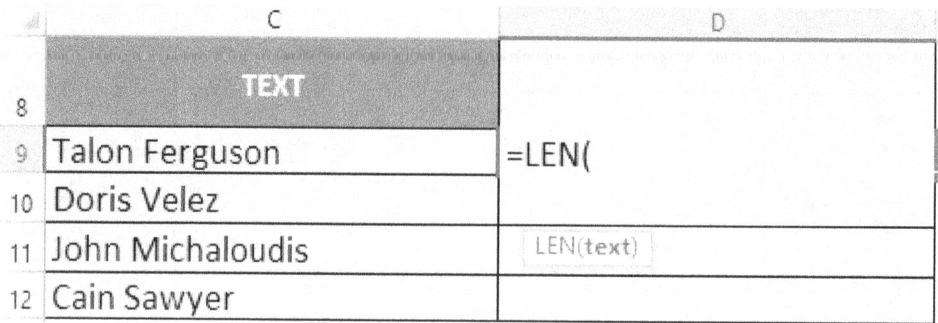

STEP 2: The **LEN** arguments:

text

Which text do we want to get the number of characters from?

Reference the cell that contains the text string:

=LEN(C9)

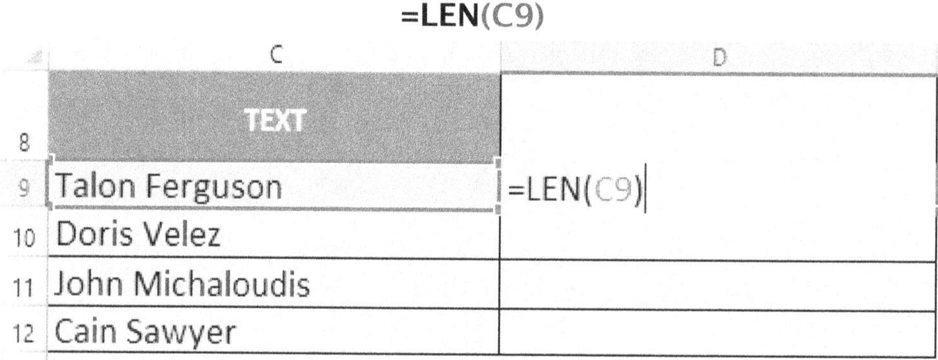

STEP 3: Do the same for the rest of the cells by dragging the **LEN** formula all the way down using the left mouse button.

Note that you are able to get the number of characters for each name. My name has 16 characters (including the space)!

	TEXT	NUMBER OF CHARACTERS
9	Talon Ferguson	14
10	Doris Velez	11
11	John Michaloudis	16
12	Cain Sawyer	11
13		

LOWER

What does it do?

Converts all characters in the text string into lowercase

Formula breakdown:

=LOWER(text)

What it means:

=LOWER(text to be converted to lower case)

Example:

=LOWER("EXCEL ROCKS!") = "excel rocks!"

We can easily change text into a lower case using the **LOWER formula** in Excel. It does not convert symbols and numbers though, which we will see in the examples.

If you want to get rid of uneven capitalization throughout the text, then this formula is perfect for you!

STEP 1: We need to **enter the *LOWER* function in a blank cell**:

=LOWER(

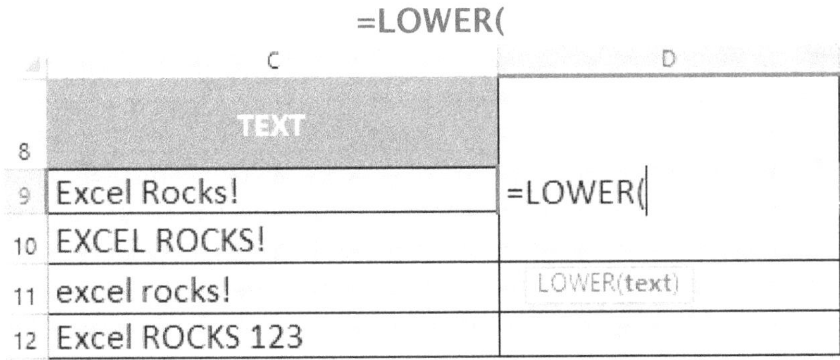

text

What is the text to be converted to lower case?

Select the cell containing the text that you want to convert:

=LOWER(C9)

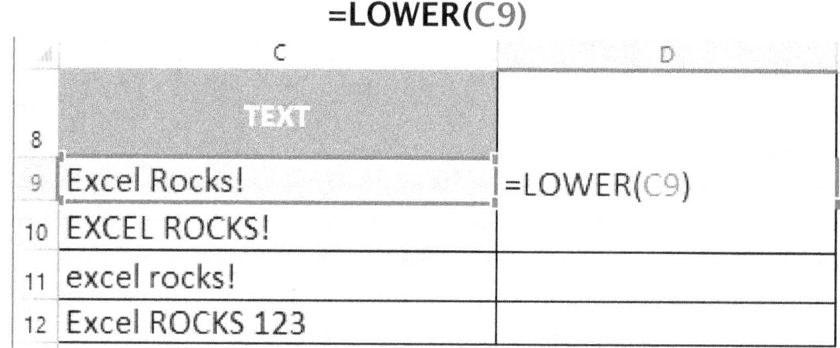

Apply the same formula to the rest of the cells by dragging the lower right corner downwards.

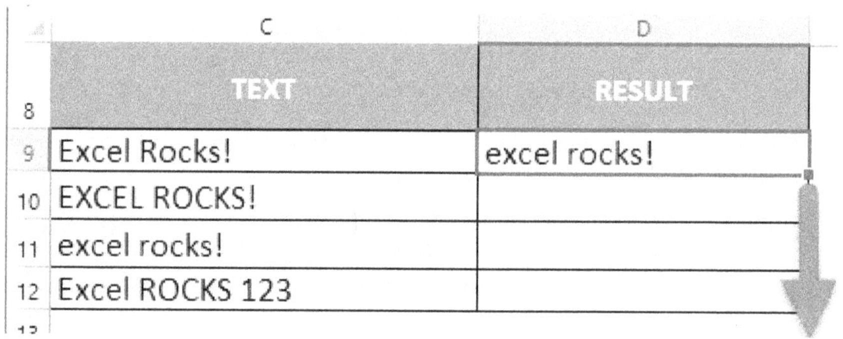

You can see that the values are all now in lower case!

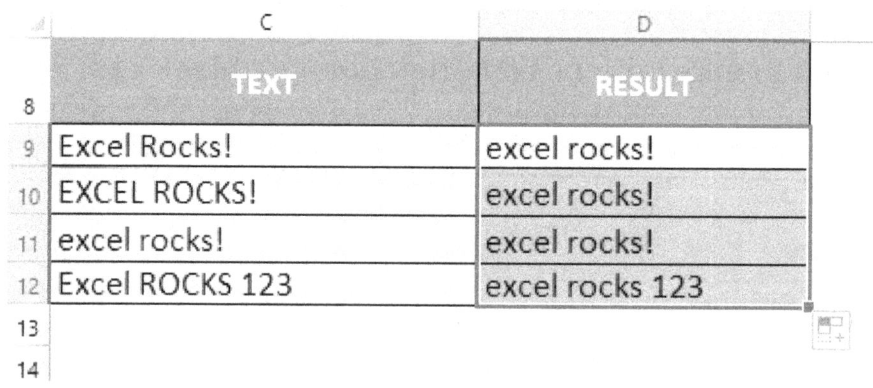

MID

What does it do?

Extracts a specific number of characters from the middle of a text

Formula breakdown:

=MID(text, start_num, num_chars)

What it means:

=MID(source text, starting position to extract text, number of characters to extract)

Example:

=MID("How are you?", 5, 3) ="are"

Ever wanted to get something in the middle of your text? And you're doing it by hand? It is very easy to do this in Excel with the **MID Formula!**

It allows you to extract any number of characters from the middle of your text!

STEP 1: We need to **enter the *MID* function in a blank cell**:

=MID(

	C	D	E	F	G	H
	SOURCE TEXT	START POSITION	NUMBER OF CHARACTERS			
9	How are you?	1	3	=MID(		
10	How are you?	5	3			
11	How are you?	9	3	MID(text, start_num, num_chars)		

text

What is the source text?

Select the cell containing the source text that you want to extract from:

=MID(C9,

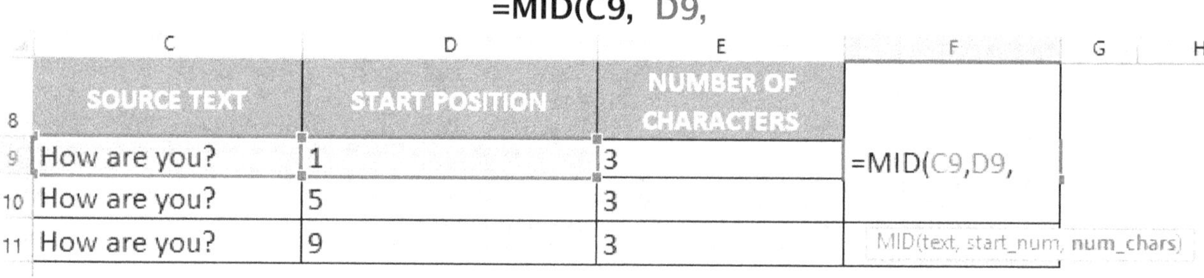

start_num

What position will we start extracting the text from?

Select the cell containing our starting position. This is where the MID formula will start extracting the text from:

=MID(C9, D9,

	SOURCE TEXT	START POSITION	NUMBER OF CHARACTERS			
	C	D	E	F	G	H
8						
9	How are you?	1	3	=MID(C9,D9,		
10	How are you?	5	3			
11	How are you?	9	3	MID(text, start_num, num_chars)		

How many characters do we want to extract?

Select the cell containing the number of characters. In our case, we want to extract 3 characters:

=MID(C9, D9, E9)

	SOURCE TEXT	START POSITION	NUMBER OF CHARACTERS		
8				F	G
9	How are you?	1	3	=MID(C9, D9, E9)	
10	How are you?	5	3		
11	How are you?	9	3		

Apply the same formula to the rest of the cells by dragging the lower right corner downwards.

	SOURCE TEXT	START POSITION	NUMBER OF CHARACTERS	EXTRACTED TEXT
9	How are you?	1	3	How
10	How are you?	5	3	
11	How are you?	9	3	

You now have your extracted text! In our scenario, we tried to extract the different words in the phrase "How are you?"

	SOURCE TEXT	START POSITION	NUMBER OF CHARACTERS	EXTRACTED TEXT
9	How are you?	1	3	How
10	How are you?	5	3	are
11	How are you?	9	3	you
12				
13				

PROPER

What does it do?

Capitalizes the first letter in a text string and any other letters in the text that follow a space. Converts all other letters to lowercase letters.

Formula breakdown:

=PROPER(text)

What it means:

=PROPER(this text cell)

Example:

=PROPER("STUART POWELL") ="Stuart Powell"

There are times when you will need to only CAPITALIZE the first letter in each word. The most common scenario would be when you receive data with employee names, countries or cities that are all in lower or uppercase.

The **PROPER** formula in Excel can help you format the text very very easily...goodbye manual adjustments!

In our example below, we have a list of names in capital letters. However we want to show the capital letters only on the first letter of each word.

STEP 1: We need to **enter the *PROPER* function** next to the cell that we want to clean the data from:

=PROPER

text

Which text do we want to change?

Reference the cell that contains the text string:

=PROPER(C10)

	C	D
9	**FULL NAME**	
10	STUART POWELL	=PROPER(C10)
11	GARY O'MALEY	
12	COLLEEN VALENTINE	
13	QUINLAN MERRILL	
14	JEREMY RUIZ	
15	YOSHIO PAUL	

STEP 3: Do the same for the rest of the cells by dragging the **PROPER** formula all the way down using the left mouse button.

Note that all of the names are now properly formatted:

	C	D
9	**FULL NAME**	**PROPER NAME**
10	STUART POWELL	Stuart Powell
11	GARY O'MALEY	Gary O'Maley
12	COLLEEN VALENTINE	Colleen Valentine
13	QUINLAN MERRILL	Quinlan Merrill
14	JEREMY RUIZ	Jeremy Ruiz
15	YOSHIO PAUL	Yoshio Paul

REPLACE

What does it do?

Replaces part of a text string (based on the number of characters you specify) with a different text string

Formula breakdown:

=REPLACE(old_text, start_num, num_chars, new_text)

What it means:

=REPLACE(this cell, starting from this number, all the way to this number, with this new text)

Example:

=REPLACE("+1-817-0000000", 1, FIND("-","+1-817-0000000"), "")

="817-0000000"

Once I was given a list of phone numbers in their international format. But for my needs, I did not want to include the country code and I just wanted the phone number.

I was looking for a quick way to remove the country code.

I discovered a cool way to do this using the **REPLACE** formula! Goodbye to manual adjustments!

STEP 1: We need to **enter the _Replace_ function** next to the cell that we want to clean the data from:

=REPLACE

	C	D	E	F
9	**PHONE NUMBER**			
10	+1-817-0000000	=REPLACE		
11	+1-817-1111111			
12	+1-817-2222222	_fx_ REPLACE Replaces part of a text string with a different text string		
13	+1-817-3333333			
14	+1-817-4444444			
15	+1-817-5555555			

STEP 2: The Replace arguments:

_old_text_

Which text do we want to change?

Reference the cell that contains the text string:

=REPLACE(C10,

	C	D	E
9	**PHONE NUMBER**		
10	+1-817-0000000	=REPLACE(C10,	
11	+1-817-1111111		
12	+1-817-2222222	REPLACE(old_text, **start_num**, num_chars, new_text)	
13	+1-817-3333333		
14	+1-817-4444444		
15	+1-817-5555555		

_start_num_

Which character do we want to start the replacement from?

We want to remove the country code, so it starts from the first character.

=REPLACE(C10, 1,

	C	D	E
9	**PHONE NUMBER**		
10	+1-817-0000000	=REPLACE(C10, 1,	
11	+1-817-1111111		
12	+1-817-2222222	REPLACE(old_text, start_num, **num_chars**, new_text)	
13	+1-817-3333333		
14	+1-817-4444444		
15	+1-817-5555555		

num_chars

How many characters do we want to replace?

We want to remove all characters up to and including the first hyphen.

We will use the **FIND** formula.

FIND("-", C10) will get the location of the first hyphen i.e. The 3rd place

=REPLACE(C10, 1, FIND("-", C10),

	C	D	E
9	**PHONE NUMBER**		
10	+1-817-0000000	=REPLACE(C10, 1, FIND("-",C10),	
11	+1-817-1111111		
12	+1-817-2222222	REPLACE(old_text, start_num, **num_chars**, new_text)	
13	+1-817-3333333		
14	+1-817-4444444		
15	+1-817-5555555		

What text will serve as the replacement?

Since we want to remove this, you guessed it! We want the value to be an empty string which is depicted by the double quotations.

=REPLACE(C10, 1, FIND("-", C10), " ")

	PHONE NUMBER	
9		
10	+1-817-0000000	=REPLACE(C10, 1, FIND("-",C10), "")
11	+1-817-1111111	
12	+1-817-2222222	
13	+1-817-3333333	
14	+1-817-4444444	
15	+1-817-5555555	

STEP 3: Do the same for the rest of the cells by dragging the **REPLACE** formula all the way down using the left mouse button.

Note that all of the phone numbers are now clean:

	PHONE NUMBER	NEW PHONE NUMBER
9		
10	+1-817-0000000	817-0000000
11	+1-817-1111111	817-1111111
12	+1-817-2222222	817-2222222
13	+1-817-3333333	817-3333333
14	+1-817-4444444	817-4444444
15	+1-817-5555555	817-5555555
16		

RIGHT

What does it do?

It returns the last character or characters in a text string, based on the number of characters you specify.

Formula breakdown:

=RIGHT(text, [num_chars])

What it means:

=RIGHT(look in this cell, extract X characters)

Example:

=RIGHT("6018 Libero St. 38390", 5) ="38390"

There are times when you will need to extract the last few characters of text within a cell, e.g. From a serial number, part number, name, address etc.

The **RIGHT** formula in Excel can help you parse and extract the needed text easily.

In our example below, we have an address which has a zip code at the end (the zip code is fixed at 5 characters long) and we want to extract all of the zip codes in our address list.

STEP 1: We need to **enter the RIGHT function** next to the cell that we want to extract the data from:

=RIGHT

text

Which text do we want to extract the last X characters from?

Reference the cell that contains the text or value:

=RIGHT(C9

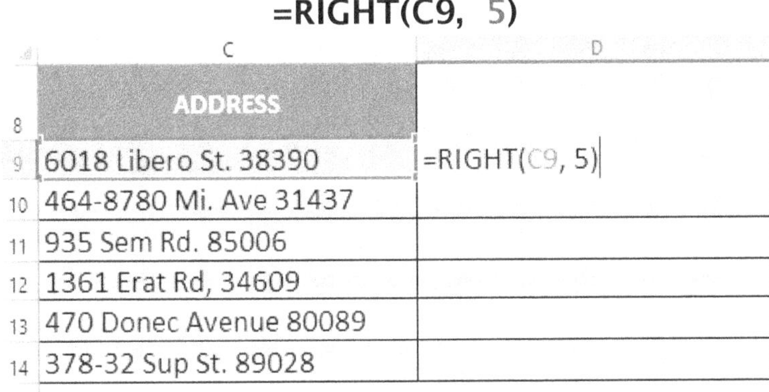

[num_chars]

How many characters from the right do we want to extract from cell C9?

Enter a positive number only:

=RIGHT(C9, 5)

STEP 3: Do the same for the rest of the cells by dragging the **RIGHT** formula all the way down. Notice all of the last 5 characters in each text are now extracted:

	C	D
8	**ADDRESS**	**ZIP CODE**
9	6018 Libero St. 38390	38390
10	464-8780 Mi. Ave 31437	31437
11	935 Sem Rd. 85006	85006
12	1361 Erat Rd, 34609	34609
13	470 Donec Avenue 80089	80089
14	378-32 Sup St. 89028	89028

SEARCH

What does it do?

Gets the position of a specific text within another text and allows wildcards * ?

Formula breakdown:

=SEARCH(find_text, within_text, [start_num])

What it means:

=SEARCH(text to be searched, the source text, [starting position of the source text])

Example:

=SEARCH("excel", "Excel with excel 2019", 1) =1

If you want to check where a specific text is located in the source text, it is very easy to search for the position using the **SEARCH Formula**!

You might be wondering on what makes it different from the FIND Formula. The **SEARCH formula** is **case-insensitive** when searching for text, and it also allows for the use of **wildcard characters like * and ?**

It is very cool when **wildcard characters** are used. The **? character** represents any single character, while * represents any number of characters.

STEP 1: We need to **enter the *SEARCH* function in a blank cell**:

=SEARCH(

	SOURCE TEXT	SEARCH TEXT	
8			=SEARCH(
9	Excel	x	
10	Excel with excel 2019	excel	SEARCH(find_text, within_text, [start_num])
11	How are you?	H?w	
12	Can you find this?	f*	

STEP 2: The **SEARCH** arguments:

find_text

What is the text to be searched for? These are the settings you can do:

- ? matches **any single character** while * matches **any number of characters**.
- For example, if we place in **H?w**, then we want to search for any 3-character text that starts with H and ends with w
- If we change it to **H*w**, then we want to search for any text that starts with H and ends with w
- If ever you want to match the question mark (?) or asterisk character (*) **literally**, you will have to add a **tilde character (~)** before the character. For example, ~? and ~*

Select the cell containing the text to be searched for. In our first example, we want to search for 'x' in the word 'Excel':

=SEARCH(D9,

	SOURCE TEXT	SEARCH TEXT	
8			
9	Excel	x	=SEARCH(D9,
10	Excel with excel 2019	excel	
11	How are you?	H?w	SEARCH(find_text, within_text, [start_num])
12	Can you find this?	f*	

within_text

What is your source text? *So let's select 'Excel' as our source text:*

=SEARCH(D9, C9,

	SOURCE TEXT	SEARCH TEXT	
8			
9	Excel	x	=SEARCH(D9, C9,
10	Excel with excel 2019	excel	
11	How are you?	H?w	SEARCH(find_text, within_text, [start_num])
12	Can you find this?	f*	
13			

Where do you want to start searching in your source text?

You can leave this blank, it will default to 1 which means it will start looking from the first character of your source text. In our case, let us put in 1 to start searching from there:

=SEARCH(D9, C9, 1)

	SOURCE TEXT	SEARCH TEXT	
8			
9	Excel	x	=SEARCH(D9, C9, 1)
10	Excel with excel 2019	excel	
11	How are you?	H?w	
12	Can you find this?	f*	

Apply the same formula to the rest of the cells by dragging the lower right corner downwards.

	SOURCE TEXT	SEARCH TEXT	POSITION
8			
9	Excel	x	2
10	Excel with excel 2019	excel	
11	How are you?	H?w	
12	Can you find this?	f*	

You can see that the matching is **case insensitive**! And you can see our **wildcard characters** matching in action!

	SOURCE TEXT	SEARCH TEXT	POSITION
8			
9	Excel	x	2
10	Excel with excel 2019	excel	1
11	How are you?	H?w	1
12	Can you find this?	f*	9

SUBSTITUTE

What does it do?

Substitutes *new text* for *old text* in a text string.

Formula breakdown:

=SUBSTITUTE(text, old_text, new_text, [instance num])

What it means:

=SUBSTITUTE(In this cell, Substitute this text, With this new text, [In the 1st, 2nd...instance it occurs])

Example:

=SUBSTITUTE("C97-27-JT", "-", "#", 2) ="C97-27#JT"

When you needed to substitute a specific text in each word, and there is a pattern, Excel has just the formula for you.

The **SUBSTITUTE** formula in Excel can help you replace one specific text with another easily.

In our example below, we have a list of part numbers.

We want to replace the second dash - with the number sign # . This formula is able to do this for us.

STEP 1: We need to **enter the *Substitute* function** next to the cell that we want to clean the data from:

=SUBSTITUTE

8	PART #	=SUBSTITUTE
9	C97-27-JT	
10	T28-24-FG	
11	F34-68-LJ	
12	S63-86-LL	
13	P73-57-UB	
14	H26-82-HH	

STEP 2: The Substitute arguments:

text

Which text do we want to change?

Reference the cell that contains the text or value:

=SUBSTITUTE(C9,

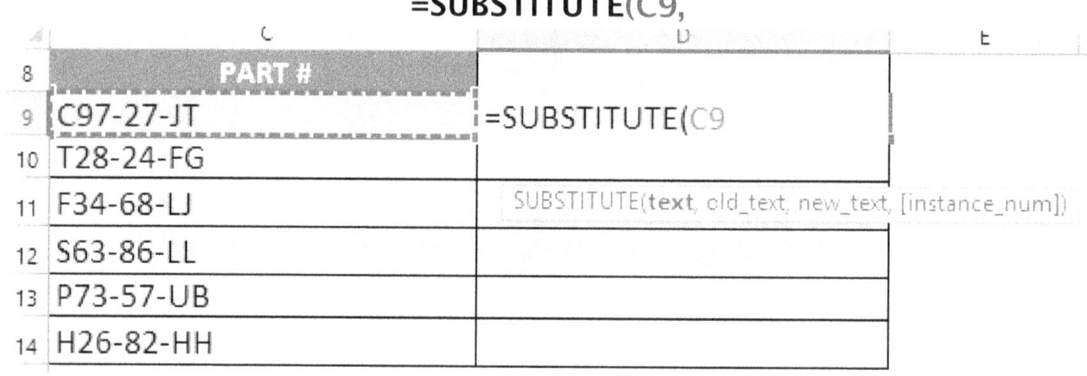

old_text

Which text / characters do we want to replace?

We want to replace the dash -   so type it in with double quotations:

=SUBSTITUTE(C9, "-",

new_text

Which text / characters do we want to replace it with?

We want to replace it with the number sign # so type it in with double quotations:

=SUBSTITUTE(C9, "-", "#",

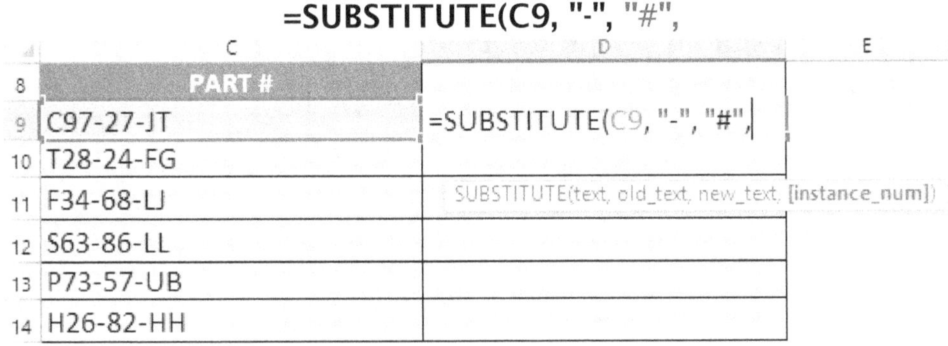

[instance num]

Which specific instance are we targeting the substitution on?

This parameter is optional. In our scenario, we want the second dash - only to be substituted. So place in the number 2:

=SUBSTITUTE(C9, "-", "#", 2)

STEP 3: Do the same for the rest of the cells by dragging the **SUBSTITUTE** formula all the way down using the left mouse button.

Note that all of the parts are now changed to your new part values:

	PART #	NEW PART #
9	C97-27-JT	C97-27#JT
10	T28-24-FG	T28-24#FG
11	F34-68-LJ	F34-68#LJ
12	S63-86-LL	S63-86#LL
13	P73-57-UB	P73-57#UB
14	H26-82-HH	H26-82#HH

TEXT

What does it do?

Converts a numeric value to text and lets you specify the display formatting by using special format strings

Formula breakdown:

=TEXT(value, format text)

What it means:

=TEXT(a numeric value or a formula, a text string enclosed in quotation marks)

Example:

=TEXT(25/12/2015 21:33:55,"dd/mm/yy") = 25/12/15

The **TEXT** function in Excel allows you to convert a numeric value to a specific format by using special format strings.

If you have a date and want to show just the month or if you have a large number and want to show it in a thousands format , then the **TEXT** function is your savior.

An example usage of the **TEXT** would be:

	A	B	C
	VALUE	**FORMAT**	**DISPLAYS AS**
23	25/12/15 9:33 PM	"dd/mm/yy"	=+TEXT(A23,"dd/mm/yy")

	A	B	C
	VALUE	**FORMAT**	**DISPLAYS AS**
23	25/12/15 9:33 PM	"dd/mm/yy"	25/12/15

Following is a demonstration and a table of the different ways you can display a value in Excel by using the **TEXT** function:

To display	As	Use this format
1234.59	1234.6	"####.#"
8.9	8.900	"#.000"
0.631	0.6	"0.#"
1234.568	1234.6	"#.0#"
5.25	5 1/4	"# ???/???"
12000	12000	"#,###"
12000	12	"#,"
12200000	12.2	"0.0,,"
Months	1–12	"m"
Months	01–12	"mm"
Months	Jan–Dec	"mmm"
Months	January–December	"mmmm"
Months	J–D	"mmmmm"
Days	1–31	"d"
Days	01–31	"dd"
Days	Sun–Sat	"ddd"
Days	Sunday–Saturday	"dddd"
Years	00–99	"yy"
Years	1900–9999	"yyyy"
Hours	0–23	"h"
Hours	00–23	"hh"
Minutes	0–59	"m"
Minutes	00–59	"mm"
Seconds	0–59	"s"
Seconds	00–59	"ss"
Time	4:00 AM	"h AM/PM"
Time	4:36 PM	"h:mm AM/PM"
Time	4:36:03 PM	"h:mm:ss A/P"
Time	36:03.8	"h:mm:ss.00"

TRIM

What does it do?

Removes unneeded spaces in your text, except single spaces in between words

Formula breakdown:

=TRIM(text)

What it means:

=TRIM(text that you want extra spaces to be removed)

Example:

=TRIM("spaces   in   the   middle") ="spaces in the middle"

In the quest for cleaner data, one of the common scenarios is removing extra spaces in our text.

Extra spaces are very difficult to spot, especially those at the end i.e. Trailing spaces.

The **TRIM** formula in Excel is one of the Data Cleansing functions and is great if you want to remove extra spaces from text whether it be from the start (leading spaces), middle or at the end (trailing spaces) of the text.

In a nutshell, the **TRIM** function in Excel removes unneeded spaces in your text, except single spaces between words.

STEP 1: We need to **enter the TRIM function**

$$=TRIM$$

STEP 2: The Trim argument - **Which text do we want to remove the extra spaces?**

This is our data source:

TEXT	TRIMMED TEXT
extra spaces in front	
spaces in the middle	
extra spaces in the end	
spaces everywhere	

Now place in the first cell as the argument for our Trim Formula.

$$=TRIM(C9)$$

TEXT	
extra spaces in front	=TRIM(C9)
spaces in the middle	
extra spaces in the end	
spaces everywhere	

STEP 3: Do the same for the rest of the cells by using the **TRIM** formula, notice all of the extra spaces have been removed:

TEXT	TRIMMED TEXT
extra spaces in front	extra spaces in front
spaces in the middle	spaces in the middle
extra spaces in the end	extra spaces in the end
spaces everywhere	spaces everywhere

UPPER

What does it do?

Converts all characters in the text string into uppercase

Formula breakdown:

=UPPER(text)

What it means:

=UPPER(text to be converted to upper case)

Example:

=UPPER("Excel Rocks!") ="EXCEL ROCKS!"

We can easily change text into upper case using the **UPPER formula** in Excel. It does not convert symbols and numbers though which we will see in the examples.

If you want to fix the uneven capitalization throughout the text, then this formula is perfect for you!

STEP 1: We need to **enter the *UPPER* function in a blank cell**:

=UPPER(

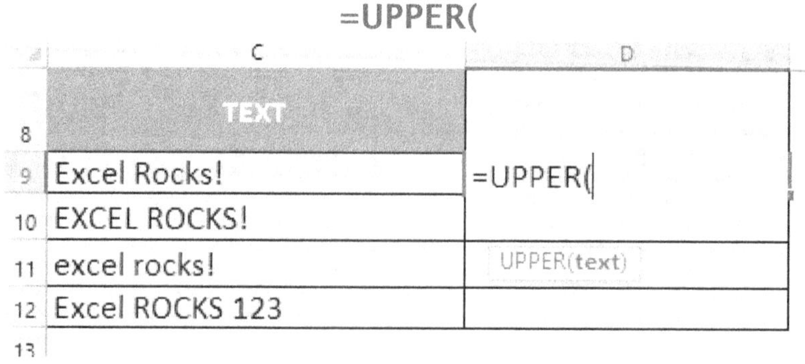

text

What is the text to be converted to upper case?

Select the cell containing the text that you want to convert:

=UPPER(C9)

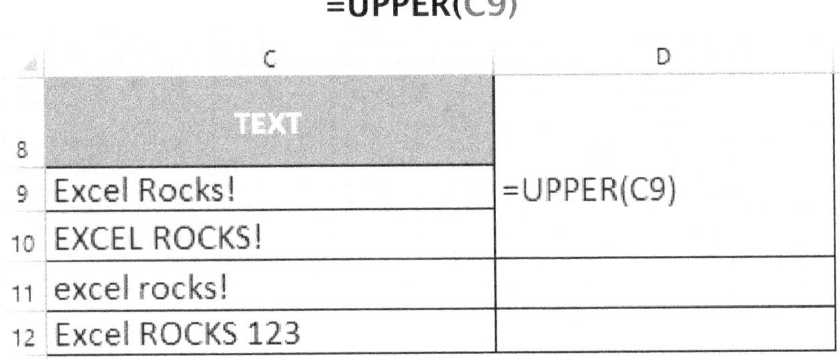

Apply the same formula to the rest of the cells by dragging the lower right corner downwards.

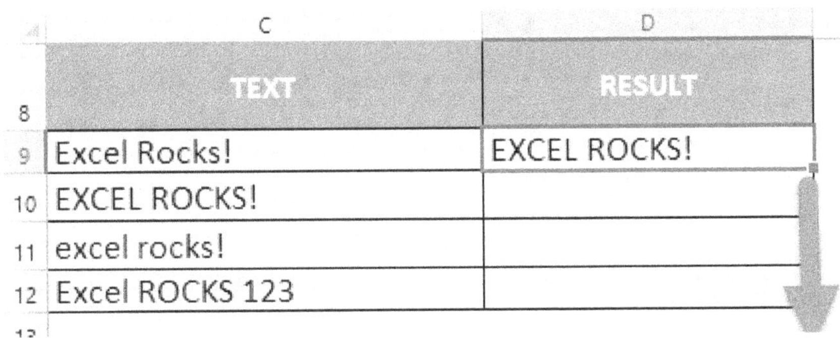

You can see that the values are all now in upper case!

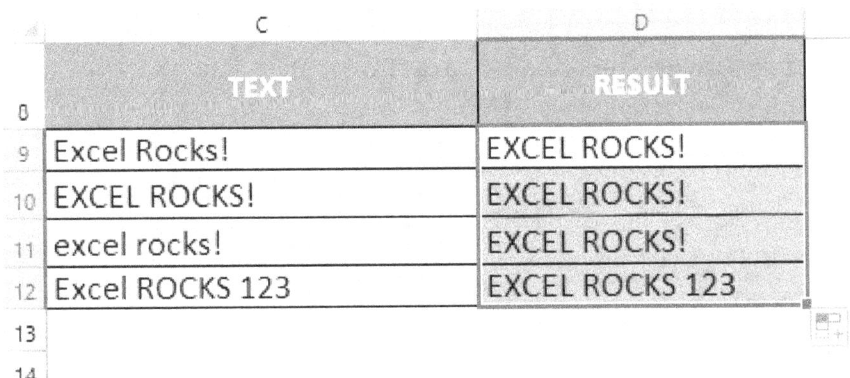

VALUE

What does it do?

Converts text into a numeric value

Formula breakdown:

=VALUE(text)

What it means:

=VALUE(text to be converted to a numeric value)

Example:

=VALUE("11/29/18") =43433

We can easily change text into its corresponding **numeric value** using the **VALUE formula** in Excel. It is also interesting as we can try out different types and see how it looks like in its numeric format.

Let us try out a couple of data types: Dates, currency, and time to name a few!

STEP 1: We need to **enter the _VALUE_ function in a blank cell**:

=VALUE(

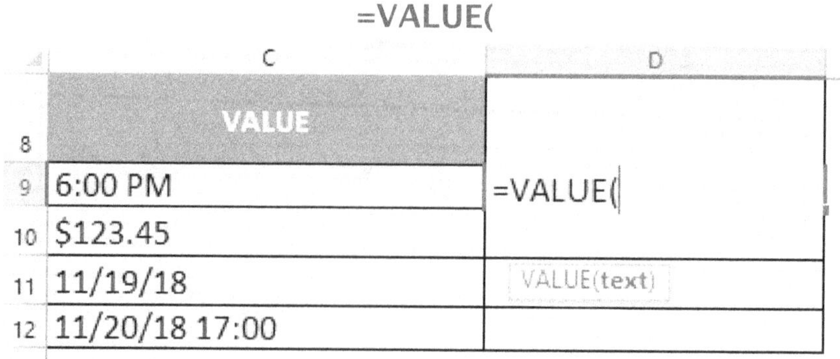

text

What is the text to be converted to a numeric value?

Select the cell containing the text that you want to convert:

=VALUE(C9)

	C	D
	VALUE	
8		
9	6:00 PM	=VALUE(C9)
10	$123.45	
11	11/19/18	
12	11/20/18 17:00	

Apply the same formula to the rest of the cells by dragging the lower right corner downwards.

	C	D
	VALUE	**RESULT**
8		
9	6:00 PM	0.75
10	$123.45	
11	11/19/18	
12	11/20/18 17:00	
13		

You can see that the text are all now in their numeric values!

	C	D
	VALUE	**RESULT**
8		
9	6:00 PM	0.75
10	$123.45	123.45
11	11/19/18	43423
12	11/20/18 17:00	43424.70833
13		
14		

DATE & TIME FUNCTIONS

DATE

What does it do?

Creates a date based on the year, month and day provided

Formula breakdown:

=DATE(year, month, day)

What it means:

=DATE(year of the date, month of the date, day of the date)

Example:

=DATE(1985, 1, 3) ="1/03/85"

If you want to create dates dynamically, Excel's **DATE formula** can do this for you! You just need to provide the year, month and day to it.

STEP 1: We need to **enter the *DATE* function in a blank cell**:

=DATE(

	YEAR	MONTH	DAY	
9	1985	1	3	=DATE(
10	1962	4	11	
11	1999	2	17	DATE(year, month, day)

year

What is the year of the date?

Select the cell containing the year:

=DATE(C9,

	C	D	E	F	G
8	YEAR	MONTH	DAY		
9	1985	1	3	=DATE(C9,	
10	1962	4	11		
11	1999	2	17	DATE(year, month, day)	
12					

month

What is the month of the date?

Select the cell containing the month:

=DATE(C9, D9,

	C	D	E	F	G
8	YEAR	MONTH	DAY		
9	1985	1	3	=DATE(C9, D9,	
10	1962	4	11		
11	1999	2	17	DATE(year, month, day)	
12					

day

What is the day of the date?

Select the cell containing the day:

=DATE(C9, D9, E9)

	C	D	E	F	G
8	YEAR	MONTH	DAY		
9	1985	1	3	=DATE(C9, D9, E9)	
10	1962	4	11		
11	1999	2	17		

Apply the same formula to the rest of the cells by dragging the lower right corner downwards.

	YEAR	MONTH	DAY	RESULT
9	1985	1	3	1/03/85
10	1962	4	11	
11	1999	2	17	

You now have your dates generated!

	YEAR	MONTH	DAY	RESULT
9	1985	1	3	1/03/85
10	1962	4	11	4/11/62
11	1999	2	17	2/17/99

DATEDIF

What does it do?

Calculates the number of Days, Months, or Years between two dates

Formula breakdown:

=DATEDIF(Start Date, End Date, Interval)

What it means:

=DATEDIF(starting date, ending date, the unit of measurement)

Where **INTERVAL** is:

"**m**" Months , "**ym**" Months Excluding Years
"**d**" Days , "**yd**" Days Excluding Years
"**y**" Years , "**md**" Days Excluding Years And Months

Example:

=DATEDIF("5/18/80","11/28/18","m") =462

The **DATEDIF** function is a mystery function within Excel. When you write it out in a workbook it doesn't give you any hints like other functions would and if you look it up in the function list you would not find it! Creepy...

The **DATEDIF** function stands for "**date difference**" and it calculates the number of Days, Months, or Years between two dates.

So if you want to find out how many days, years or months have passed since you were born, well this is the formula for you!   Well you can also extend this to project start and end dates, but you get my point.

 Enter the **Start Date**

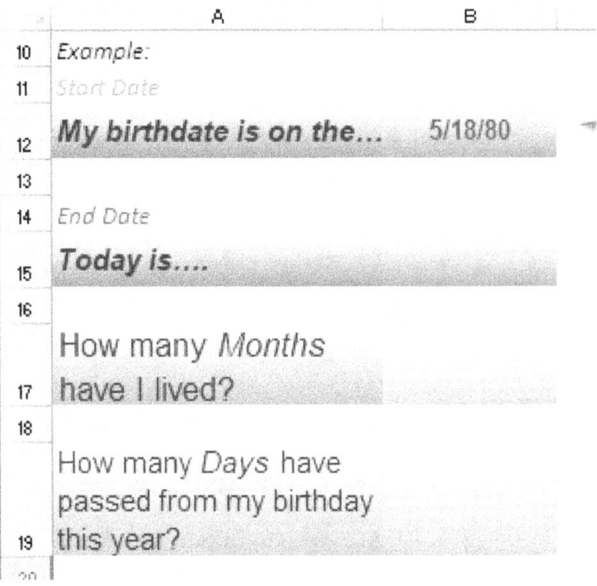

 Enter the **End Date**

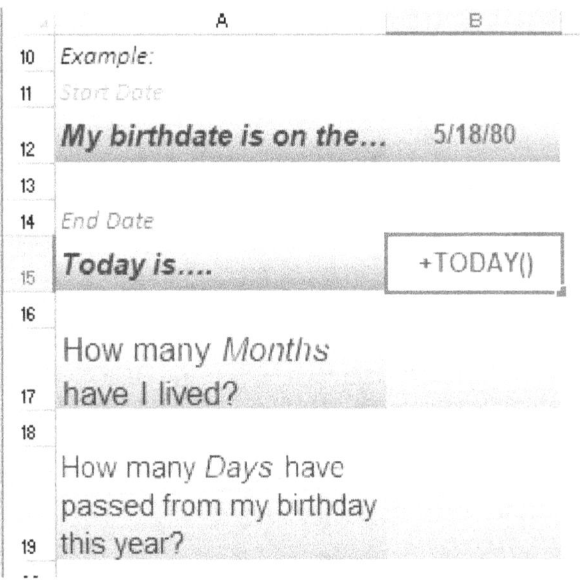

 To get the **number of months** as a difference, type in the following formula

$$=\text{DATEDIF(B12, B15, "m")}$$

The **DATEDIF** arguments:

B12 is the **startdate**
B15 is the **enddate**
m tells it to **count in total months**

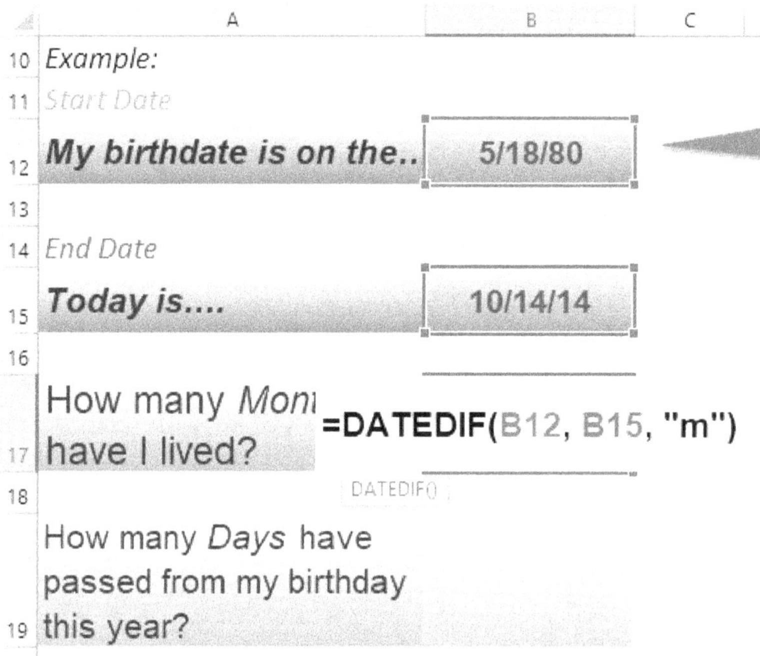

STEP 4: To get the **number of days on this year** from your birthday, type in the following formula

$$=\text{DATEDIF(B12, B15, "yd")}$$

The **DATEDIF** arguments:

B12 is the **startdate**
B15 is the **enddate**
yd tells it to **count in days but excluding the year portion**

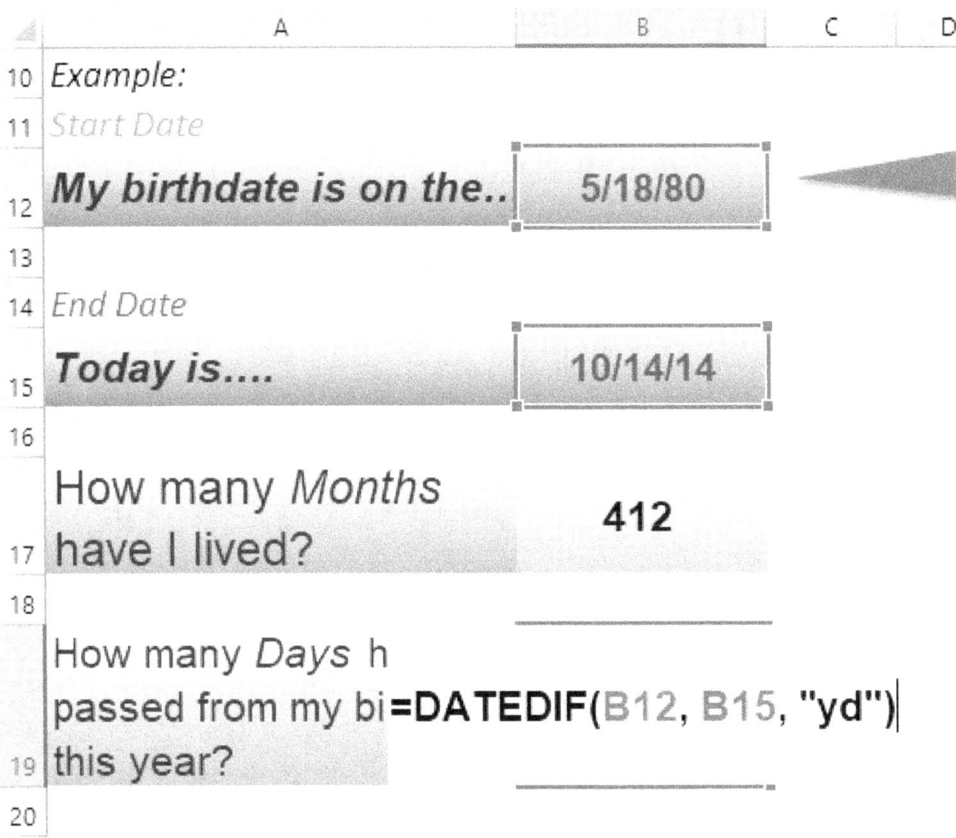

And you have your calculated differences!

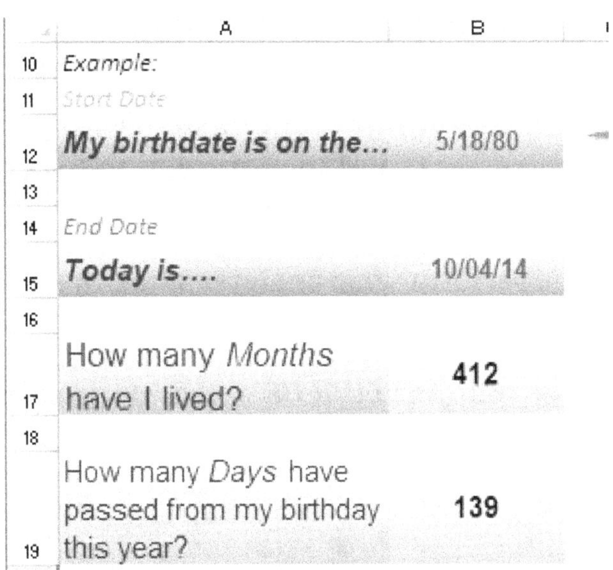

DATEVALUE

What does it do?

Converts a date that is in text format, into Excel's date serial number format

Formula breakdown:

=DATEVALUE(date_text)

What it means:

=DATEVALUE(the date to be converted)

Example:

=DATEVALUE("December 12, 2018") =43446

Ever had a lot of dates in different textual formats? These are a pain to deal with! Thankfully there is the **DATEVALUE Formula** in Excel that converts these text dates into the proper Excel date values.

Once converted, you can perform your analysis since they are now in the Excel date format.

STEP 1: We need to **enter the *DATEVALUE* function in a blank cell**:

=DATEVALUE(

	C	D
8	**DATE**	
9	4/11/1999	=DATEVALUE(
10	December 12, 2018	
11	12 December 2018	DATEVALUE(date_text)
12	Dec 12, 2018	

 The **DATEVALUE** arguments:

date_text

What is the textual date that you want to convert to the proper Excel date?

Select the cell containing the date:

=DATEVALUE(C9)

	C	D
	DATE	
8		
9	4/11/1999	=DATEVALUE(C9)
10	December 12, 2018	
11	12 December 2018	
12	Dec 12, 2018	
13		

Apply the same formula to the rest of the cells by dragging the lower right corner downwards.

	C	D
	DATE	**DATEVALUE**
8		
9	4/11/1999	36261
10	December 12, 2018	
11	12 December 2018	
12	Dec 12, 2018	

You now have your proper dates! Notice the December 12 dates all resulted to the same **DATEVALUE**!

	C	D
	DATE	**DATEVALUE**
8		
9	4/11/1999	36261
10	December 12, 2018	43446
11	12 December 2018	43446
12	Dec 12, 2018	43446

DAY

What does it do?

Gets the day from the date

Formula breakdown:

=DAY(serial_number)

What it means:

=DAY(date where the day will be extracted from)

Example:

=DAY("4/11/85") =11

I recall where I had a lot of dates and I wanted to extract the day of the dates one-by-one... It was too much of a hassle! Thankfully there is Excel's **DAY Formula** to do that for me!

STEP 1: We need to **enter the *DAY* function in a blank cell**:

=DAY(

	DATE	=DAY(
9	4/11/85	
10	3/06/62	
11	2/17/50	DAY(serial_number)
12	12/28/90	

serial_number

What is the date that you want to extract the day from?

Select the cell containing the date:

=DAY(C9)

	C	D
	DATE	
8		
9	4/11/85	=DAY(C9)
10	3/06/62	
11	2/17/50	
12	12/28/90	
13		

Apply the same formula to the rest of the cells by dragging the lower right corner downwards.

	C	D
	DATE	DAY
8		
9	4/11/85	11
10	3/06/62	
11	2/17/50	
12	12/28/90	
13		

You now have your days extracted!

	C	D
	DATE	DAY
8		
9	4/11/85	11
10	3/06/62	6
11	2/17/50	17
12	12/28/90	28
13		
14		

DAY360

What does it do?

Gets the number of days between two dates using 30-day months

Formula breakdown:

=DAYS360(start_date, end_date, [method])

What it means:

=DAYS360(starting date, ending date, [US or European Method])

Example:

=DAYS360("1/01/18", "12/31/18") =360

If you need to get the difference of two dates, but want to use **30-day months** in calculating the difference, Excel has you covered! We can use the **DAYS360 Formula** to do this. It can be useful in the accounting world and there are two modes that are used to count the number of days:

US Method (Default)

- If your start date is the last day of the month, then it is treated as the 30th day of the same month
- If your end date is the last day of the month and your start date is earlier than the 30th day of the month, then the end date is treated as the 1st day of the NEXT month, otherwise the end date is treated as the 30th day of the same month

European Method

- If your start date or end date is the 31st day of the month, then it is treated as the 30th day of the same month

We will be using the Default US Method in our examples below!

I explain how you can do this below:

 We need to **enter the *DAYS360* function in a blank cell**:

=DAYS360(

	START DATE	END DATE	=DAYS360(		
	C	D	E	F	G
8					
9	1/01/18	12/31/18			
10	1/01/20	12/31/20			
11	2/01/19	3/01/19	*DAYS360(start_date, end_date, [method])*		
12	1/15/17	3/15/19			

STEP 2: The **DAYS360** arguments:

start_date
What is the start date?

Select the cell containing the starting date:

=DAYS360(C9,

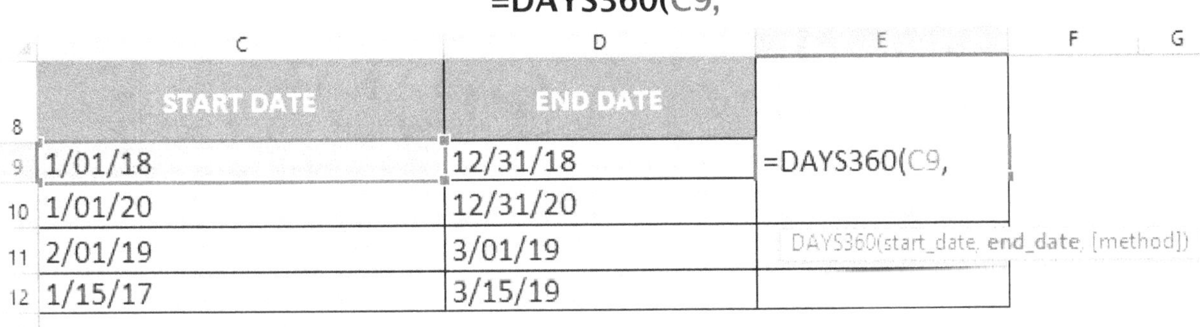

=DAYS360(C9, D9)

end_date
What is the end date?

Select the cell containing the ending date:

=DAYS360(C9, D9)

	START DATE	END DATE	
8			
9	1/01/18	12/31/18	=DAYS360(C9, D9)
10	1/01/20	12/31/20	
11	2/01/19	3/01/19	
12	1/15/17	3/15/19	
13			

We will leave the method as blank, which will use the default US method. Apply the same formula to the rest of the cells by dragging the lower right corner downwards.

	START DATE	END DATE	NUMBER OF DAYS
8			
9	1/01/18	12/31/18	360
10	1/01/20	12/31/20	
11	2/01/19	3/01/19	
12	1/15/17	3/15/19	

You now have your differences using 30-day months! Notice that 1 year is treated as 360 days (30 days x 12 months).

	START DATE	END DATE	NUMBER OF DAYS	
8				
9	1/01/18	12/31/18	360	
10	1/01/20	12/31/20	360	
11	2/01/19	3/01/19	30	
12	1/15/17	3/15/19	780	
13				

DAYS

What does it do?

Gets the number of days between two dates

Formula breakdown:

=DAYS(end_date, start_date)

What it means:

=DAYS(ending date, starting date)

Example:

=DAYS("12/31/18", "1/01/18") =364

Have two dates that you want to check what is the difference in days? No problem! Excel's **DAYS Formula** will compute this easily for you!

STEP 1: We need to **enter the _DAYS_ function in a blank cell**:

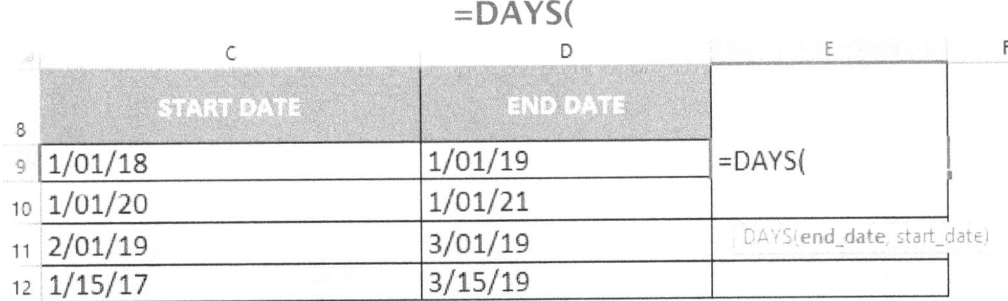

	START DATE	END DATE		F
8				
9	1/01/18	1/01/19	=DAYS(	
10	1/01/20	1/01/21		
11	2/01/19	3/01/19	DAYS(end_date, start_date)	
12	1/15/17	3/15/19		

STEP 2: The **DAYS** arguments:

_end_date_

What is the ending date?

Select the cell containing the ending date:

=DAYS(D9,

	START DATE	END DATE	
9	1/01/18	1/01/19	=DAYS(D9,
10	1/01/20	1/01/21	
11	2/01/19	3/01/19	DAYS(end_date, start_date)
12	1/15/17	3/15/19	

start_date

What is the starting date?

Select the cell containing the starting date:

=DAYS(D9, C9)

	START DATE	END DATE	
9	1/01/18	1/01/19	=DAYS(D9, C9)
10	1/01/20	1/01/21	
11	2/01/19	3/01/19	
12	1/15/17	3/15/19	

Apply the formula to the rest by dragging the lower right corner downwards.

	START DATE	END DATE	NUMBER OF DAYS
9	1/01/18	1/01/19	365
10	1/01/20	1/01/21	
11	2/01/19	3/01/19	
12	1/15/17	3/15/19	
13			

You now have your differences in days!

	START DATE	END DATE	NUMBER OF DAYS
9	1/01/18	1/01/19	365
10	1/01/20	1/01/21	366
11	2/01/19	3/01/19	28
12	1/15/17	3/15/19	789

ENDOFMONTH

What does it do?

Returns the last day of the month after a start date

Formula breakdown:

=EOMONTH(start_date, months)

What it means:

= EOMONTH (Your Start Date, enter 0 for current end of month, 1 for the next end of month, and so on...)

Example:

=EOMONTH("1/13/15",1) ="2/28/15"

The **EOMONTH (EndOfMonth)** function in Excel is one that most people do not use because they just don't know that It exists.

It is a great Excel function to use if you want to see when the month end date is from a current date's value.

So if you have sales reps who make a sale during the month and their commission is due to be paid at the end of the next month, the **EOMONTH** function will help you determine the total sales due.

STEP 1: We need to enter the **EOMONTH** function in a blank cell:

=EOMONTH(

	SALES REPRESENTATIVE	SALE DATE	SALES AMOUNT	COMMISSION DUE DATE
12	Homer Simpson	1/13/15	$78,782	=EOMONTH(
13	Ian Wright	1/25/15	$72,602	
14	John Michaloudis	2/06/15	$48,503	
15	Michael Jackson	2/18/15	$44,316	
16	Homer Simpson	3/02/15	$47,810	
17	Ian Wright	3/14/15	$77,361	
18	John Michaloudis	3/26/15	$51,146	
19	Michael Jackson	4/07/15	$28,673	
20	Homer Simpson	4/19/15	$31,810	
21	Ian Wright	5/01/15	$52,916	
22	John Michaloudis	5/13/15	$71,305	
23	Michael Jackson	5/25/15	$27,757	
24	Homer Simpson	6/06/15	$47,404	
25	Ian Wright	6/18/15	$77,547	

STEP 2: The **EOMONTH** arguments:

start_date

What is your start_date?

=EOMONTH(B12,

	SALES REPRESENTATIVE	SALE DATE	SALES AMOUNT	COMMISSION DUE DATE
12	Homer Simpson	1/13/15	$78,782	=EOMONTH(B12,
13	Ian Wright	1/25/15	$72,602	
14	John Michaloudis	2/06/15	$48,503	
15	Michael Jackson	2/18/15	$44,316	
16	Homer Simpson	3/02/15	$47,810	
17	Ian Wright	3/14/15	$77,361	
18	John Michaloudis	3/26/15	$51,146	
19	Michael Jackson	4/07/15	$28,673	
20	Homer Simpson	4/19/15	$31,810	
21	Ian Wright	5/01/15	$52,916	
22	John Michaloudis	5/13/15	$71,305	
23	Michael Jackson	5/25/15	$27,757	
24	Homer Simpson	6/06/15	$47,404	
25	Ian Wright	6/18/15	$77,547	

Which end of month do you want?

We can type in 0 for the current End of Month, or 1 for the next End of Month, and so on.

=EOMONTH(B12, 1)

	A	B	C	D
11	**SALES REPRESENTATIVE**	**SALE DATE**	**SALES AMOUNT**	**COMMISSION DUE DATE**
12	Homer Simpson	1/13/15	$78,782	=EOMONTH(B12, 1)
13	Ian Wright	1/25/15	$72,602	
14	John Michaloudis	2/06/15	$48,503	
15	Michael Jackson	2/18/15	$44,316	
16	Homer Simpson	3/02/15	$47,810	
17	Ian Wright	3/14/15	$77,361	
18	John Michaloudis	3/26/15	$51,146	
19	Michael Jackson	4/07/15	$28,673	
20	Homer Simpson	4/19/15	$31,810	
21	Ian Wright	5/01/15	$52,916	
22	John Michaloudis	5/13/15	$71,305	
23	Michael Jackson	5/25/15	$27,757	
24	Homer Simpson	6/06/15	$47,404	
25	Ian Wright	6/18/15	$77,547	

Apply the same formula to the rest of the cells by dragging the lower right corner downwards.

	A	B	C	D
11	**SALES REPRESENTATIVE**	**SALE DATE**	**SALES AMOUNT**	**COMMISSION DUE DATE**
12	Homer Simpson	1/13/15	$78,782	2/28/15
13	Ian Wright	1/25/15	$72,602	
14	John Michaloudis	2/06/15	$48,503	
15	Michael Jackson	2/18/15	$44,316	
16	Homer Simpson	3/02/15	$47,810	
17	Ian Wright	3/14/15	$77,361	
18	John Michaloudis	3/26/15	$51,146	
19	Michael Jackson	4/07/15	$28,673	
20	Homer Simpson	4/19/15	$31,810	
21	Ian Wright	5/01/15	$52,916	
22	John Michaloudis	5/13/15	$71,305	
23	Michael Jackson	5/25/15	$27,757	
24	Homer Simpson	6/06/15	$47,404	
25	Ian Wright	6/18/15	$77,547	

You now have all of results!

	A	B	C	D
	SALES REPRESENTATIVE	**SALE DATE**	**SALES AMOUNT**	**COMMISSION DUE DATE**
12	Homer Simpson	1/13/15	$78,782	2/28/15
13	Ian Wright	1/25/15	$72,602	2/28/15
14	John Michaloudis	2/06/15	$48,503	3/31/15
15	Michael Jackson	2/18/15	$44,316	3/31/15
16	Homer Simpson	3/02/15	$47,810	4/30/15
17	Ian Wright	3/14/15	$77,361	4/30/15
18	John Michaloudis	3/26/15	$51,146	4/30/15
19	Michael Jackson	4/07/15	$28,673	5/31/15
20	Homer Simpson	4/19/15	$31,810	5/31/15
21	Ian Wright	5/01/15	$52,916	6/30/15
22	John Michaloudis	5/13/15	$71,305	6/30/15
23	Michael Jackson	5/25/15	$27,757	6/30/15
24	Homer Simpson	6/06/15	$47,404	7/31/15
25	Ian Wright	6/18/15	$77,547	7/31/15

HOUR

What does it do?

Gets the hour from the time

Formula breakdown:

=HOUR(serial_number)

What it means:

=HOUR(time where the hour will be extracted from)

Example:

=HOUR("6:00 PM") =18

I recall wherein I had a lot of times and I wanted to extract the hour of the times one-by-one... It was too much of a hassle! Thankfully there is Excel's **HOUR Formula** to do that for me!

A couple of interesting things on the **HOUR Formula**:

- The hour it returns to you is similar to military time ranging from 0 - 23
- If it's a date time, then the date gets ignored
- If the time is greater than 24 hours, then it simply converts it to days and hours, then returns the hour component only

STEP 1: We need to **enter the *HOUR* function in a blank cell**:

=HOUR(

	C	D
8	**DATE**	
9	12:00 AM	=HOUR(
10	6:00 AM	
11	12:00 PM	HOUR(serial_number)
12	6:00 PM	
13	1/01/18 9:30	
14	36:00	
15	6:30 AM	

 The **HOUR** arguments:

serial_number

What is the time that you want to extract the hour from?

Select the cell containing the time:

=HOUR(C9)

	C	D
8	**DATE**	
9	12:00 AM	=HOUR(C9)
10	6:00 AM	
11	12:00 PM	
12	6:00 PM	
13	1/01/18 9:30	
14	36:00	
15	6:30 AM	

Apply the same formula to the rest of the cells by dragging the lower right corner downwards.

	DATE	HOUR
8		
9	12:00 AM	0
10	6:00 AM	
11	12:00 PM	
12	6:00 PM	
13	1/01/18 9:30	
14	36:00	
15	6:30 AM	

You now have your years extracted!

	DATE	HOUR
8		
9	12:00 AM	0
10	6:00 AM	6
11	12:00 PM	12
12	6:00 PM	18
13	1/01/18 9:30	9
14	36:00	12
15	6:30 AM	6
16		
17		

MONTH

What does it do?

Gets the month from the date

Formula breakdown:

=MONTH(serial_number)

What it means:

=MONTH(date where the month will be extracted from)

Example:

=MONTH("4/11/85") =4

I recall wherein I had a lot of dates and I wanted to extract the month of the dates one-by-one... It was too much of a hassle! Thankfully there is Excel's **MONTH Formula** to do that for me!

STEP 1: We need to **enter the *MONTH* function in a blank cell:**

=MONTH(

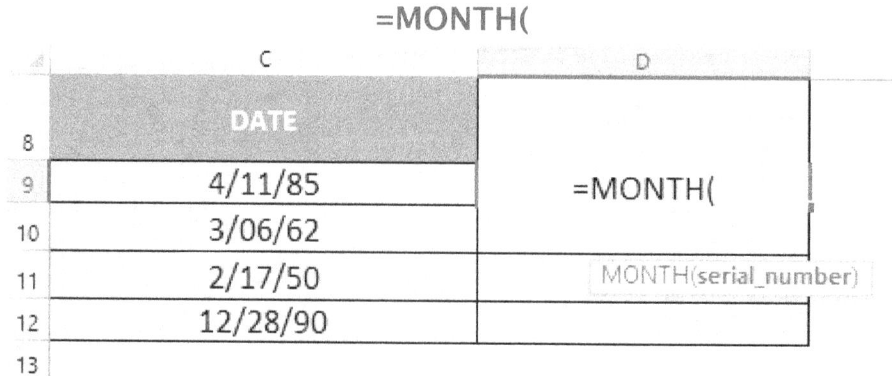

serial_number

What is the date that you want to extract the month from?

Select the cell containing the date:

=MONTH(C9)

	C DATE	D
8		
9	4/11/85	=MONTH(C9)
10	3/06/62	
11	2/17/50	
12	12/28/90	
13		

Apply the same formula to the rest of the cells by dragging the lower right corner downwards.

	C DATE	D MONTH
8		
9	4/11/85	4
10	3/06/62	
11	2/17/50	
12	12/28/90	

You now have your months extracted!

	C DATE	D MONTH
8		
9	4/11/85	4
10	3/06/62	3
11	2/17/50	2
12	12/28/90	12
13		

NETWORKDAYS

What does it do?

Gets the number of working days between two dates

Formula breakdown:

=NETWORKDAYS(start_date, end_date, [holidays])

What it means:

=NETWORKDAYS(starting date, ending date, [holidays to exclude])

Example:

=NETWORKDAYS("1/01/18","1/07/18",A9:A11) =number of days minus holidays

If you want to calculate the number of working days, it is very difficult to do by hand! Imagine going through your calendar and counting the weekdays week per week. Thankfully there is Excel's **NETWORKDAYS Formula!**

The **NETWORKDAYS Formula** will exclude the weekends in the count, and you can also provide it a list of holidays for it to exclude as well in the count!

Let us try out in our example below from **January 1, 2018 to January 28, 2018,** for these 4 weeks it should be a **total of 20 working days**. Let us add in **3 holidays** during this period, so that total working days will be reduced to **17 working days**.

I explain how you can do this below:

STEP 1: We need to **enter the *NETWORKDAYS* function in a blank cell**:

=NETWORKDAYS(

	A	B	C	D	E	F	G	H
8	HOLIDAYS		START DATE	END DATE				
9	1/01/18		1/01/18	1/07/18	=NETWORKDAYS(			
10	1/08/18		1/01/18	1/14/18				
11	1/09/18		1/01/18	1/21/18	NETWORKDAYS(**start_date**, end_date, [holidays])			
12			1/01/18	1/28/18				

STEP 2: The **NETWORKDAYS** arguments:

start_date

What is the start date?

Select the cell containing the starting date:

=NETWORKDAYS(C9,

	A	B	C	D	E	F	G	H
8	HOLIDAYS		START DATE	END DATE				
9	1/01/18		1/01/18	1/07/18	=NETWORKDAYS(C9,			
10	1/08/18		1/01/18	1/14/18				
11	1/09/18		1/01/18	1/21/18	NETWORKDAYS(start_date, **end_date**, [holidays])			
12			1/01/18	1/28/18				
13								

end_date

What is the end date?

Select the cell containing the ending date:

=NETWORKDAYS(C9, D9,

	A	B	C	D	E	F	G	H
8	HOLIDAYS		START DATE	END DATE				
9	1/01/18		1/01/18	1/07/18	=NETWORKDAYS(C9, D9,			
10	1/08/18		1/01/18	1/14/18				
11	1/09/18		1/01/18	1/21/18	NETWORKDAYS(start_date, end_date, **[holidays]**)			
12			1/01/18	1/28/18				
13								

Any holidays that you want to be excluded from the total count?

*Select the range of cells containing your holidays. Ensure to press **F4** to make your cell reference absolute:*

=NETWORKDAYS(C9, D9, $A$9:$A$11)

	HOLIDAYS		START DATE	END DATE	
9	1/01/18		1/01/18	1/07/18	=NETWORKDAYS(C9, D9, $A$9:$A$11)
10	1/08/18		1/01/18	1/14/18	
11	1/09/18		1/01/18	1/21/18	
12			1/01/18	1/28/18	

Apply the same formula to the rest of the cells by dragging the lower right corner downwards.

	HOLIDAYS		START DATE	END DATE	NUMBER OF DAYS
9	1/01/18		1/01/18	1/07/18	4
10	1/08/18		1/01/18	1/14/18	
11	1/09/18		1/01/18	1/21/18	
12			1/01/18	1/28/18	
13					

You now have the number of working days and the holidays are excluded!

	HOLIDAYS		START DATE	END DATE	NUMBER OF DAYS
9	1/01/18		1/01/18	1/07/18	4
10	1/08/18		1/01/18	1/14/18	7
11	1/09/18		1/01/18	1/21/18	12
12			1/01/18	1/28/18	17
13					
14					

TODAY

What does it do?

Returns today's date

Formula breakdown:

=TODAY()

What it means:

=TODAY()

Example:

=TODAY() ="11/29/2018"

Have a dynamic formula that needs the current date and you are tired of changing the date everyday? Use Excel's **TODAY Formula** to have it update dynamically!

STEP 1: We need to **enter the *TODAY* function in a blank cell:**

=TODAY()

	C
8	
9	=TODAY()
10	

And just like that, you already have today's date!

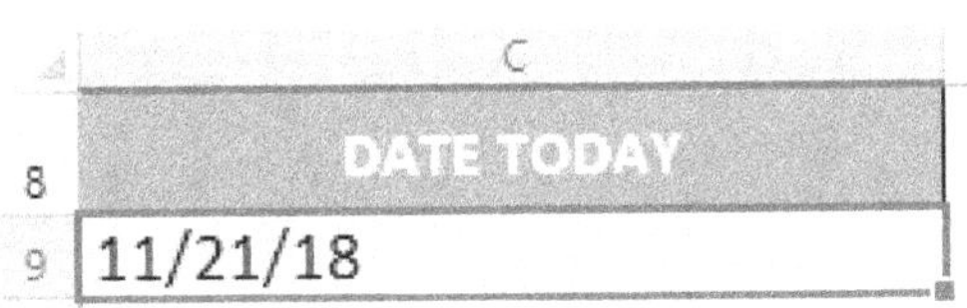

	C
8	**DATE TODAY**
9	11/21/18

WEEKDAY

What does it do?

Returns the day of the week corresponding to a date. The day is given as an integer, ranging from 1 (Sunday) to 7 (Saturday), by default.

Formula breakdown:

=WEEKDAY(Serial_Number, [Return_Type])

What it means:

=WEEKDAY(Date, [Numbers 1 (Sunday) through 7 (Saturday)])

Example:

=WEEKDAY("5/18/85",1) =7

The **WEEKDAY** function returns the day of the week corresponding to a date. The day is given as an integer, ranging from 1 (Sunday) to 7 (Saturday).

So if you want to find out on what day you were born, then the **WEEKDAY** function will remind you.

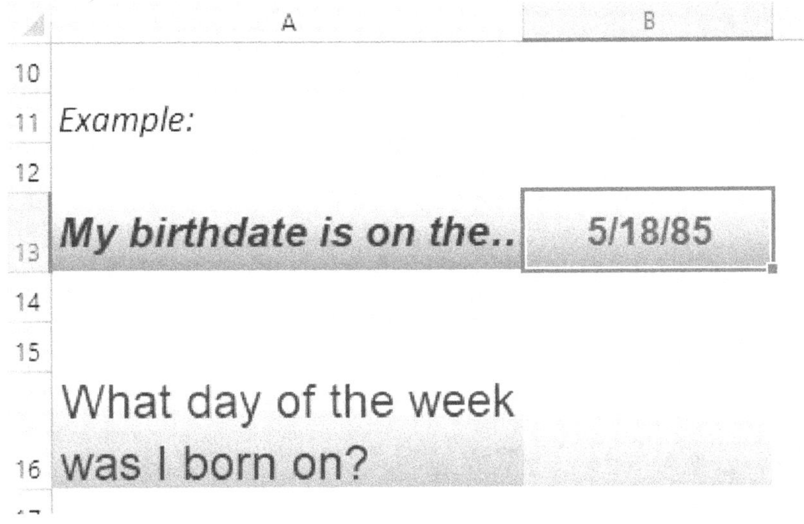

STEP 2: The **WEEKDAY** arguments:

date

What is the date?

Select the date you have entered

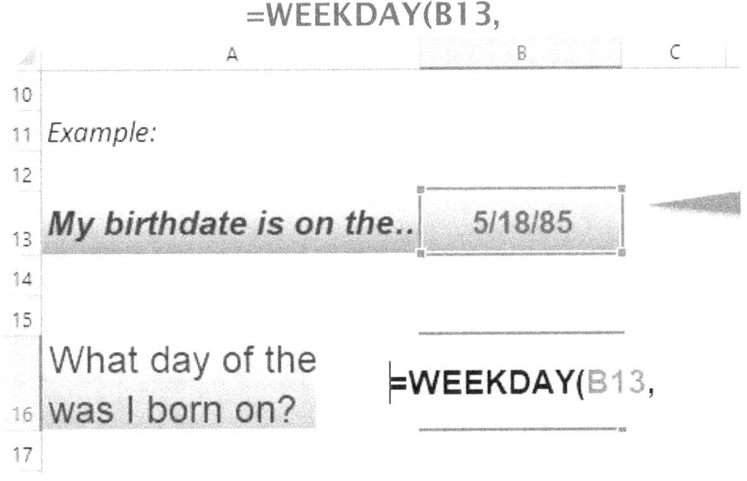

return_Type

What kind of output do you want to show?

For Sunday=1 through to Saturday=7, use 1

For Monday=1 through to Sunday=7, use 2

Type in **1** to get the number of the day of the week

We get a result of 7 here, which signifies a **Saturday**. As Type 1 represents days **ranging from 1 (Sunday) to 7 (Saturday).**

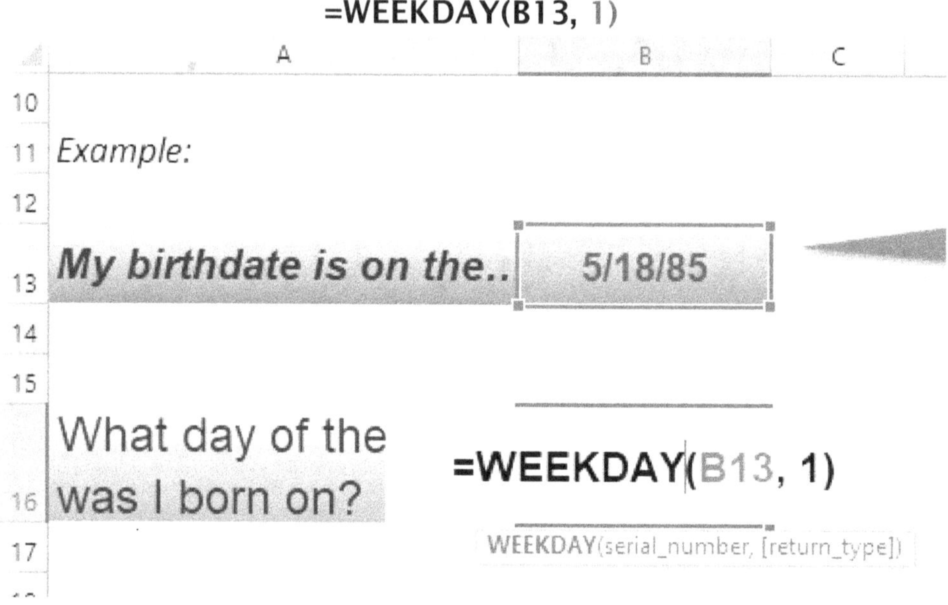

Now we know the day in an instant!

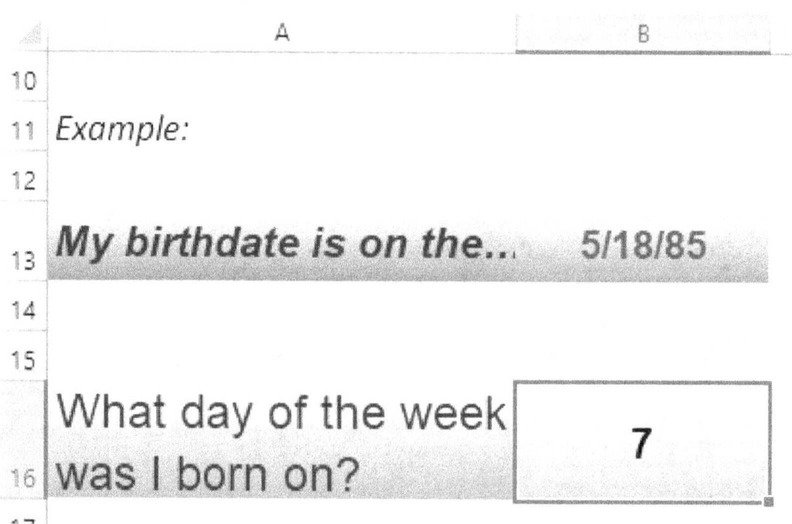

WEEKNUM

What does it do?

Gets the week number from the date

Formula breakdown:

=WEEKNUM(serial_number, [return_type])

What it means:

=WEEKNUM(date where the week number will be retrieved, [day when the week will begin])

Example:

=WEEKNUM("4/11/1985") =15

Do you need to retrieve the week number from a given date? The **WEEKNUM Formula** in Excel is perfect for this!

There are a couple of interesting points to take note of the **WEEKNUM Formula**:

- The return type parameter specifies which day of the week is used to start a new week number. For our examples, we will be using the default. But there are a number of settings that you can use:
  - 1 (default) - Sunday
  - 2 - Monday
  - 11 - Monday
  - 12 - Tuesday
  - 13 - Wednesday
  - 14 - Thursday
  - 15 - Friday
  - 16 - Saturday
  - 17 - Sunday

- o 21 - Monday, the difference here Is it uses the European week numbering system, week 1 is the week containing the first Thursday of the year as specified in ISO 8601

I explain how you can do this below:

STEP 1: We need to **enter the _WEEKNUM_ function in a blank cell**:

=WEEKNUM(

	C	D	E
	DATE		
8			
9	4/11/85	=WEEKNUM(	
10	3/06/62		
11	1/01/50	WEEKNUM(serial_number, [return_type])	
12	12/28/90		
13			

STEP 2: The **WEEKNUM** arguments:

_serial_number_

What is the date to extract the week number from?

Select the cell containing the date:

=WEEKNUM(C9)

	C	D
	DATE	
8		
9	4/11/85	=WEEKNUM(C9)
10	3/06/62	
11	1/01/50	
12	12/28/90	
13		

Apply the same formula to the rest of the cells by dragging the lower right corner downwards.

DATE	WEEK NUMBER
4/11/85	15
3/06/62	
1/01/50	
12/28/90	

You now have your week numbers!

DATE	WEEK NUMBER
4/11/85	15
3/06/62	10
1/01/50	1
12/28/90	52

WORKDAY

What does it do?

Adds/Subtracts a specified number of workdays to a Date, which will give you a Future/Past Date

Formula breakdown:

=WORKDAY(start_date, days, [holidays])

What it means:

=WORKDAY(specified date, number of work days to add/subtract, [holidays to be considered])

Example:

=WORKDAY("2/12/2010",10) ="2/26/2010"

If you want to calculate the future date based on a number of working days added, it will be difficult to manually calculate this! Let me show you the easy way!

STEP 1: We need to **enter the *WORKDAY* function in a blank cell:**

=WORKDAY(

	DATE	# OF WORKDAYS ADDED		F	
8					
9	2/12/10	10	=WORKDAY(		
10	1/15/18	150			
11	3/05/09	23	WORKDAY(start_date, days, [holidays])		
12	5/15/15	55			

start_date

What is the specified date?

Select the cell containing the date you want to add the number of workdays to:

=WORKDAY(C9,

	DATE	# OF WORKDAYS ADDED		
8				
9	2/12/10	10	=WORKDAY(C9,	
10	1/15/18	150		
11	3/05/09	23	WORKDAY(start_date, days, [holidays])	
12	5/15/15	55		

days

How many work days to be added?

Select the cell containing the number of work days to be added (i.e The number of non-weekend and non-holiday days after the start date):

=WORKDAY(C9, D9)

	DATE	# OF WORKDAYS ADDED	
8			
9	2/12/10	10	=WORKDAY(C9,D9)
10	1/15/18	150	
11	3/05/09	23	
12	5/15/15	55	

Apply the same formula to the rest of the cells by dragging the lower right corner downwards.

You now have your future dates with the work days added!

	DATE	# OF WORKDAYS ADDED	RESULT	
8				
9	2/12/10	10	2/26/10	
10	1/15/18	150	8/13/18	
11	3/05/09	23	4/07/09	
12	5/15/15	55	7/31/15	

YEAR

What does it do?

Extracts the Year from the Date

Formula breakdown:

=YEAR(serial_number)

What it means:

=YEAR(date where the year will be extracted from)

Example:

=YEAR("4/11/85") =1985

I recall wherein I had a lot of dates and I wanted to extract the year of the dates one-by-one... It was too much of a hassle! Thankfully there is Excel's **YEAR Formula** to do that for me!

STEP 1: We need to **enter the *YEAR* function in a blank cell**:

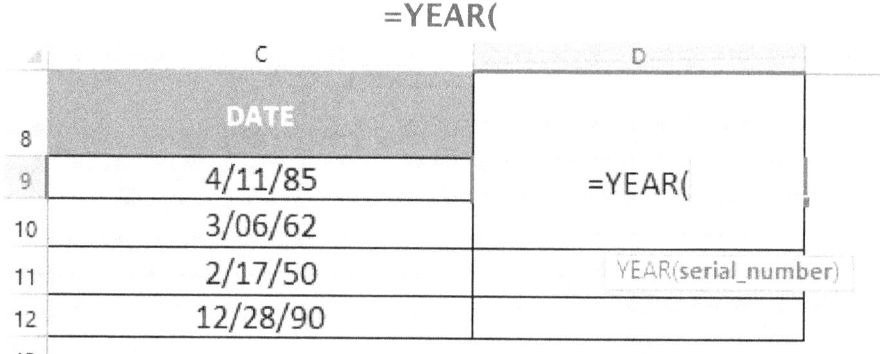

serial_number

What is the Date that you want to extract the Year from?

Select the cell containing the date:

=YEAR(C9)

	DATE	=YEAR(C9)
9	4/11/85	
10	3/06/62	
11	2/17/50	
12	12/28/90	

Apply the same formula to the rest of the cells by dragging the lower right corner downwards.

	DATE	YEAR
9	4/11/85	1985
10	3/06/62	
11	2/17/50	
12	12/28/90	

You now have your years extracted!

	DATE	YEAR
9	4/11/85	1985
10	3/06/62	1962
11	2/17/50	1950
12	12/28/90	1990

INFORMATION FUNCTIONS

ISBLANK

What does it do?

Checks if the cell value is empty or not

Formula breakdown:

=ISBLANK(value)

What it means:

=ISBLANK(value to be checked to see if it is empty or not)

Example:

=ISBLANK("abc") =FALSE

Have a bunch of empty values and you need to check all of your cells?
The **ISBLANK Formula** in Excel is perfect for this!

STEP 1: We need to **enter the *ISBLANK* function in a blank cell**:

=ISBLANK(

	C	D
	VALUE	
8		
9	4/11/85	=ISBLANK(
10		
11	How are you?	ISBLANK(value)
12	12.50	

 The **ISBLANK** arguments:

value

What is the value to be checked?

Select the cell containing the value you want to be checked if it's blank:

=ISBLANK(C9)

	VALUE	
8		
9	4/11/85	=ISBLANK(C9)
10		
11	How are you?	
12	12.50	

Apply the same formula to the rest of the cells by dragging the lower right corner downwards.

	VALUE	IS IT BLANK?
8		
9	4/11/85	FALSE
10		
11	How are you?	
12	12.50	
13		

You can now see which ones are the blank values!

	VALUE	IS IT BLANK?
8		
9	4/11/85	FALSE
10		TRUE
11	How are you?	FALSE
12	12.50	FALSE
13		

ISERROR

What does it do?

Checks if the cell value is an error or not

Formula breakdown:

=ISERROR(value)

What it means:

=ISERROR(value to be checked to see if it is an error or not)

Example:

=ISERROR(0/0) =TRUE

Have a bunch of values and you need to check which ones are errors?
The **ISERROR Formula** in Excel is perfect for this!

There are a couple of interesting points to take note of the **ISERROR Formula**:

- The following are treated as errors by the **ISERROR Formula**
    - #N/A
    - #VALUE!
    - #REF!
    - #DIV/0!
    - #NUM!
    - #NAME?
    - #NULL!

I explain how you can do this below:

 We need to **enter the *ISERROR* function in a blank cell**:

=ISERROR(

	C	D
8	**VALUE**	
9	#N/A	=ISERROR(
10	#VALUE!	
11	#REF!	ISERROR(value)
12	#DIV/0!	
13	#NUM!	
14	#NAME?	

STEP 2: The **ISERROR** arguments:

value

What is the value to be checked?

Select the cell containing the value you want to be checked if it is an error:

=ISERROR(C9)

	C	D
8	**VALUE**	
9	#N/A	=ISERROR(C9)
10	#VALUE!	
11	#REF!	
12	#DIV/0!	
13	#NUM!	
14	#NAME?	

Apply the same formula to the rest of the cells by dragging the lower right corner downwards.

	VALUE	IS IT AN ERROR?
8		
9	#N/A	TRUE
10	#VALUE!	
11	#REF!	
12	#DIV/0!	
13	#NUM!	
14	#NAME?	

You can now see which ones are errors!

	VALUE	IS IT AN ERROR?
8		
9	#N/A	TRUE
10	#VALUE!	TRUE
11	#REF!	TRUE
12	#DIV/0!	TRUE
13	#NUM!	TRUE
14	#NAME?	TRUE
15		
16		

ISNUMBER

What does it do?

Checks if the cell value is numeric or not

Formula breakdown:

=ISNUMBER(value)

What it means:

=ISNUMBER(value to be checked to see if it is a number or not)

Example:

=ISNUMBER(12.5) =TRUE

Have a bunch of values and you need to check which ones are numbers?
The **ISNUMBER Formula** in Excel is perfect for this!

There are a couple of interesting points to take note of the **ISNUMBER Formula**:

- Dates are also treated as numerical values, so the **ISNUMBER Formula** will return **TRUE**
- If the number is stored as text, then the **ISNUMBER Formula** will return **FALSE**

I explain how you can do this below:

STEP 1: We need to **enter the *ISNUMBER* function in a blank cell**:

=ISNUMBER(

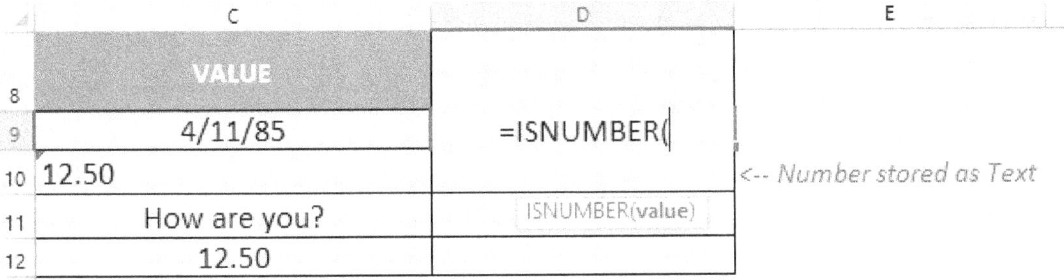

 The **ISNUMBER** arguments:

value

What is the value to be checked?

Select the cell containing the value you want to be checked

=ISNUMBER(C9)

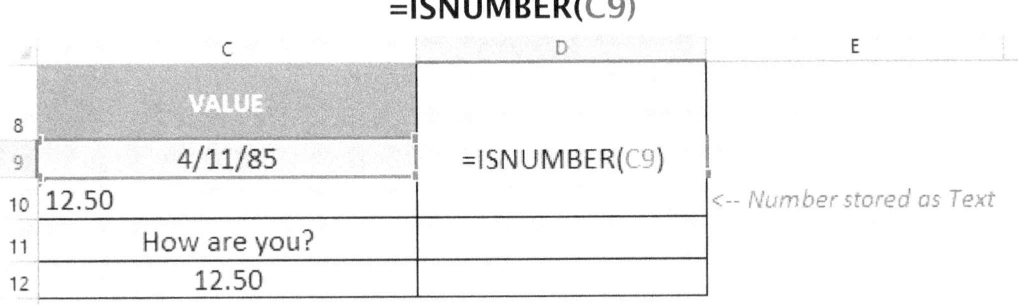

Apply the same formula to the rest of the cells by dragging the lower right corner downwards.

You can now see which ones are the numbers!

ISTEXT

What does it do?

Checks if the cell value is text or not

Formula breakdown:

=ISTEXT(value)

What it means:

=ISTEXT(value to be checked to see if it is a text or not)

Example:

=ISTEXT("abc") =TRUE

Have a bunch of values and you need to check which ones are text? The **ISTEXT Formula** in Excel is perfect for this!

There are a couple of interesting points to take note of the **ISTEXT Formula**:

- Dates are also treated as numerical values, so the **ISTEXT Formula** will return **FALSE**
- If a number is stored as text, then the **ISTEXT Formula** will return **TRUE**

STEP 1: We need to **enter the *ISTEXT* function in a blank cell**:

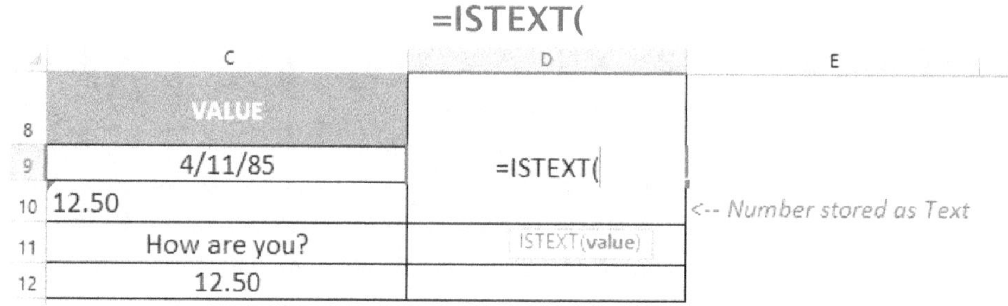

value
What is the value to be checked?

Select the cell containing the value you want to be checked:

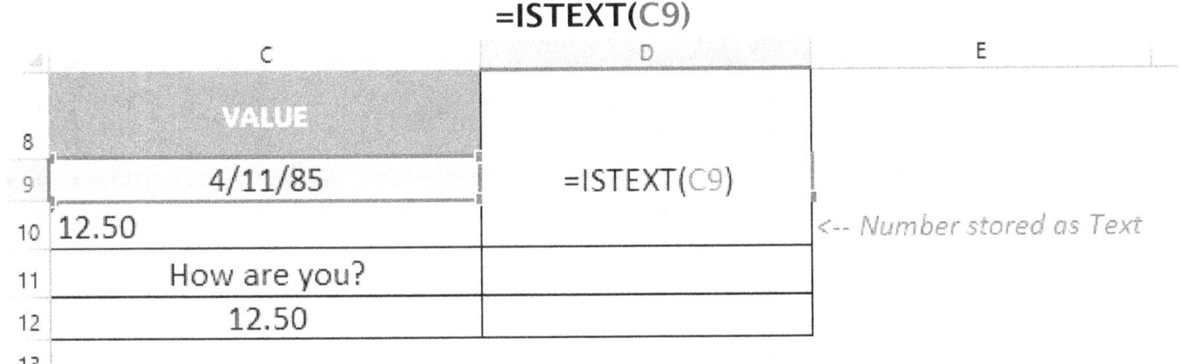

Apply the same formula to the rest of the cells by dragging the lower right corner downwards.

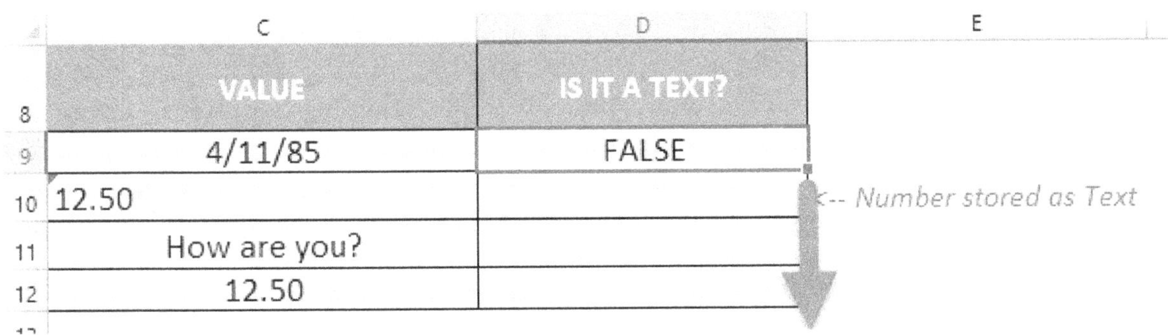

You can now see which ones are text!

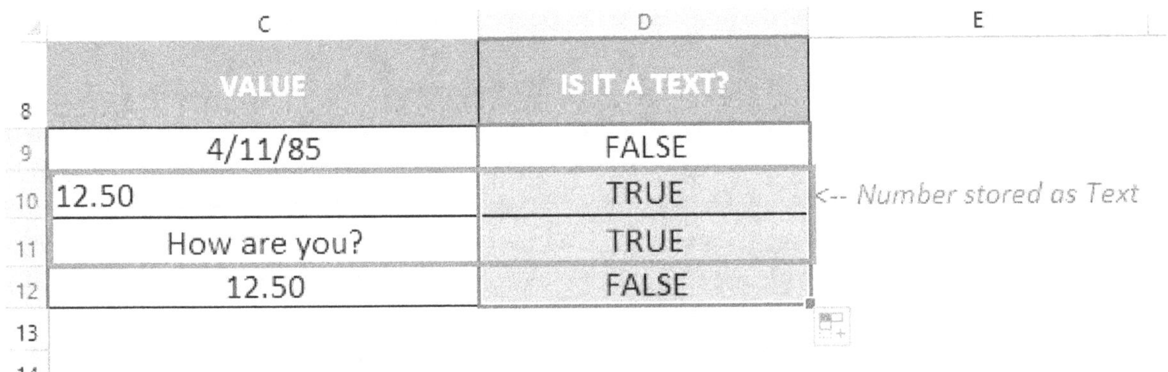

TYPE

What does it do?

Returns the data type from a cell's value

Formula breakdown:

=TYPE(value)

What it means:

=TYPE(value to be checked for its data type)

Example:

=TYPE(FALSE) =4

Do you need to check the data type of your values? The **TYPE Formula** in Excel is perfect for this!

The **TYPE- Formula** checks for the following data types:

- 1 - number
- 2 - text
- 4 - logical value
- 16 - error value
- 64 - array

I explain how you can do this below:

=TYPE(

C		D
VALUE		
12.50		=TYPE(|
How are you?		
FALSE		TYPE(value)
#NAME?		
1/01/10		

STEP 2: The **TYPE** arguments:

value

What is the value to get the data type from?

Select the cell containing the value:

=TYPE(C9)

C		D
VALUE		
12.50		=TYPE(C9)
How are you?		
FALSE		
#NAME?		
1/01/10		

Apply the same formula to the rest of the cells by dragging the lower right corner downwards.

C		D
VALUE		**TYPE**
12.50		1
How are you?		
FALSE		
#NAME?		
1/01/10		

You now have your data types!

	VALUE	TYPE
9	12.50	1
10	How are you?	2
11	FALSE	4
12	#NAME?	16
13	1/01/10	1

OTHER FUNCTIONS

CONVERT

What does it do?

Converts a number from one measurement system to another

Formula breakdown:

=CONVERT(number, from_unit, to_unit)

What it means:

=CONVERT(number, starting measurement system, target measurement system)

Example:

=CONVERT(12, "in", "ft") =1

Did you know that Excel can convert numbers from one measurement system to another measurement system? Yes you can with the **CONVERT Formula!** You will be surprised at what units it can convert for you!

I explain how you can do this below:

STEP 1: We need to **enter the *CONVERT* function in a blank cell**:

=CONVERT(

	NOTES	NUMBER	FROM UNIT	TO UNIT		
9	kilometer to mile	1000.00	km	mi	=CONVERT(	
10	tablespoon to teaspoon	2.00	tbs	tsp		
11	inch to feet	12.00	in	ft	CONVERT(number, from_unit, to_unit)	
12	year to day	10.00	yr	day		
13	bit to byte	1024.00	bit	byte		

number

What is the numeric measurement?

Select the cell containing the number that you want to convert

=CONVERT(C9,

	NOTES	NUMBER	FROM UNIT	TO UNIT	
8					
9	kilometer to mile	1000.00	km	mi	=CONVERT(C9,
10	tablespoon to teaspoon	2.00	tbs	tsp	
11	inch to feet	12.00	in	ft	CONVERT(number, from_unit, to_unit)
12	year to day	10.00	yr	day	
13	bit to byte	1024.00	bit	byte	

from_unit

What is the starting measurement system?

Select the cell containing the starting measurement system.

=CONVERT(C9, D9,

	NOTES	NUMBER	FROM UNIT	TO UNIT	
8					
9	kilometer to mile	1000.00	km	mi	=CONVERT(C9, D9,
10	tablespoon to teaspoon	2.00	tbs	tsp	
11	inch to feet	12.00	in	ft	CONVERT(number, from_unit, to_unit)
12	year to day	10.00	yr	day	
13	bit to byte	1024.00	bit	byte	

to_unit

What is the target measurement system?

Select the cell containing the target measurement system.

=CONVERT(C9, D9, E9)

	NOTES	NUMBER	FROM UNIT	TO UNIT	
8					
9	kilometer to mile	1000.00	km	mi	=CONVERT(C9, D9, E9)
10	tablespoon to teaspoon	2.00	tbs	tsp	
11	inch to feet	12.00	in	ft	
12	year to day	10.00	yr	day	
13	bit to byte	1024.00	bit	byte	

Apply the same formula to the rest of the cells by dragging the lower right corner downwards.

	NOTES	NUMBER	FROM UNIT	TO UNIT	RESULT
9	kilometer to mile	1000.00	km	mi	621.371192
10	tablespoon to teaspoon	2.00	tbs	tsp	
11	inch to feet	12.00	in	ft	
12	year to day	10.00	yr	day	
13	bit to byte	1024.00	bit	byte	

You now have your conversions completed!

	NOTES	NUMBER	FROM UNIT	TO UNIT	RESULT
9	kilometer to mile	1000.00	km	mi	621.371192
10	tablespoon to teaspoon	2.00	tbs	tsp	6.000000
11	inch to feet	12.00	in	ft	1.000000
12	year to day	10.00	yr	day	3652.500000
13	bit to byte	1024.00	bit	byte	128.000000

Here is an extensive list of all of the units that you can use:

Category	Unit	Usage in CONVERT FORMULA
Weight and mass	Gram	"g"
Weight and mass	Slug	"sg"
Weight and mass	Pound mass (avoirdupois)	"lbm"
Weight and mass	U (atomic mass unit)	"u"
Weight and mass	Ounce mass (avoirdupois)	"ozm"
Weight and mass	Grain	"grain"
Weight and mass	U.S. (short) hundredweight	"cwt" or "shweight"
Weight and mass	Imperial hundredweight	"uk_cwt" or "lcwt" ("hweight")
Weight and mass	Stone	"stone"
Weight and mass	Ton	"ton"
Weight and mass	Imperial ton	"uk_ton" or "LTON" ("brton")
Distance	Meter	"m"
Distance	Statute mile	"mi"
Distance	Nautical mile	"Nmi"
Distance	Inch	"in"
Distance	Foot	"ft"
Distance	Yard	"yd"
Distance	Angstrom	"ang"
Distance	Ell	"ell"
Distance	Light-year	"ly"
Distance	Parsec	"parsec" or "pc"
Distance	Pica (1/72 inch)	"Picapt" or "Pica"
Distance	Pica (1/6 inch)	"pica"

Distance	U.S survey mile (statute mile)	"survey_mi"
Time	Year	"yr"
Time	Day	"day" or "d"
Time	Hour	"hr"
Time	Minute	"mn" or "min"
Time	Second	"sec" or "s"
Pressure	Pascal	"Pa" (or "p")
Pressure	Atmosphere	"atm" (or "at")
Pressure	mm of Mercury	"mmHg"
Pressure	PSI	"psi"
Pressure	Torr	"Torr"
Force	Newton	"N"
Force	Dyne	"dyn" (or "dy")
Force	Pound force	"lbf"
Force	Pond	"pond"
Energy	Joule	"J"
Energy	Erg	"e"
Energy	Thermodynamic calorie	"c"
Energy	IT calorie	"cal"
Energy	Electron volt	"eV" (or "ev")
Energy	Horsepower-hour	"HPh" (or "hh")
Energy	Watt-hour	"Wh" (or "wh")
Energy	Foot-pound	"flb"
Energy	BTU	"BTU" (or "btu")
Power	Horsepower	"HP" (or "h")
Power	Pferdestärke	"PS"
Power	Watt	"W" (or "w")
Magnetism	Tesla	"T"
Magnetism	Gauss	"ga"
Temperature	Degree Celsius	"C" (or "cel")
Temperature	Degree Fahrenheit	"F" (or "fah")
Temperature	Kelvin	"K" (or "kel")
Temperature	Degrees Rankine	"Rank"
Temperature	Degrees Réaumur	"Reau"
Volume	Teaspoon	"tsp"
Volume	Modern teaspoon	"tspm"
Volume	Tablespoon	"tbs"
Volume	Fluid ounce	"oz"
Volume	Cup	"cup"
Volume	U.S. pint	"pt" (or "us_pt")
Volume	U.K. pint	"uk_pt"
Volume	Quart	"qt"
Volume	Imperial quart (U.K.)	"uk_qt"
Volume	Gallon	"gal"
Volume	Imperial gallon (U.K.)	"uk_gal"
Volume	Liter	"l" or "L" ("lt")
Volume	Cubic angstrom	"ang3" or "ang^3"

Volume	U.S. oil barrel	"barrel"
Volume	U.S. bushel	"bushel"
Volume	Cubic feet	"ft3" or "ft^3"
Volume	Cubic inch	"in3" or "in^3"
Volume	Cubic light-year	"ly3" or "ly^3"
Volume	Cubic meter	"m3" or "m^3"
Volume	Cubic Mile	"mi3" or "mi^3"
Volume	Cubic yard	"yd3" or "yd^3"
Volume	Cubic nautical mile	"Nmi3" or "Nmi^3"
Volume	Cubic Pica	"Picapt3", "Picapt^3", "Pica3" or "Pica^3"
Volume	Gross Registered Ton	"GRT" ("regton")
Volume	Measurement ton (freight ton)	"MTON"
Area	International acre	"uk_acre"
Area	U.S. survey/statute acre	"us_acre"
Area	Square angstrom	"ang2" or "ang^2"
Area	Are	"ar"
Area	Square feet	"ft2" or "ft^2"
Area	Hectare	"ha"
Area	Square inches	"in2" or "in^2"
Area	Square light-year	"ly2" or "ly^2"
Area	Square meters	"m2" or "m^2"
Area	Morgen	"Morgen"
Area	Square miles	"mi2" or "mi^2"
Area	Square nautical miles	"Nmi2" or "Nmi^2"
Area	Square Pica	"Picapt2", "Pica2", "Pica^2" or "Picapt^2"
Area	Square yards	"yd2" or "yd^2"
Information	Bit	"bit"
Information	Byte	"byte"
Speed	Admiralty knot	"admkn"
Speed	Knot	"kn"
Speed	Meters per hour	"m/h" or "m/hr"
Speed	Meters per second	"m/s" or "m/sec"
Speed	Miles per hour	"mph"

The following abbreviated unit prefixes can be added in front of any **metric** from_unit or to_unit.

Prefix	Multiplier	Abbreviation
yotta	1.00E+24	"Y"
zetta	1.00E+21	"Z"
exa	1.00E+18	"E"
peta	1.00E+15	"P"
tera	1.00E+12	"T"
giga	1.00E+09	"G"
mega	1.00E+06	"M"
kilo	1.00E+03	"k"
hecto	1.00E+02	"h"
dekao	1.00E+01	"da" or "e"
deci	1.00E-01	"d"
centi	1.00E-02	"c"
milli	1.00E-03	"m"
micro	1.00E-06	"u"
nano	1.00E-09	"n"
pico	1.00E-12	"p"
femto	1.00E-15	"f"
atto	1.00E-18	"a"
zepto	1.00E-21	"z"
yocto	1.00E-24	"y"

FV – Compound Interest

What does it do?

Calculates the compound interest of an initial investment

Formula breakdown:

=FV(rate, nper, pmt, [pv])

What it means:

=FV(interest rate, number of periods, periodic payment, initial amount)

Example:

=FV(0.1,2,0,1000*-1) =$1210

Say that you turn 18 years today (CONGRATS!) and you find out that your parents deposited an amount with their bank when you were born.

Now that you are 18 years old you can collect this money and go spend it all in one day!

How much would be available for you to spend?

Thankfully there is an easy way to calculate this with Excel's **FV formula!** **FV** stands for **Future Value.**

The future value (FV) is the value of a current asset at a specified date in the future based on an assumed rate of growth over time.

In our example below, we have the table of values that we need to get the compound interest or Future Value from:

*(Change the **NUMBER OF YEARS** column to 18 to see the results on your 18th birthday)*

	A	B	C	D
	INITIAL AMOUNT	INTEREST RATE	NUMBER OF YEARS	TOTAL AMOUNT WITH INTEREST
9	$1,000.00	10%	2	
10	$5,000.00	4%	10	
11	$300.00	22%	5	
12	$3,500.00	15%	25	

STEP 1: We need to **enter the *FV* function in a blank cell**:

=FV(

	A	B	C	D
	INITIAL AMOUNT	INTEREST RATE	NUMBER OF YEARS	
9	$1,000.00	10%	2	=FV(
10	$5,000.00	4%	10	
11	$300.00	22%	5	FV(rate, nper, pmt, [pv], [type])
12	$3,500.00	15%	25	

STEP 2: The **FV** arguments:

rate

What is the rate of the interest?

Select the cell containing the interest rate (make sure that this is in a percentage):

=FV(B9,

	A	B	C	D
8	INITIAL AMOUNT	INTEREST RATE	NUMBER OF YEARS	
9	$1,000.00	10%	2	=FV(B9,
10	$5,000.00	4%	10	
11	$300.00	22%	5	FV(rate, **nper**, pmt, [pv], [type])
12	$3,500.00	15%	25	

nper

How many periods?

Select the cell containing the number of years:

=FV(B9, C9,

	A	B	C	D
8	INITIAL AMOUNT	INTEREST RATE	NUMBER OF YEARS	
9	$1,000.00	10%	2	=FV(B9,C9,
10	$5,000.00	4%	10	
11	$300.00	22%	5	FV(rate, nper, **pmt**, [pv], [type])
12	$3,500.00	15%	25	

pmt

What is the periodic payment?

We have no periodic payment, only an initial amount, so let us put in 0:

=FV(B9, C9, 0,

	A	B	C	D
8	INITIAL AMOUNT	INTEREST RATE	NUMBER OF YEARS	
9	$1,000.00	10%	2	=FV(B9,C9,0,
10	$5,000.00	4%	10	
11	$300.00	22%	5	FV(rate, nper, pmt, **[pv]**, [type])
12	$3,500.00	15%	25	

pv

What is the initial amount?

PV stands for present value, the initial amount. We need to change this to a negative value by multiplying -1.

The reason why we need this as a negative value as Excel treats this as "money out" for your investment.

=FV(B9, C9, 0, A9 * -1)

	A	B	C	D
8	INITIAL AMOUNT	INTEREST RATE	NUMBER OF YEARS	
9	$1,000.00	10%	2	=FV(B9,C9,0,A9*-1)
10	$5,000.00	4%	10	
11	$300.00	22%	5	
12	$3,500.00	15%	25	

Apply the same formula to the rest of the cells by dragging the lower right corner downwards.

You now have all of the compound interest results! GO OUT & SPEND!

	A	B	C	D
8	INITIAL AMOUNT	INTEREST RATE	NUMBER OF YEARS	TOTAL AMOUNT WITH INTEREST
9	$1,000.00	10%	2	$1,210.00
10	$5,000.00	4%	10	$7,401.22
11	$300.00	22%	5	$810.81
12	$3,500.00	15%	25	$115,216.33
13				

FV – Monthly Investment

What does it do?

Calculates the compound interest when you have monthly contributions

Formula breakdown:

=FV(rate, nper, pmt, [pv])

What it means:

=FV(interest rate, number of periods, periodic payment, initial amount)

Example:

=FV(0.1/12,2*12,500,0) * -1 =$13,223.46

Computing the compound interest of an initial investment is easy for a fixed number of years. But let's add an additional challenge.

What if you are also putting in **monthly contributions** to your investment? Now that's a lot more challenging to compute now!

How much would be available for you at the end of your investment?

Thankfully there is an easy way to calculate this with Excel's **FV formula!** **FV** stands for **Future Value.**

In our example below, we have the table of values that we need to get the compound interest or Future Value from:

	A	B	C	D	E
8	INITIAL AMOUNT	INTEREST RATE	NUMBER OF YEARS	MONTHLY CONTRIBUTIONS	TOTAL AMOUNT WITH INTEREST
9	$ -	10%	2	$ 500.00	
10	$ 5,000.00	4%	10	$ 1,000.00	
11	$ 300.00	22%	5	$ 50.00	
12	$ 3,500.00	15%	25	$ 120.00	

There are two important concepts we need to use since we are using monthly contributions:

- Since our interest rate is the annual rate, we will have to **divide it by 12** to make it monthly
- We will need to convert our number of years into number of months by **multiplying it by 12**

STEP 1: We need to **enter the _FV_ function in a blank cell**:

$$=FV($$

	A	B	C	D	E	F
8	INITIAL AMOUNT	INTEREST RATE	NUMBER OF YEARS	MONTHLY CONTRIBUTIONS		
9	$ -	10%	2	$ 500.00	=FV(	
10	$ 5,000.00	4%	10	$ 1,000.00		
11	$ 300.00	22%	5	$ 50.00	FV(rate, nper, pmt, [pv], [type])	
12	$ 3,500.00	15%	25	$ 120.00		

STEP 2: The **FV** arguments:

rate

What is the rate of the interest?

Select the cell containing the interest rate and divide it by 12 to get the monthly interest rate (make sure that this is in a percentage):

$$=FV(B9/12,$$

	A	B	C	D	E	F
8	INITIAL AMOUNT	INTEREST RATE	NUMBER OF YEARS	MONTHLY CONTRIBUTIONS		
9	$ -	10%	2	$ 500.00	=FV(B9/12,	
10	$ 5,000.00	4%	10	$ 1,000.00		
11	$ 300.00	22%	5	$ 50.00	FV(rate, **nper**, pmt, [pv], [type])	
12	$ 3,500.00	15%	25	$ 120.00		

nper

How many periods?

Select the cell containing the number of years and multiply it by 12 to get the number of months:

$$=FV(B9/12,\ C9*12,$$

	A	B	C	D	E	F
8	INITIAL AMOUNT	INTEREST RATE	NUMBER OF YEARS	MONTHLY CONTRIBUTIONS		
9	$ -	10%	2	$ 500.00	=FV(B9/12,C9*12,	
10	$ 5,000.00	4%	10	$ 1,000.00		
11	$ 300.00	22%	5	$ 50.00	FV(rate, nper, **pmt**, [pv], [type])	
12	$ 3,500.00	15%	25	$ 120.00		

pmt

What is the periodic payment?

Select the cell that contains your monthly contribution (this is your periodic payment):

$$=FV(B9/12,\ C9*12,\ D9,$$

	A	B	C	D	E	F
8	INITIAL AMOUNT	INTEREST RATE	NUMBER OF YEARS	MONTHLY CONTRIBUTIONS		
9	$ -	10%	2	$ 500.00	=FV(B9/12,C9*12,D9,	
10	$ 5,000.00	4%	10	$ 1,000.00		
11	$ 300.00	22%	5	$ 50.00	FV(rate, nper, pmt, [pv], [type])	
12	$ 3,500.00	15%	25	$ 120.00		

What is the initial amount?

PV stands for present value, the initial amount. Multiply the entire result by -1.

=FV(B9/12, C9*12, D9, A9) * -1

	A	B	C	D	E	F
8	INITIAL AMOUNT	INTEREST RATE	NUMBER OF YEARS	MONTHLY CONTRIBUTIONS		
9	$ -	10%	2	$ 500.00	=FV(B9/12,C9*12,D9,A9)*-1	
10	$ 5,000.00	4%	10	$ 1,000.00		
11	$ 300.00	22%	5	$ 50.00		
12	$ 3,500.00	15%	25	$ 120.00		

Apply the same formula to the rest of the cells by dragging the lower right corner downwards.

You now have all of the compound interest results!

	A	B	C	D	E	F
8	INITIAL AMOUNT	INTEREST RATE	NUMBER OF YEARS	MONTHLY CONTRIBUTIONS	TOTAL AMOUNT WITH INTEREST	
9	$ -	10%	2	$ 500.00	$13,223.46	
10	$ 5,000.00	4%	10	$ 1,000.00	$154,703.97	
11	$ 300.00	22%	5	$ 50.00	$6,277.01	
12	$ 3,500.00	15%	25	$ 120.00	$534,627.97	
13						

CONCAT

What does it do?

Concatenates a list together without a delimiter

Formula breakdown:

=CONCAT(text1, [text2], ...)

What it means:

=CONCAT(first text to combine, [second text to combine], ...)

Example:

=CONCAT("Hello", " ", "World") ="Hello World"

Do you want to combine text or a range of cells together easily? The **CONCAT Formula** in Excel will do this for you in a flash!

It will simply combine the text you specify together into a single text.

STEP 1: We need to **enter the *CONCAT* function in a blank cell**:

=CONCAT(

	C	D	E	F
	TEXT 1	**TEXT 2**	**TEXT 3**	
8				
9	Combine	us	together	=CONCAT(
10	Hello		World	
11	Hi			CONCAT(text1, ...)

text1, …

Which cells do you want to combine together?

Select the range of cells that you want to combine together

=CONCAT(C9:E9)

	TEXT 1	TEXT 2	TEXT 3	
8				
9	Combine	us	together	=CONCAT(C9:E9)
10	Hello		World	
11	Hi			
12				

Apply the same formula to the rest of the cells by dragging the lower right corner downwards.

	TEXT 1	TEXT 2	TEXT 3	COMBINED TEXT
8				
9	Combine	us	together	Combineustogether
10	Hello		World	
11	Hi			

You now have your combined text!

	TEXT 1	TEXT 2	TEXT 3	COMBINED TEXT	
8					
9	Combine	us	together	Combineustogether	
10	Hello		World	HelloWorld	
11	Hi			Hi	
12					
13					

If we were to do this the old way it would look something like this using the CONCATENATE FORMULA:

=CONCATENATE(C9,D9,E9)

It is way easier using the **CONCAT Formula**!

IFS

What does it do?

Checks multiple conditions and returns the value of the first TRUE condition

Formula breakdown:

=IFS(logical_test1, value_if_true1, [logical_test2, value_if_true2], ...)

What it means:

=IFS(first condition to check, value to return, [succeeding conditions to check], ...)

Example:

=IFS(10000<8456, 13%, 10000<15874, 18%, 10000>=15874, 22%)

=18%

If you have multiple logical conditions to check, instead of creating Nested IF Formulas, we can use **Excel's IFS Formula!** It allows us to specify multiple conditions to check, then the **IFS Formula** will look for the first condition that gets satisfied!

Let us try it out on a simple tax table, then we will create an **IFS Formula** that will simulate the exact same logic of the table!

=IFS(

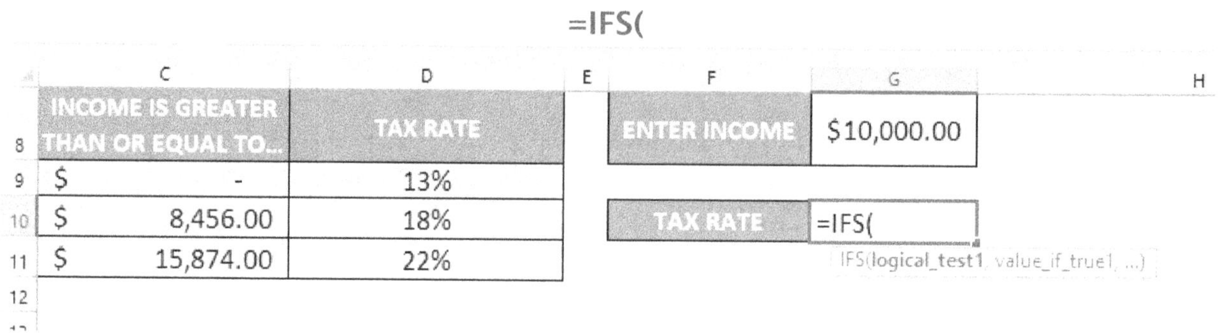

STEP 2: The **IFS** arguments:

logical_test1, value_if_true1

What is the first condition and value to return if the condition is met?

Let us start from the minimum value of the tax table. If the income is less than $8456, then the tax rate is 13%

=IFS(G8<8456, 13%,

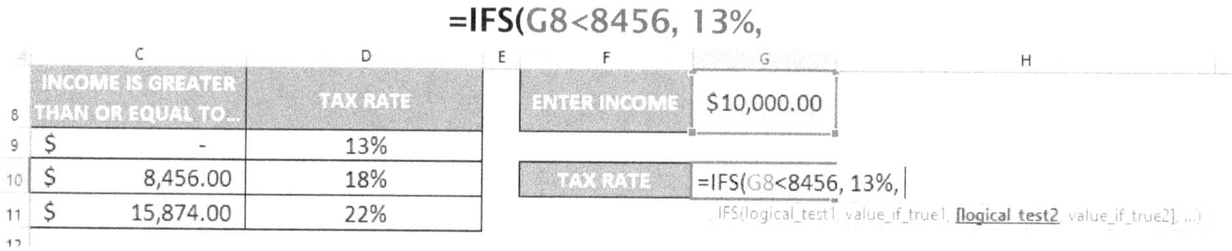

logical_test2, value_if_true2

What is the second condition and value to return if the condition is met?

Going to the second row, if the income is less than $15874, then the tax rate is 18%

=IFS(G8<8456, 13%, G8<15874, 18%,

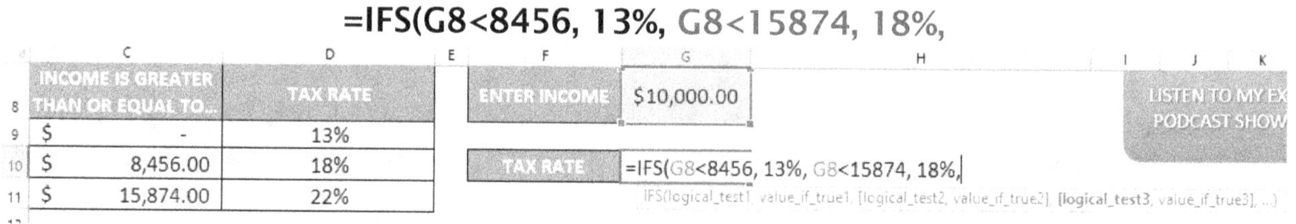

What is the third condition and value to return if the condition is met?

Going to the last row, if the income is greater than or equal to $15874, then the tax rate is 22%

=IFS(G8<8456, 13%, G8<15874, 18%, G8>=15874, 22%)

	INCOME IS GREATER THAN OR EQUAL TO...	TAX RATE		ENTER INCOME	$10,000.00		
9	$ -	13%					
10	$ 8,456.00	18%		TAX RATE	=IFS(G8<8456, 13%, G8<15874, 18%, G8>=15874, 22%)		
11	$ 15,874.00	22%					

You now have your correct tax rate!

	INCOME IS GREATER THAN OR EQUAL TO...	TAX RATE		ENTER INCOME	$10,000.00
9	$ -	13%			
10	$ 8,456.00	18%		TAX RATE	18%
11	$ 15,874.00	22%			
12					

If we were to do this the old way it would look something like this using Nested IF Formulas:

=IF(G8<8456, 13%, IF(G8<15874, 18%, 22%))

It is much neater & easier to read using the **IFS Formula**, especially if you have lots of conditions!

MAXIFS

What does it do?

Gets the max value based on the cells that matches certain criteria

Formula breakdown:

=MAXIFS(max_range, criteria_range1, criteria1, ...)

What it means:

=MAXIFS(cells that contains the values, first set of cells to base the filtering on, filtering condition of first set of cells, ...)

Example:

=MAXIFS(D9:D13, C9:C13, "John") = $3,500

i.e. John's largest sale was $3,500

If you need to get the max value based on certain criteria, the **MAXIFS Formula** will do this for you in Excel!

STEP 1: We need to **enter the *MAXIFS* function in a blank cell**:

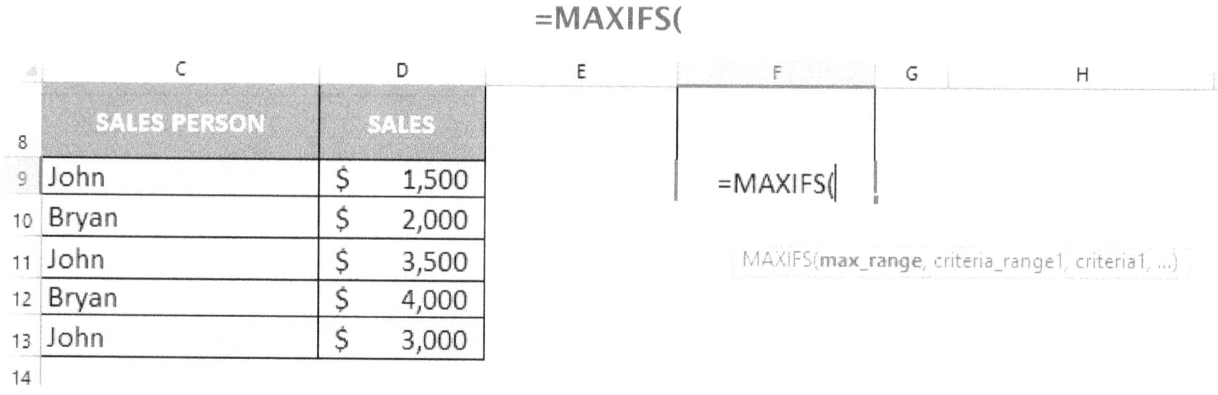

max_range

What is the range that contains the values to get the max value from?

Select the cells containing the sales numbers that you want to get the maximum value from:

=MAXIFS(D9:D13,

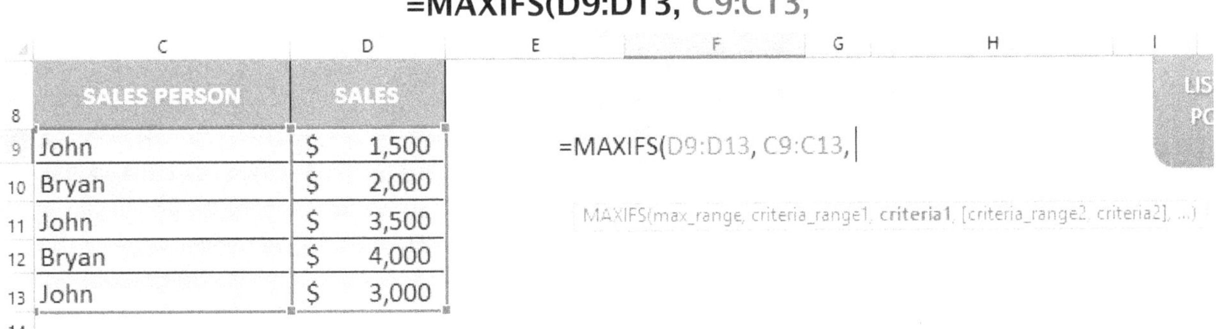

criteria_range1

What is the range that contains the values for filtering?

Select the cells containing the sales person names:

=MAXIFS(D9:D13, C9:C13,

What is your filtering criteria?

Since we want to filter the sales numbers for John, type in "John":

=MAXIFS(D9:D13, C9:C13, "John")

	SALES PERSON	D
8		
9	John	=MAXIFS(D9:D13, C9:C13, "John")
10	Bryan	$
11	John	$ 3,500
12	Bryan	$ 4,000
13	John	$ 3,000

You now have John's largest sales number!

	SALES PERSON	SALES		MAX SALES OF JOHN
8				
9	John	$ 1,500		$ 3,500
10	Bryan	$ 2,000		
11	John	$ 3,500		
12	Bryan	$ 4,000		
13	John	$ 3,000		

MINIFS

What does it do?

Gets the minimum value based on the cells that matches certain criteria

Formula breakdown:

=MINIFS(min_range, criteria_range1, criteria1, ...)

What it means:

=MINIFS(cells that contains the values, first set of cells to base the filtering on, filtering condition of first set of cells, ...)

Example:

=MINIFS(D9:D13,C9:C13,"John") = $1,500

i.e. John's smallest sale was $1,500

If you need to get the minimum value based on certain criteria, the **MINIFS Formula** will do this for you in Excel!

STEP 1: We need to **enter the *MINIFS* function in a blank cell:**

=MINIFS(

	SALES PERSON	SALES			=MINIFS(
8					
9	John	$ 1,500			
10	Bryan	$ 100			
11	John	$ 3,500			
12	Bryan	$ 4,000			
13	John	$ 3,000			

MINIFS(min_range, criteria_range1, criteria1, ...)

min_range

What is the range that contains the values to get the min value from?

Select the cells containing the sales numbers that you want to get the minimum value from:

=MINIFS(D9:D13,

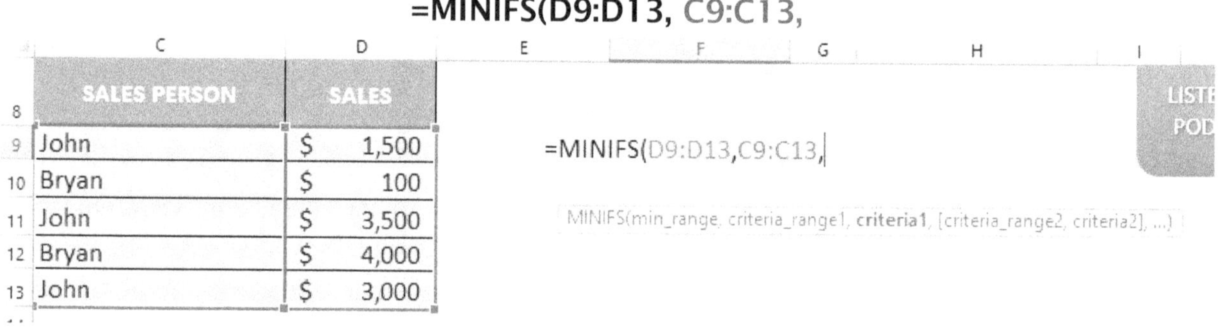

criteria_range1

What is the range that contains the values for filtering?

Select the cells containing the sales person names:

=MINIFS(D9:D13, C9:C13,

What is your filtering criteria?

Since we want to filter the sales numbers for John, type in "John":

=MINIFS(D9:D13, C9:C13, "John")

	C	D	E	F
	SALES PERSON			
8				
9	John	=MINIFS(D9:D13,C9:C13,"John")		
10	Bryan	$		
11	John	$ 3,500		
12	Bryan	$ 4,000		
13	John	$ 3,000		

You now have John's smallest sales number!

	C	D	E	F
	SALES PERSON	SALES		MIN SALES OF JOHN
8				
9	John	$ 1,500		$ 1,500
10	Bryan	$ 100		
11	John	$ 3,500		
12	Bryan	$ 4,000		
13	John	$ 3,000		

SWITCH

What does it do?

Matches multiple values and returns the first value that has a match

Formula breakdown:

=SWITCH(expression, value1, result1, [value2 / default, result2], ...)

What it means:

=SWITCH(value to check, value to match against, result to return, [succeeding values to match or the default value if nothing gets matched], ...)

Example:

=SWITCH(3, 1, "Bad", 2, "Average", 3, "Great", "Unknown") ="Great"

If you have multiple values to check, we can use **Excel's SWITCH Formula!** It allows us to specify multiple values to check, then the **SWITCH Formula** will look for the first value that gets matched!

Let us try it out on a simple ratings table (e.g. 1 = Bad, 2 = Average, 3 = Great), then we will create a **SWITCH Formula** that will simulate the exact same logic of the table!

STEP 1: We need to **enter the SWITCH function in a blank cell**:

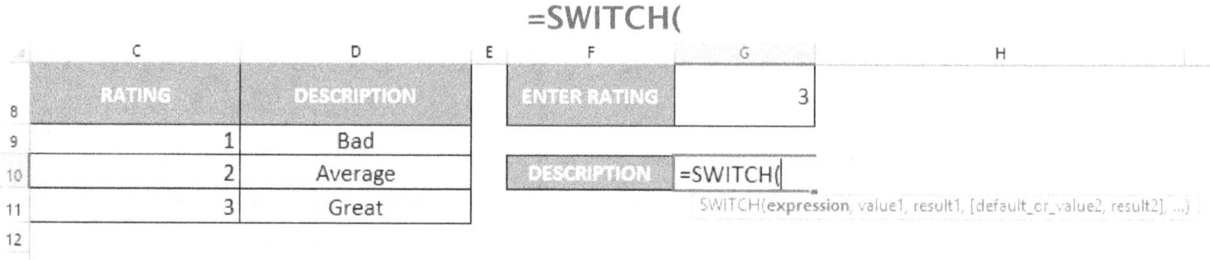

expression

What is the value to check?

Select the cell containing the rating that you want to translate to the correct description

=SWITCH(G8,

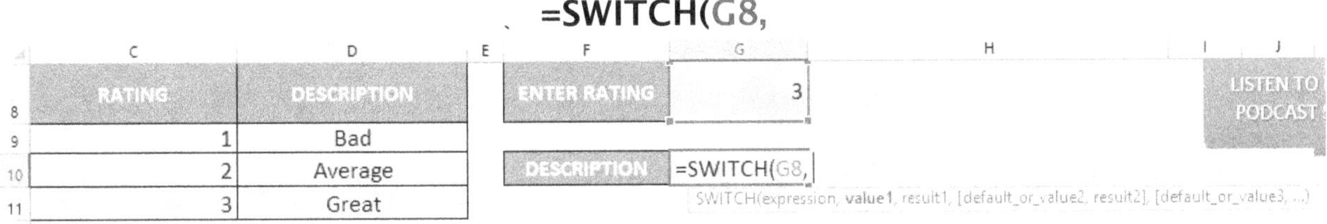

value1, result1

What is the first lookup value and value to return if it is matched?

Let us start from the first value of the rating table. If the value is 1, then the description is "Bad"

=SWITCH(G8, 1, "Bad"

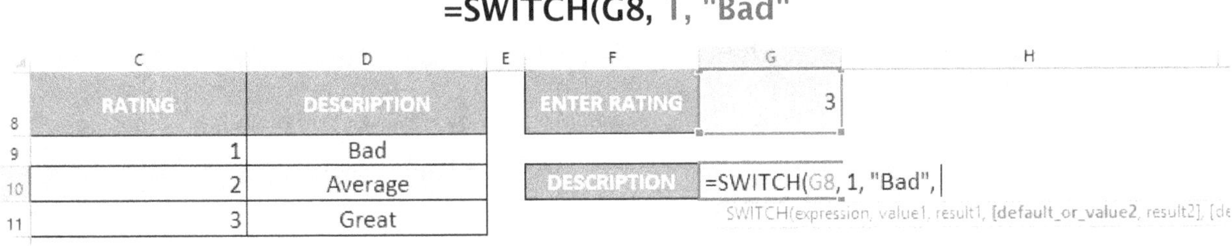

value2, result2

What is the second lookup value and value to return if it is matched?

Let us start from the second value of the rating table. If the value is 2, then the description is "Average"

=SWITCH(G8, 1, "Bad", 2, "Average",

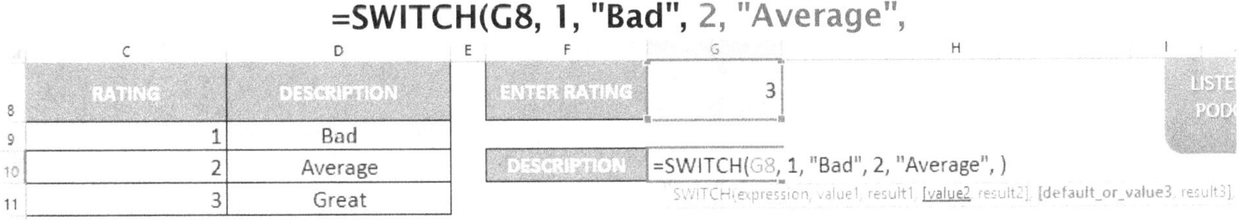

value3, result3

What is the third lookup value and value to return if it is matched?

Let us start from the third value of the rating table. If the value is 3, then the description is "Great"

=SWITCH(G8, 1, "Bad", 2, "Average", 3, "Great",

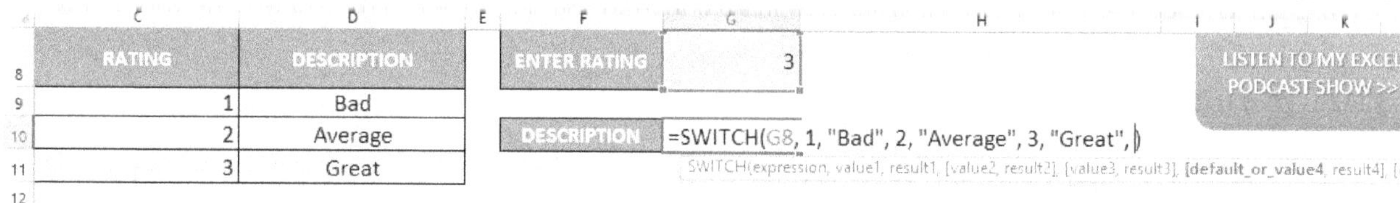

default

What is the default value to return if nothing gets matched?

We want to show the value "Unknown", if an unknown rating is specified.

=SWITCH(G8, 1, "Bad", 2, "Average", 3, "Great", "Unknown")

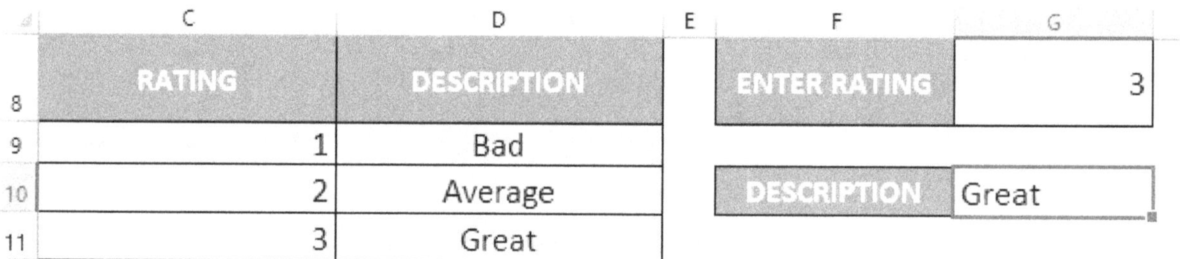

You now have your correct rating description!

	RATING	DESCRIPTION		ENTER RATING	3
9	1	Bad			
10	2	Average		DESCRIPTION	Great
11	3	Great			

Let us try an unknown rating (40) and see the resulting description:

	RATING	DESCRIPTION		ENTER RATING	40
9	1	Bad			
10	2	Average		DESCRIPTION	Unknown
11	3	Great			

If we were to do this the old way it would look something like this using Nested IF Formulas:

=IF(G8= 1, "Bad", IF(G8=2, "Average", IF(G8=3, "Great", "Unknown")))

It is way easier using the **SWITCH Formula**!

TEXTJOIN

What does it do?

Concatenates a list with a specified delimiter

Formula breakdown:

=TEXTJOIN(delimiter, ignore_empty, text1, ...)

What it means:

=TEXTJOIN(the delimiter, ignore empty cells in combining text, first text/range to combine, ...)

Example:

=TEXTJOIN(",",TRUE,"Hello","World") ="Hello,World"

Do you want to combine text or a range of cells together easily? The **TEXTJOIN Formula** in Excel will do this for you in a flash! The **TEXTJOIN Formula** was introduced in Excel 2016.

It can even let you specify a **delimiter** to use to combine the text together and **ignore empty cells** for you!

I explain how you can do this below:

=TEXTJOIN(

	TEXT 1	TEXT 2	TEXT 3			
	C	D	E	F	G	H
8						
9	Combine	us	together	=TEXTJOIN(		
10	Hello		World			
11			Hi	TEXTJOIN(delimiter, ignore_empty, text1, ...)		
12						

STEP 2: The **TEXTJOIN** arguments:

delimiter

What is the delimiter to use in combining the text?

We want to have the text combined together and separated by a comma:

=TEXTJOIN(",",

	TEXT 1	TEXT 2	TEXT 3			
	C	D	E	F	G	H
8						
9	Combine	us	together	=TEXTJOIN(",",		
10	Hello		World			
11			Hi	TEXTJOIN(delimiter, ignore_empty, text1, [text2], ...)		
12				TRUE - Ignore empty cells		
				FALSE - Include empty cells		

ignore_empty

Do you want to ignore the empty cells?

Let us set this to TRUE to ignore the empty cells when combining them together:

=TEXTJOIN(",", TRUE,

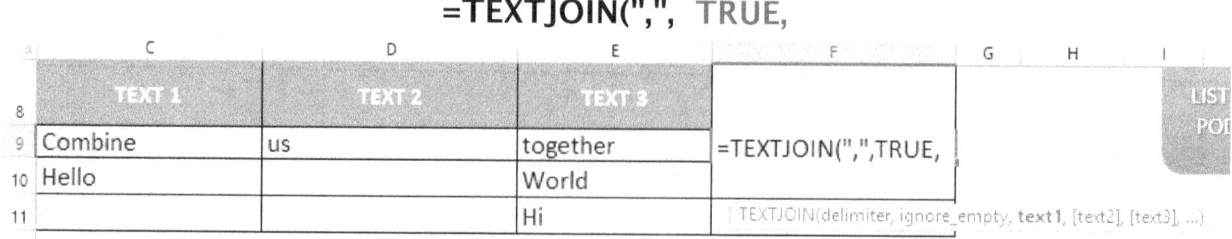

	TEXT 1	TEXT 2	TEXT 3				LIST
	C	D	E	F	G	H	I
8							POI
9	Combine	us	together	=TEXTJOIN(",",TRUE,			
10	Hello		World				
11			Hi	TEXTJOIN(delimiter, ignore_empty, **text1**, [text2], [text3], ...)			

text1, ...

Which cells do you want to combine together?

Select the range of cells that you want to combine together

=TEXTJOIN(",", TRUE, C9:E9)

	TEXT 1	TEXT 2	TEXT 3		
8					
9	Combine	us	together	=TEXTJOIN(",",TRUE,C9:E9)	
10	Hello		World		
11			Hi		

Apply the same formula to the rest of the cells by dragging the lower right corner downwards.

	TEXT 1	TEXT 2	TEXT 3	COMBINED TEXT
8				
9	Combine	us	together	Combine,us,together
10	Hello		World	
11			Hi	
12				

You now have your combined text!

	TEXT 1	TEXT 2	TEXT 3	COMBINED TEXT	
8					
9	Combine	us	together	Combine,us,together	
10	Hello		World	Hello,World	
11			Hi	Hi	
12					
13					

If we were to do this the old way it would look something like this using the CONCATENATE FORMULA:

=CONCATENATE(C9,",",D9,",",E9)

And it does not even have the capability to ignore empty cells. It is way easier using the **TEXTJOIN Formula**!

OFFICE 365
(AS OF SEPTEMBER 2018)

FILTER

What does it do?

Filters a table array based on the filtering condition given

Formula breakdown:

=FILTER(array, include, [if_empty])

What it means:

=FILTER(data to be filtered, the filtering condition, [value to display if nothing gets matched])

Example:

=FILTER(C9:D14,D9:D14>0.33,"") = Shows all the data that has a tax rate > 33%

Did you know that you can now filter your table data with an Excel Formula? Yes you can! It is definitely possible now with **Excel's FILTER Formula**.

We have a tax table that we want to dynamically filter with a given rate.

STEP 1: We need to **enter the FILTER function in a blank cell**:

=FILTER(

	C	D	E	F	G
8	INCOME IS GREATER THAN OR EQUAL TO...	TAX RATE		ENTER TAX RATE FILTER (GREATER THAN)	
9	$ -	13%			
10	$ 8,456.00	18%		INCOME IS GREATER THAN OR EQUAL TO...	TAX RATE
11	$ 15,874.00	22%		=FILTER(	
12	$ 36,897.00	30%		FILTER(array, include, [if_empty])	
13	$ 87,458.00	39%			
14	$ 141,569.00	45%			
15					
16					
17					

STEP 2: The **FILTER** arguments:

array

What is the data to be filtered?

Select the cells containing the tax data, do not include the headers:

$$=FILTER(C9:D14,$$

	C	D	E	F	G
8	INCOME IS GREATER THAN OR EQUAL TO...	TAX RATE		ENTER TAX RATE FILTER (GREATER THAN)	
9	$ -	13%			
10	$ 8,456.00	18%		INCOME IS GREATER THAN OR EQUAL TO...	TAX RATE
11	$ 15,874.00	22%		=FILTER(C9:D14,	
12	$ 36,897.00	30%		FILTER(array, include, [if_empty])	
13	$ 87,458.00	39%			
14	$ 141,569.00	45%			
15					
16					
17					

include

What is your filtering condition?

We want to filter the tax rate that is greater than the specified rate. Type in the condition as the tax rate column > the specific tax rate.

=FILTER(C9:D14, D9:D14>G8

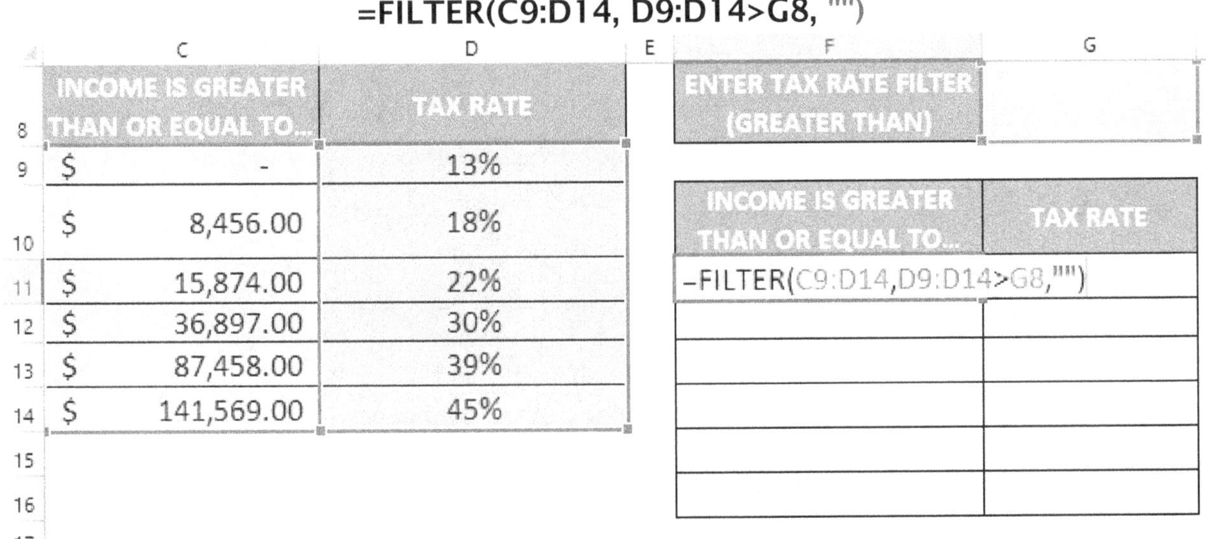

[if_empty]

What is the value to display in case nothing gets matched?

Just place an empty string to be displayed if nothing gets matched.

=FILTER(C9:D14, D9:D14>G8, "")

Try it out now with different values and see it get filtered magically!

	INCOME IS GREATER THAN OR EQUAL TO...	TAX RATE
9	$ -	13%
10	$ 8,456.00	18%
11	$ 15,874.00	22%
12	$ 36,897.00	30%
13	$ 87,458.00	39%
14	$ 141,569.00	45%

ENTER TAX RATE FILTER (GREATER THAN)	15%

INCOME IS GREATER THAN OR EQUAL TO...	TAX RATE
$ 8,456.00	18%
$ 15,874.00	22%
$ 36,897.00	30%
$ 87,458.00	39%
$ 141,569.00	45%

	INCOME IS GREATER THAN OR EQUAL TO...	TAX RATE
9	$ -	13%
10	$ 8,456.00	18%
11	$ 15,874.00	22%
12	$ 36,897.00	30%
13	$ 87,458.00	39%
14	$ 141,569.00	45%

ENTER TAX RATE FILTER (GREATER THAN)	33%

INCOME IS GREATER THAN OR EQUAL TO...	TAX RATE
$ 87,458.00	39%
$ 141,569.00	45%

RANDARRAY

What does it do?

Creates an array of random numbers between 0 and 1

Formula breakdown:

=RANDARRAY([rows], [columns])

What it means:

=RANDARRAY(number of rows, number of columns)

Example:

=RANDARRAY(6,2)

=Random numbers in a table of 6 rows and 2 columns

Ever wondered how to create an array of random numbers easily? It is definitely possible now with **Excel's RANDARRAY Formula.**

We want to fill up a table of 6 rows and 2 columns with random numbers between 0 and 1.

STEP 1: We need to **enter the *RANDARRAY* function in a blank cell:**

=RANDARRAY(

	RANDOM VALUE	RANDOM VALUE
8		
9	=RANDARRAY(	
	RANDARRAY([rows], [columns])	
10		
11		
12		
13		
14		

[rows]

How many rows are going to be populated?

We want 6 so input that as the number of rows:

=RANDARRAY(6,

	C	D	E
	RANDOM VALUE	RANDOM VALUE	
8			
9	=RANDARRAY(6,		
	RANDARRAY([rows], [columns])		
10			
11			
12			
13			
14			

[columns]

How many columns are going to be populated?

We want 2 so input that as the number of columns

=RANDARRAY(6, 2)

	C	D	I
	RANDOM VALUE	RANDOM VALUE	
8			
9	=RANDARRAY(6, 2)		
10			
11			
12			
13			
14			

Now you have your random array of values!

	C	D	E
	RANDOM VALUE	RANDOM VALUE	
8			
9	0.35	0.16	
10	0.37	0.38	
11	0.25	0.32	
12	0.82	0.91	
13	0.51	0.91	
14	0.12	0.74	

SEQUENCE

What does it do?

Creates an array of sequential numbers

Formula breakdown:

=SEQUENCE(rows, [columns], [start], [step])

What it means:

=SEQUENCE(number of rows, [number of columns], [starting number], [increment per number])

Example:

=SEQUENCE(6,2,0,2)

=Even numbers starting from 0 in a table of 6 rows and 2 columns

Ever wondered how to create an array of sequential numbers easily? It is definitely possible now with **Excel's SEQUENCE Formula.**

We want to fill up 6 rows and 2 columns with even numbers starting from 0.

STEP 1: We need to **enter the *SEQUENCE* function in a blank cell**:

=SEQUENCE(

	VALUE	VALUE
9	=SEQUENCE(	
	SEQUENCE(rows, [columns], [start], [step])	
10		
11		
12		
13		
14		

rows

How many rows are going to be populated?

We want 6 so input that as the number of rows.

=SEQUENCE(6,

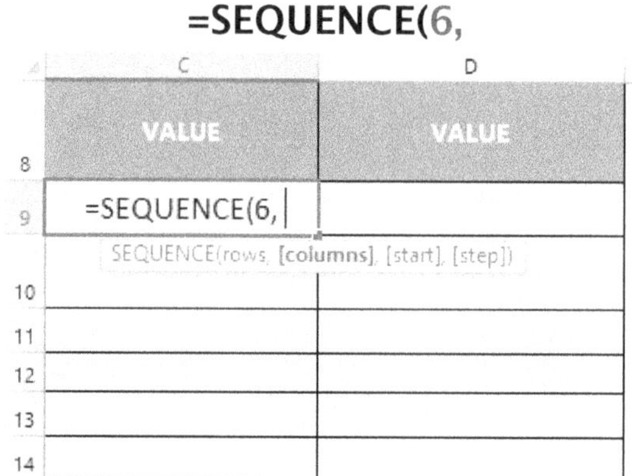

[columns]

How many columns are going to be populated?

We want 2 so input that as the number of columns.

=SEQUENCE(6, 2,

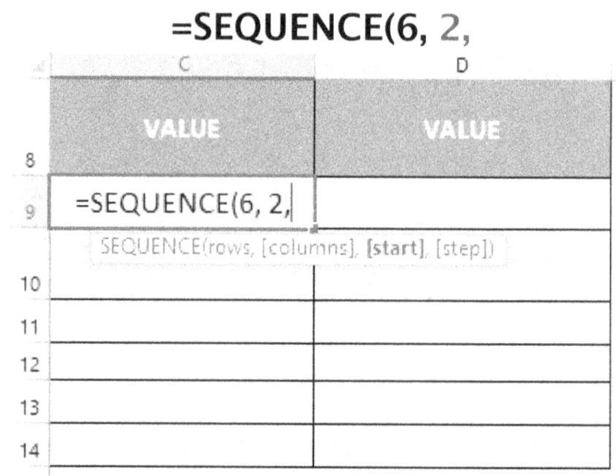

[start]

What is the starting number?

We want the first number to be 0.

=SEQUENCE(6, 2, 0,

	C	D
8	VALUE	VALUE
9	=SEQUENCE(6, 2, 0,	
	SEQUENCE(rows, [columns], [start], [step])	
10		
11		
12		
13		
14		

[step]

What is the interval for each succeeding number?

We want even numbers, so the increment should be 2 for each succeeding number.

=SEQUENCE(6, 2, 0, 2)

	C	D
8	VALUE	VALUE
9	=SEQUENCE(6, 2, 0, 2)	
10		
11		
12		
13		
14		

Now you have your even numbers filled up!

	C	D
8	VALUE	VALUE
9	0	2
10	4	6
11	8	10
12	12	14
13	16	18
14	20	22

SORT

What does it do?

Sorts a table based on a column and order specified

Formula breakdown:

=SORT(array, [sort_index], [sort_order])

What it means:

=SORT(data to be sorted, [which column to be used for sorting], [ascending or descending order])

Example:

=SORT(C9:D14, 2, -1)

Did you know that you can now sort your table data with an Excel Formula? Yes you can! It is definitely possible now with **Excel's SORT Formula**. It is a new formula introduced in **Excel 2019**!

We have a tax table that we want to sort by the tax rate in a **descending order**.

I explain how you can do this below:

STEP 1: We need to **enter the SORT function in a blank cell**:

=SORT(

INCOME IS GREATER THAN OR EQUAL TO…	TAX RATE		SORTED TABLE	
			INCOME IS GREATER THAN OR EQUAL TO…	TAX RATE
$ -	13%		=SORT(	
			SORT(array, [sort_index], [sort_order], [by_col])	
$ 87,458.00	39%			
$ 15,874.00	22%			
$ 36,897.00	30%			
$ 141,569.00	45%			
$ 8,456.00	18%			

STEP 2: The **SORT** arguments:

array

What is the data to be sorted?

Select the cells containing the tax data, do not include the headers:

=SORT(C9:D14,

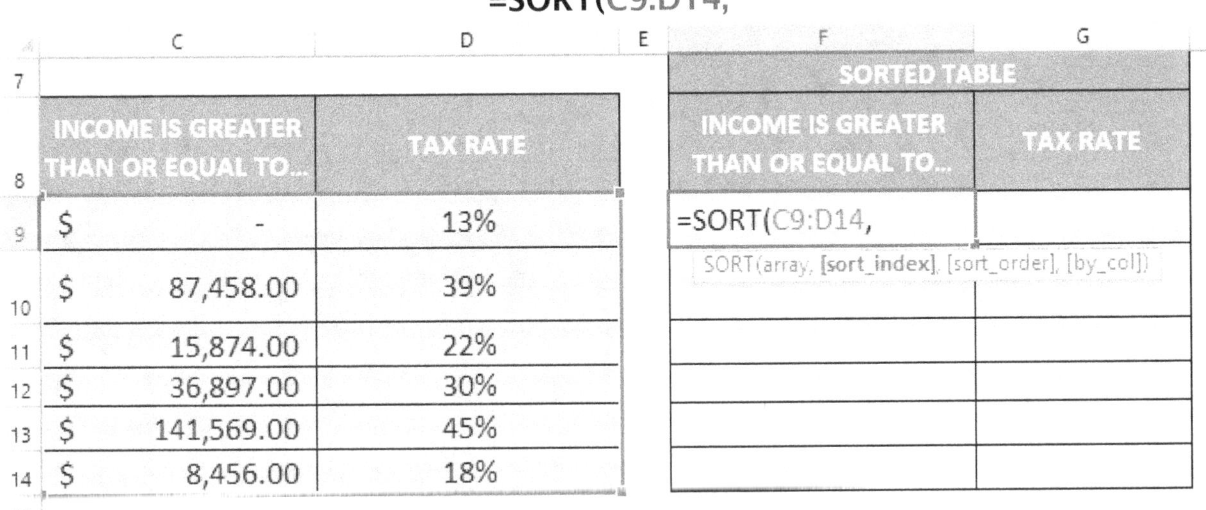

[sort_index]

What is the column to be used for sorting?

We specify the column number here. Since the tax rate column is the second column, place in 2.

=SORT(C9:D14, 2,

	INCOME IS GREATER THAN OR EQUAL TO...	TAX RATE		SORTED TABLE	
				INCOME IS GREATER THAN OR EQUAL TO...	TAX RATE
9	$ -	13%		=SORT(C9:D14, 2,	
				SORT(array, [sort_index], [sort_order], [by_col])	
10	$ 87,458.00	39%			
11	$ 15,874.00	22%			
12	$ 36,897.00	30%			
13	$ 141,569.00	45%			
14	$ 8,456.00	18%			

[sort_order]

What is the sort order? 1 for Ascending, -1 for Descending order.

Since we want descending order, place in -1.

=SORT(C9:D14, 2, -1)

	INCOME IS GREATER THAN OR EQUAL TO...	TAX RATE		SORTED TABLE	
				INCOME IS GREATER THAN OR EQUAL TO...	TAX RATE
9	$ -	13%		=SORT(C9:D14, 2, -1)	
10	$ 87,458.00	39%			
11	$ 15,874.00	22%			
12	$ 36,897.00	30%			
13	$ 141,569.00	45%			
14	$ 8,456.00	18%			

Now it gets sorted magically!

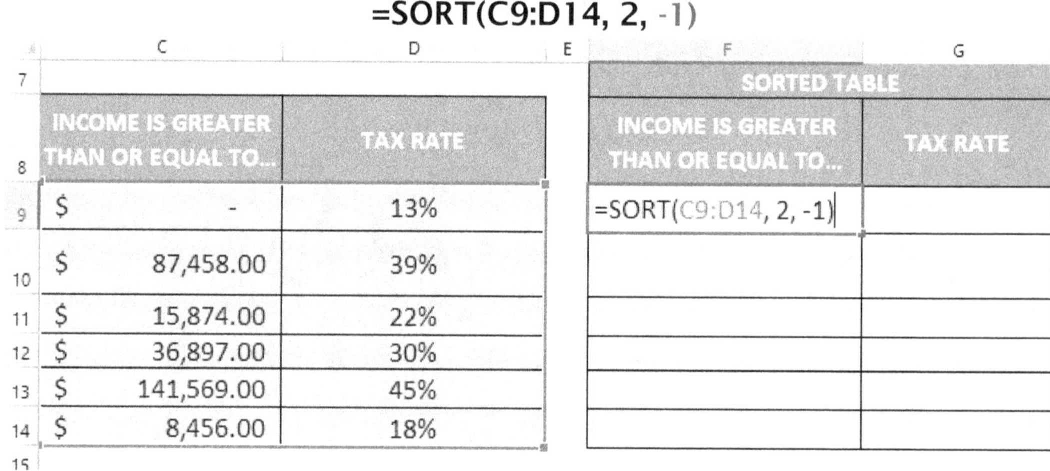

	INCOME IS GREATER THAN OR EQUAL TO...	TAX RATE		SORTED TABLE	
				INCOME IS GREATER THAN OR EQUAL TO...	TAX RATE
9	$ -	13%		$ 141,569.00	45%
10	$ 87,458.00	39%		$ 87,458.00	39%
11	$ 15,874.00	22%		$ 36,897.00	30%
12	$ 36,897.00	30%		$ 15,874.00	22%
13	$ 141,569.00	45%		$ 8,456.00	18%
14	$ 8,456.00	18%		$ -	13%

SORTBY

What does it do?

Sorts a table based on the column(s) specified

Formula breakdown:

=SORTBY(array, by_array1, sort_order1, [by_array2, sort_order2], ...)

What it means:

=SORTBY(data to be sorted, by which column to sort first, [by which column to sort afterwards], ...)

Example:

=SORTBY(B9:D14, B9:B14, 1, D9:D14, 1)

Did you know that you can now sort your table data with an Excel Formula? Yes you can! It is definitely possible now with **Excel's SORTBY Formula**. It also allows you to sort by multiple columns as well. It is a new formula introduced in **Excel 2019**!

We have a person list that we want to sort by Gender (ascending order) and then by Age (ascending order).

Do take note that in specifying the sorting order, 1 represents ascending order, -1 represents descending order.

I explain how you can do this below:

=SORTBY(

	B	C	D	E	F	G	H
7						SORTED TABLE	
8	GENDER	NAME	AGE		GENDER	NAME	AGE
9	M	John	32		=SORTBY(		
10	M	Bryan	35		SORTBY(array, by_array1, sort_order1], ...)		
11	F	Kay	25				
12	M	Michael	30				
13	F	Cess	32				
14	F	Jill	44				

STEP 2: The **SORTBY** arguments:

array

What is the data to be sorted?

Select the cells containing the personal data, do not include the headers:

=SORTBY(B9:D14,

	B	C	D	E	F	G	H
7						SORTED TABLE	
8	GENDER	NAME	AGE		GENDER	NAME	AGE
9	M	John	32	=SORTBY(B9:D14,			
10	M	Bryan	35		SORTBY(array, by_array1, sort_order1], [by_array2, ...)		
11	F	Kay	25				
12	M	Michael	30				
13	F	Cess	32				
14	F	Jill	44				

by_array1, sort_order1

Which column will be used to sort first?

Select the cells containing the gender column, then type in 1 for it to be ascending order.

=SORTBY(B9:D14, B9:B14, 1,

B	C	D	E	F	G	H
					SORTED TABLE	
GENDER	NAME	AGE		GENDER	NAME	AGE
M	John	=SORTBY(B9:D14, B9:B14, 1,				
M	Bryan	35				
F	Kay	25				
M	Michael	30				
F	Cess	32				
F	Jill	44				

SORTBY(array, by_array1, sort_order1], [by_array2, sort_order2], [by_array3, …)

by_array2, sort_order2

Which column will be used to sort next?

Select the cells containing the age column, then type in 1 for it to be ascending order.

=SORTBY(B9:D14, B9:B14, 1, D9:D14, 1)

B	C	D	E	F	G	H
					SORTED TABLE	
GENDER	NAME	AGE		GENDER	NAME	AGE
M	John	32		=SORTBY(B9:D14, B9:B14, 1, D9:D14, 1)		
M	Bryan	35				
F	Kay	25				
M	Michael	30				
F	Cess	32				
F	Jill	44				

Now it gets sorted magically!

B	C	D	E	F	G	H
					SORTED TABLE	
GENDER	NAME	AGE		GENDER	NAME	AGE
M	John	32		F	Kay	25
M	Bryan	35		F	Cess	32
F	Kay	25		F	Jill	44
M	Michael	30		M	Michael	30
F	Cess	32		M	John	32
F	Jill	44		M	Bryan	35

UNIQUE

What does it do?

Gets the unique values of a list

Formula breakdown:

=UNIQUE(array)

What it means:

=UNIQUE(data to have duplicates removed)

Example:

=UNIQUE(C9:C14)

Want to remove duplicate values from your list? It is definitely possible now with **Excel's UNIQUE Formula**. It is a new formula introduced in **Excel 2019**!

We have a list of names and we want to remove the duplicates from it. The **UNIQUE Formula** will make this very quick to do!

STEP 1: We need to **enter the *UNIQUE* function in a blank cell**:

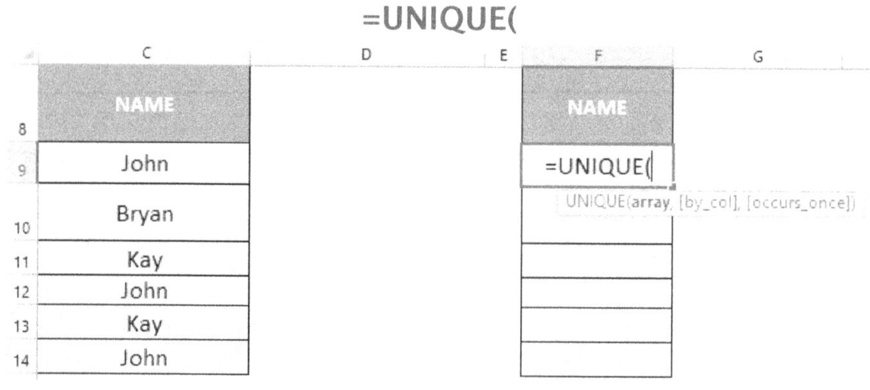

array

What is the data to be cleared of duplicate values?

Select the cells containing the names, do not include the headers:

=UNIQUE(C9:C14)

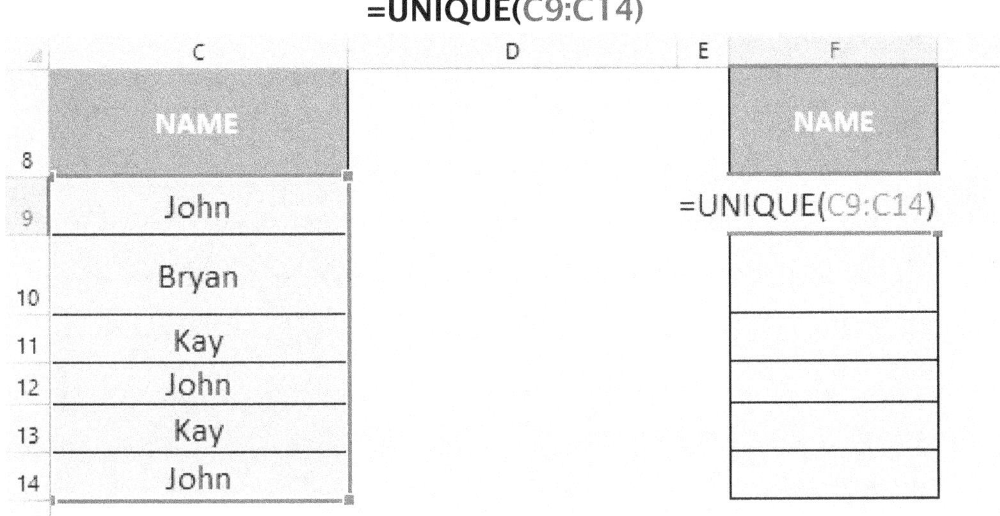

Now the duplicate names are all gone!

ADVANCED FORMULAS

3D Formulas

What does it do?

3D Formulas or References in Excel are a great way to consolidate data from multiple sheets.

3D Formulas reference several worksheets that have the same structure which allows you to consolidate by using the SUM function.

Formula breakdown:

=SUM(Sheet1:Sheet4!A1)

What it means:

=SUM(from this Sheet#:up to this Sheet#!return the sum of these cells)

Example:

=SUM(MARKETING:ADMIN!C13)

STEP 1: Make sure you have a SUMMARY *Sheet* and several sheets where you want to sum your data from;

STEP 2: All *Sheets* have to have the same structure...so the same number of columns, rows and cells;

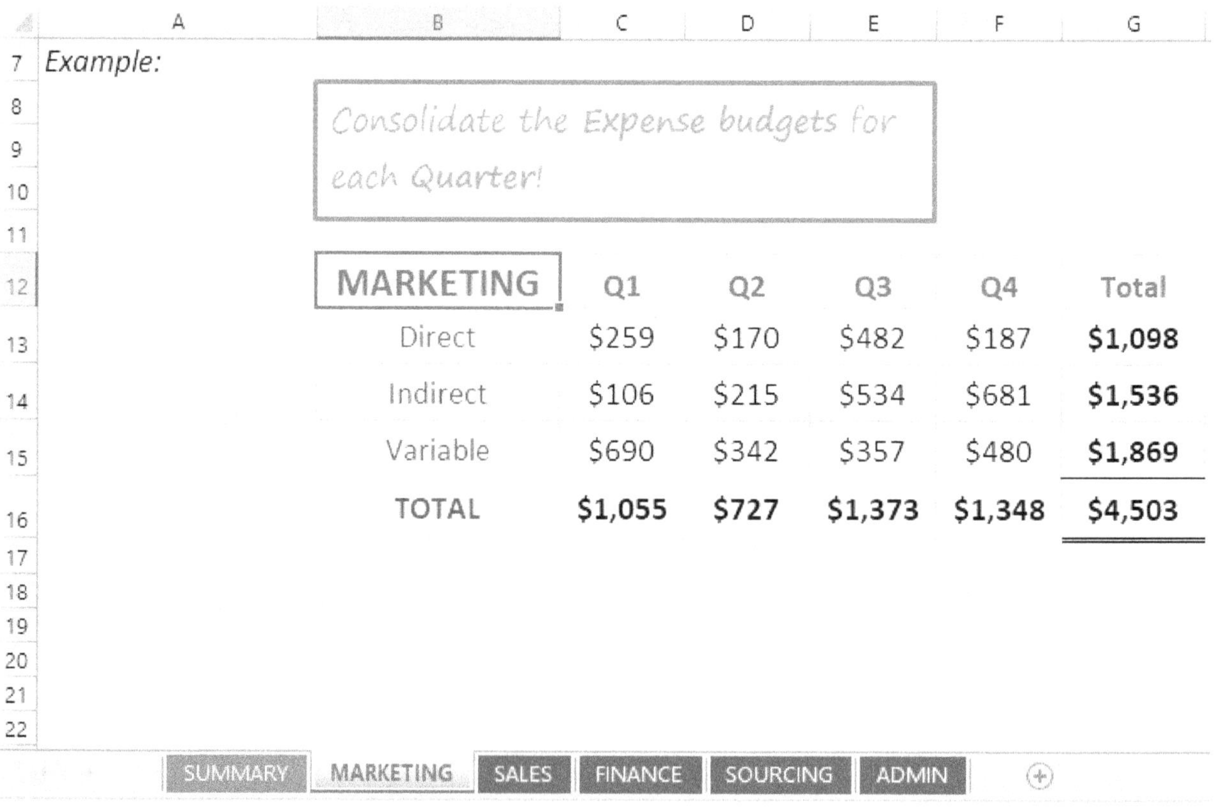

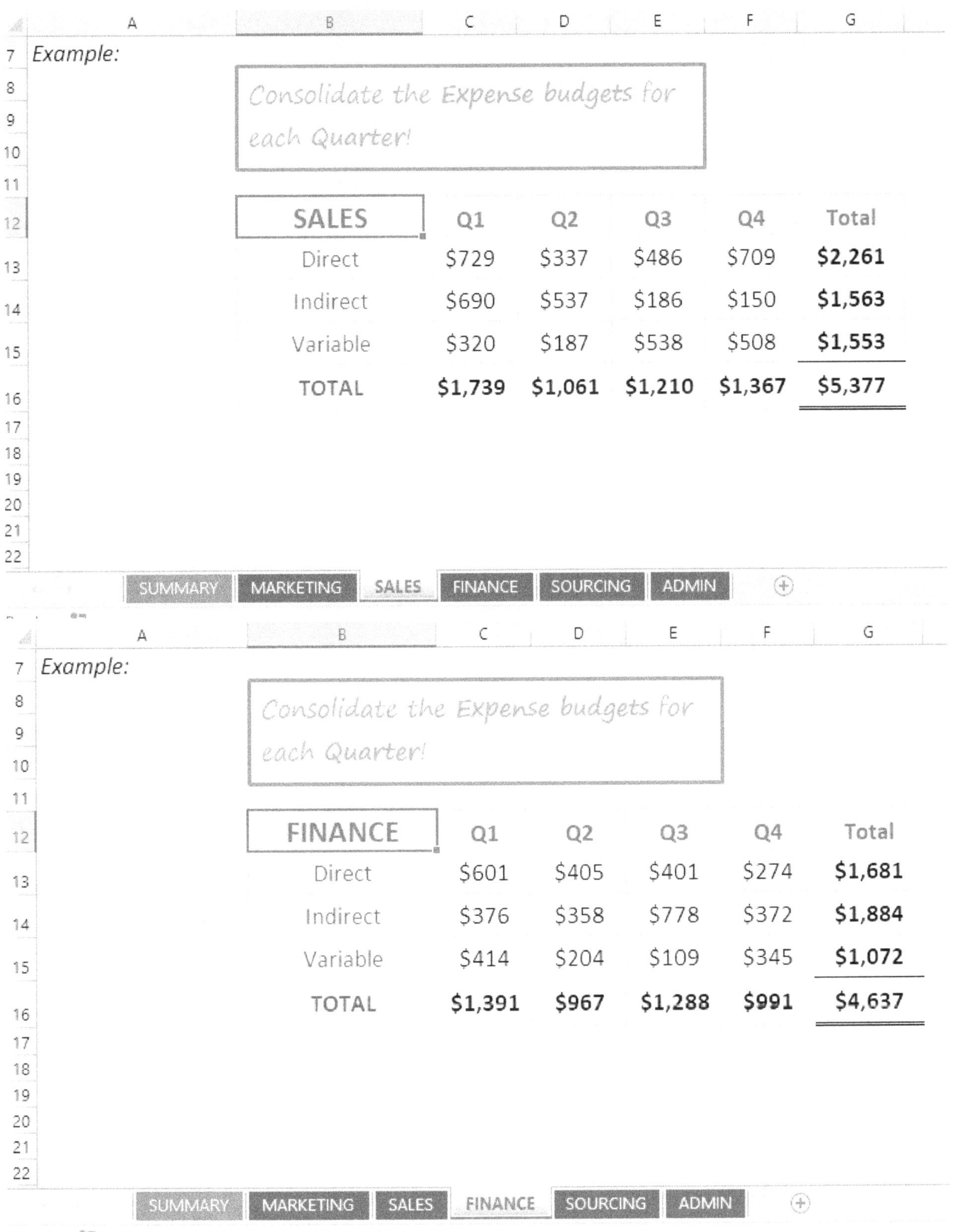

SALES	Q1	Q2	Q3	Q4	Total
Direct	$729	$337	$486	$709	$2,261
Indirect	$690	$537	$186	$150	$1,563
Variable	$320	$187	$538	$508	$1,553
TOTAL	$1,739	$1,061	$1,210	$1,367	$5,377

FINANCE	Q1	Q2	Q3	Q4	Total
Direct	$601	$405	$401	$274	$1,681
Indirect	$376	$358	$778	$372	$1,884
Variable	$414	$204	$109	$345	$1,072
TOTAL	$1,391	$967	$1,288	$991	$4,637

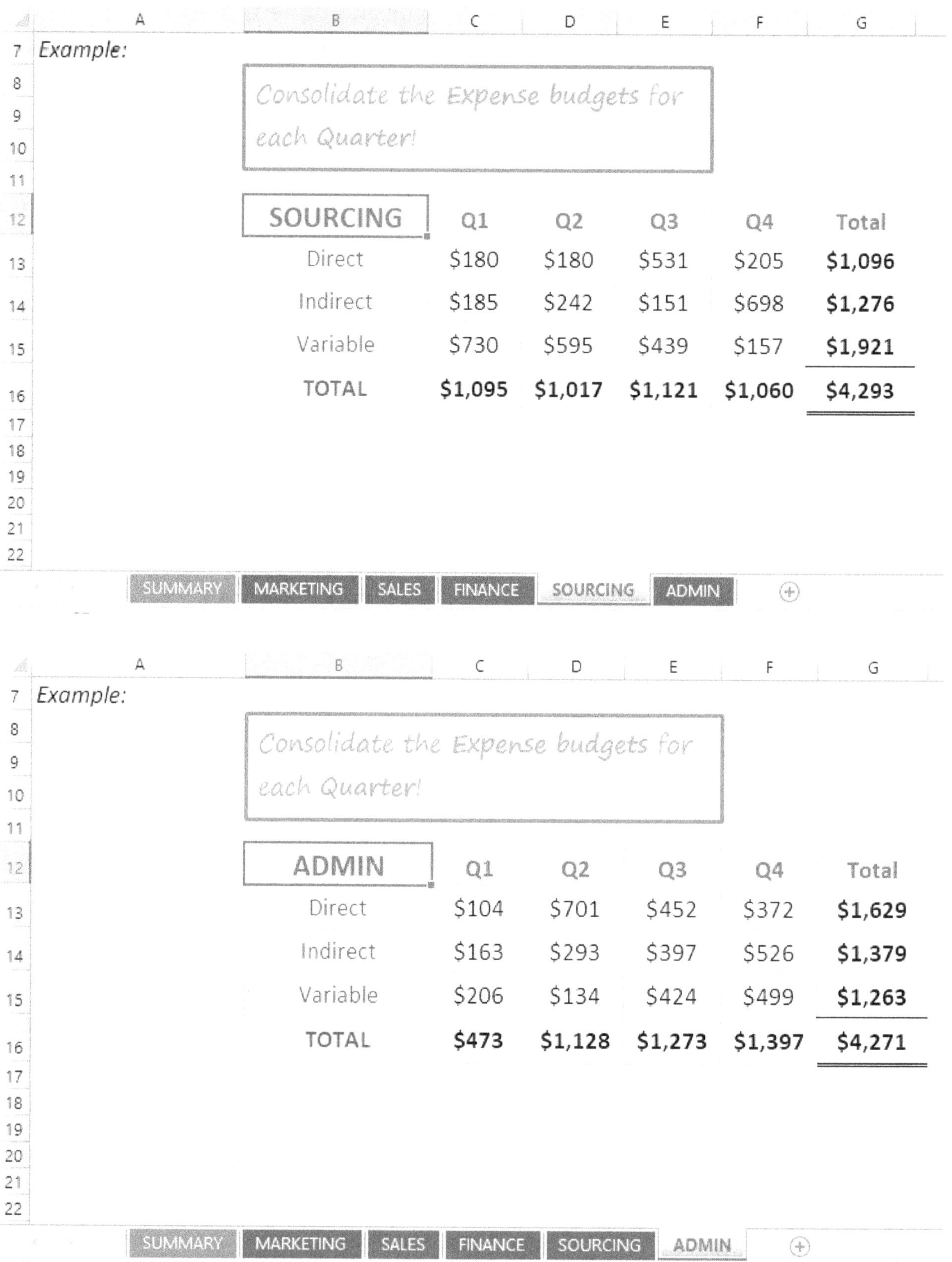

Example:

SOURCING	Q1	Q2	Q3	Q4	Total
Direct	$180	$180	$531	$205	**$1,096**
Indirect	$185	$242	$151	$698	**$1,276**
Variable	$730	$595	$439	$157	**$1,921**
TOTAL	**$1,095**	**$1,017**	**$1,121**	**$1,060**	**$4,293**

Example:

ADMIN	Q1	Q2	Q3	Q4	Total
Direct	$104	$701	$452	$372	**$1,629**
Indirect	$163	$293	$397	$526	**$1,379**
Variable	$206	$134	$424	$499	**$1,263**
TOTAL	**$473**	**$1,128**	**$1,273**	**$1,397**	**$4,271**

STEP 3: Enter a SUM formula in your SUMMARY *Sheet*, preferably in the top left hand corner;

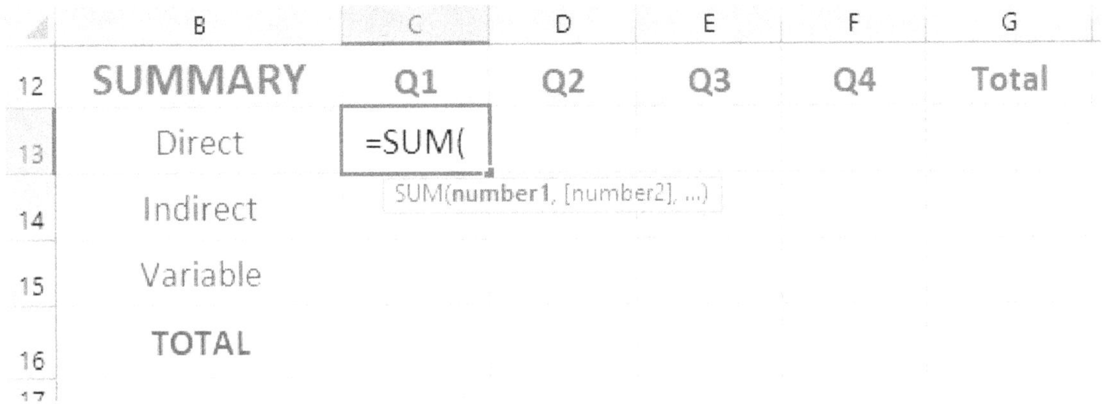

STEP 4: With your mouse select the first *Sheet* you want to consolidate;

STEP 5: Hold down the SHIFT key;

STEP 6: Whilst holding the SHIFT key, select the last *Sheet* you want to consolidate with your mouse key;

STEP 7: In the formula bar, type in the active cell that you are in (from Step 3) after the ! and press *Enter*

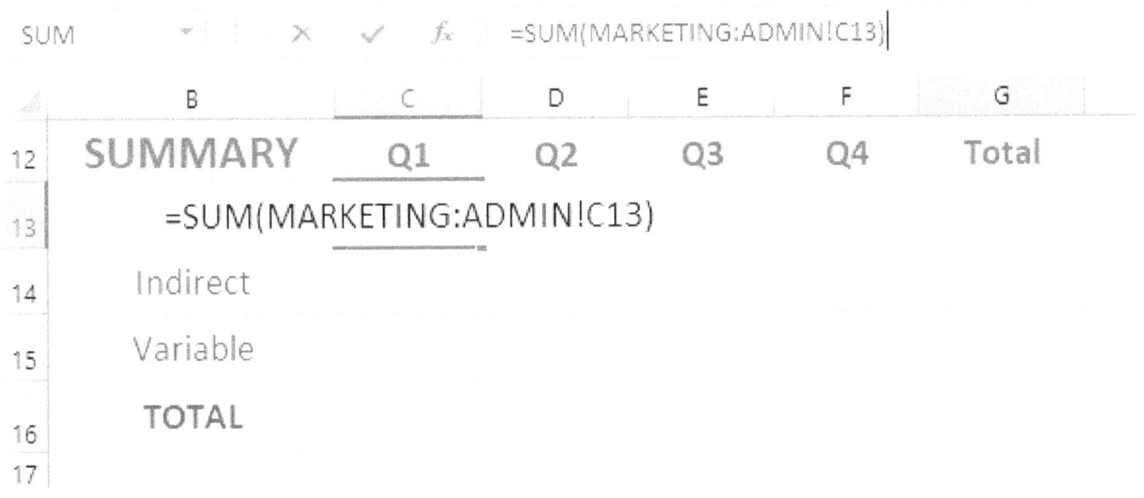

{ 303 }

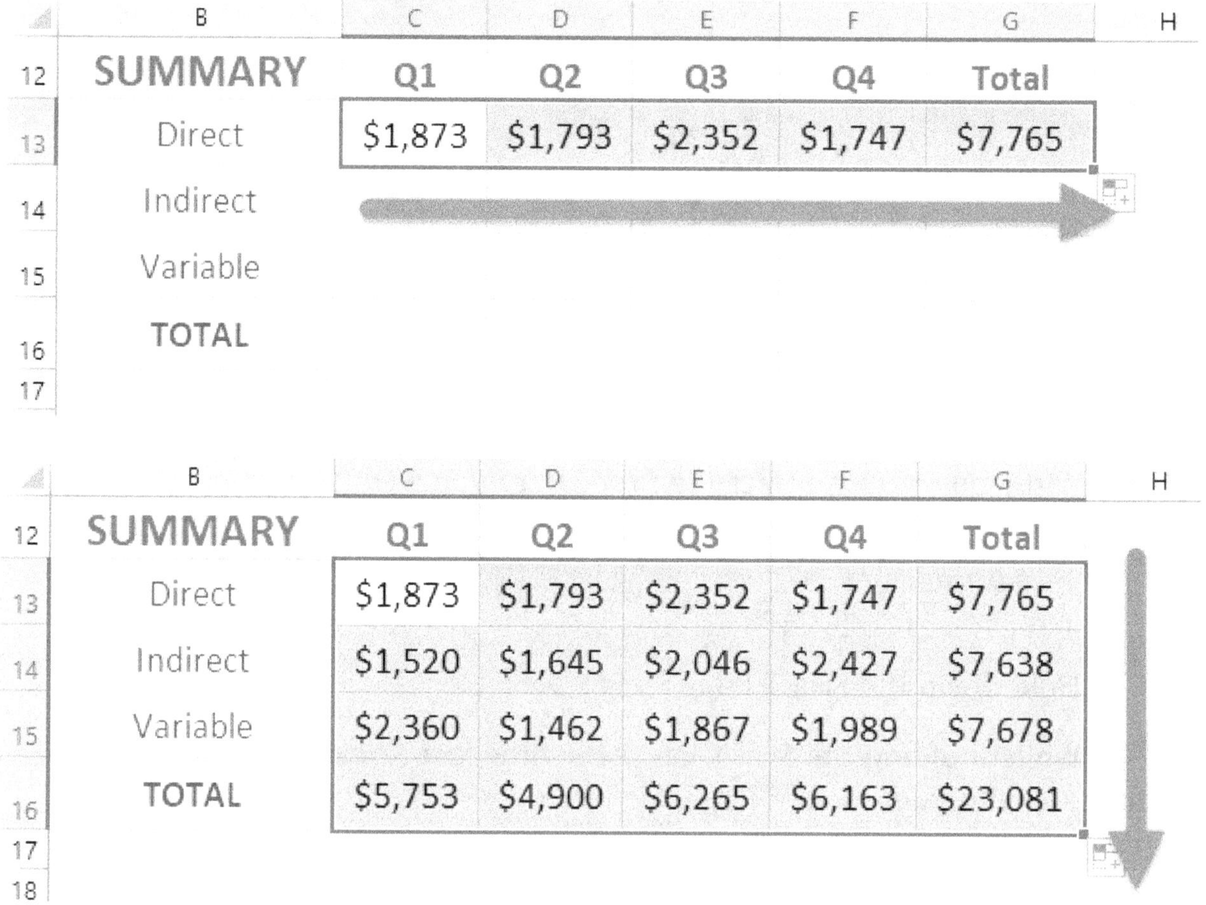

Note: You can change the **Sheet** names and this will be reflected in your 3D formula.

You cannot move the positioning of the **Sheets** after you create the 3D formula as this throw out the formula.

ARRAY Formulas

What does it do?

An Array Formula performs an Excel operation (math, comparative, join or function argument) on an array or range of data. This could be a range of cells, a worksheet reference or a defined name.

An Array contains more than one cell, so you cannot perform an Array Formula on a single cell.

To turn your formula into an Array Formula, you will need to press **CTRL+SHIFT+ENTER** which will put the squiggly brackets {} outside the formula: **{=MAX(D13:D16-C13:C16)}**

Let's break down the different Excel operations that you can use to create an Array Formula:

MATH: +-*/()

COMPARATIVE: =<>

JOIN: &

FUNCTIONS: MAX, MIN, IF, INDEX, VLOOKUP etc

Creates a cell reference based on the row and column numbers

Example:

{=MAX(D13:D16-C13:C16)}

Let's do an example of an Array Formula that calculates the maximum stock value change over a four day period:

STEP 1: Enter the MAX formula

$$=MAX($$

STEP 2: Subtract one array/range of data from another array/range of data

=MAX(D13:D16-C13:C16)

FACEBOOK STOCK PRICES

DATE	OPEN	CLOSE
18/02/2015	105	109
19/02/2015	108	95
20/02/2015	99	104
21/02/2015	106	120

=MAX(D13:D16-C13:C16**)**

STEP 3: Instead of pressing ENTER to evaluate the formula, you need to press **CTRL+SHIFT+ENTER** to turn the formula into an Array Formula which will look like this:

{=MAX(D13:D16-C13:C16)}

fx	{=MAX(D13:D16-C13:C16)}

	B	C	D

FACEBOOK STOCK PRICES

DATE	OPEN	CLOSE
18/02/2015	105	109
19/02/2015	108	95
20/02/2015	99	104
21/02/2015	106	120

MAX	14

 By **pressing F9 on the selected formula array** will give you the resulting array of numbers (press CTRL+Z to get out of this mode when you are done checking the formula results):

$$=MAX(D13:D16-C13:C16)$$

$$=MAX(\{4;-13;5;14\})$$

If we had to get the above result using a non-Array Formula we would have to create a helper column which subtracts the Open & Close cells and then enter the MAX formula to reference these results. This is double the work!

BETWEEN

What does it do?

There is no explicit **Between formula** in Excel, however we can come up with creative ways to create this functionality. Our goal is to evaluate if a given value is between a range, for example, is 6 between 1 and 10?

We have three possible scenarios: **numbers, dates, and text.**

We want to check if a value is in between two other values.

There are different creative ways so be sure to view them all below!

STEP 1: For **numbers**, we have a creative use of the **MEDIAN formula**:

$$=IF(C7=MEDIAN(A7:C7), \text{"Yes"}, \text{"No"})$$

	A	B	C	D	E
	START OF RANGE	**END OF RANGE**	**VALUE TO BE EVALUATED**	**IS THE VALUE IN BETWEEN?**	**FORMULA**
7	20	60	50	Yes	=IF(C7=MEDIAN(A7:C7), "Yes", "No")
8	10	40	50	No	=IF(C8=MEDIAN(A8:C8), "Yes", "No")
9	70	100	50	No	=IF(C9=MEDIAN(A9:C9), "Yes", "No")

In our first example above, the range is 20-60, upon checking the value 50, it is in between this range.

The median formula will return the value in the middle of these 3 values when arranged in increasing order: 20, 50, 60. The median value is 50. Since it matches the value we are evaluating, then the answer we get is a **Yes,** this value (50) is in between the range.

STEP 2: For **dates,** we have the same application of the **MEDIAN formula.** Because Excel treats dates as numbers too:

$$=IF(C10=MEDIAN(A10:C10), "Yes", "No")$$

	START OF RANGE	END OF RANGE	VALUE TO BE EVALUATED	IS THE VALUE IN BETWEEN?	FORMULA
10	2016-05-01	2016-07-01	2016-06-01	Yes	=IF(C10=MEDIAN(A10:C10), "Yes", "No")
11	2016-01-30	2016-05-30	2016-06-01	No	=IF(C11=MEDIAN(A11:C11), "Yes", "No")

In our first example above, the range is May 1 - July 1, upon checking the date June 1, it is in between this range.

The median formula will return the value in the middle of these 3 dates when arranged in increasing order: May 1, June 1, July 1. The median value is June 1. Since it matches the value we are evaluating, then the answer we get is a **Yes,** this value (June 1) is in between the range.

STEP 3: For text, we are checking if the value is alphabetically in the middle. We will be using the **AND formula:**

$$=IF(AND(C12>=A12, C12<=B12, "Yes", "No")$$

	START OF RANGE	END OF RANGE	VALUE TO BE EVALUATED	IS THE VALUE IN BETWEEN?	FORMULA
12	Cat	Dog	Cow	Yes	=IF(AND(C12>=A12, C12<=B12), "Yes", "No")
13	Dog	Mouse	Cow	No	=IF(AND(C13>=A13, C13<=B13), "Yes", "No")

Interestingly enough, you can compare texts using the **>= and <= operators.** Excel is able to compare them which goes alphabetically first or last.

In our first example above, the range is Cat - Dog, upon checking the text Cow, it is in between this range. As when arranged alphabetically, it would be: Cat, Cow, Dog.

The And formula checks if **Cow >= Cat,** and **Cow <= Dog.** You will see that both of these are true, as **Cow** is alphabetically later than **Cat,** while **Cow** is alphabetically ahead of **Dog.** Which is why we get a **Yes** result.

Extract First Name from Full Name

What does it do?

Gets the first name from a full name

Formula breakdown:

=LEFT(full_name, FIND(space, full name) -1)

What it means:

=LEFT(the full name, location of the last character in the first name)

Example:

=LEFT("John Michaloudis", FIND(" ", "John Michaloudis") -1)

There were countless times when I had a list of full names, and all I needed was the First Name. It would be time-consuming to manually get the first names one by one. Thank goodness there are formulas to make my life easier!

In Excel, it's very easy to do that with the **LEFT and FIND formula!**

	C	D	E
	FULL NAME	**FIRST NAME**	
6			
7	Talon Ferguson		
8	Doris Velez		
9	John Michaloudis		
10	Cain Sawyer		
11	Giacomo Trujillo		
12	Holly Coffey		

Here is the gameplan:

- Use the **FIND** formula to find the location of the space that separates the **First Name** and the **Last Name**
- However we need to deduct this numerical location by 1, so that we have the location of the **end of the First Name**
- With this number, we will use the **LEFT** formula to retrieve the **First Name**!

STEP 1: We need to **enter the *LEFT* function** and **select the Full Name**:

=LEFT(C7

	C	D	E
	FULL NAME	**FIRST NAME**	
6			
7	Talon Ferguson	=LEFT(C7	
8	Doris Velez	LEFT(text, [num_chars])	
9	John Michaloudis		
10	Cain Sawyer		
11	Giacomo Trujillo		
12	Holly Coffey		

STEP 2: We need to enter the **FIND formula to get the empty space location between the first and last name:**

=LEFT(C7, FIND(" "

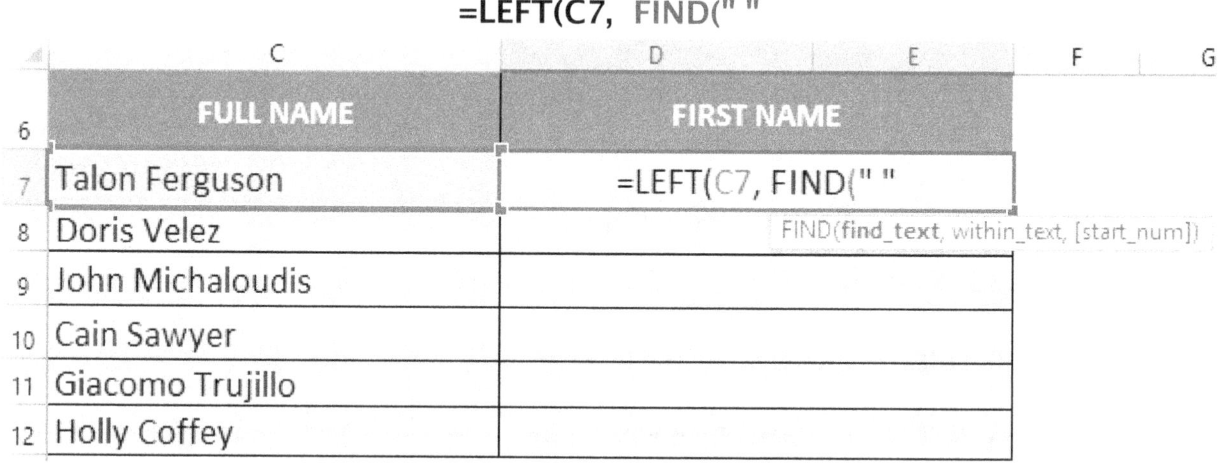

STEP 3: Select the **Full Name** again for the **FIND formula's 2nd argument:**

=LEFT(C7, FIND(" ", C7)

STEP 4: **Deduct 1** from the **FIND formula** so that our result will return us the text up to the last letter of the first name:

=LEFT(C7, FIND(" ", C7) -1)

	FULL NAME	FIRST NAME
6		
7	Talon Ferguson	=LEFT(C7, FIND(" ",C7) -1)
8	Doris Velez	
9	John Michaloudis	
10	Cain Sawyer	
11	Giacomo Trujillo	
12	Holly Coffey	

STEP 5: Do the same for the rest of the cells by dragging the formula all the way down using the left mouse button.

Now you are able to extract all the **First Names from your FULL NAME using the FIND formula in Excel!**

	FULL NAME	FIRST NAME
6		
7	Talon Ferguson	Talon
8	Doris Velez	Doris
9	John Michaloudis	John
10	Cain Sawyer	Cain
11	Giacomo Trujillo	Giacomo
12	Holly Coffey	Holly
13		

Extract Last Name - REPLACE Function

What does it do?

Replaces part of a text string, based on the number of characters you specify, with a different text string

Formula breakdown:

=REPLACE(old_text, start_num, num_chars, new_text)

What it means:

=REPLACE(this cell, starting from this number, all the way to this number, with this new text)

Example:

=REPLACE("Bryan Hong",1,SEARCH(" ", "Bryan Hong"),"") ="Hong"

I had a scenario where I wanted to extract the last names from a list of names using a formula.

Did you know that we can creatively use the **REPLACE formula** to replace the first name with an empty string, leaving us with the SURNAME?

Here is what we want to happen:

	FULL NAME	SURNAME
11	Talon Ferguson	Ferguson
12	Doris Velez	Velez
13	John Michaloudis	Michaloudis
14	Cain Sawyer	Sawyer
15	Giacomo Trujillo	Trujillo
16	Holly Coffey	Coffey

STEP 1: To start off, let us try the **Search function** and see what it will give us. We want to search on which character the space resides on.   Type in:

$$=SEARCH("\ ", C11)$$

	FULL NAME	
11	Talon Ferguson	=SEARCH(" ", C11)
12	Doris Velez	
13	John Michaloudis	
14	Cain Sawyer	
15	Giacomo Trujillo	
16	Holly Coffey	

You will see that it returned **6**.

This means our space is on the 6th character of the name *Talon Ferguson*.

We will use this in our **Replace function** later in **STEP 3**.

	C	D
10	**FULL NAME**	**SURNAME**
11	Talon Ferguson	6
12	Doris Velez	
13	John Michaloudis	
14	Cain Sawyer	
15	Giacomo Trujillo	
16	Holly Coffey	

STEP 2: Clear the Search function. We need to **enter the *Replace* function** next to the cell that we want to clean the data from:

=REPLACE

STEP 3: The Replace arguments:

old_text

Which text do we want to change?

Reference the cell that contains the text string:

=REPLACE(C11,

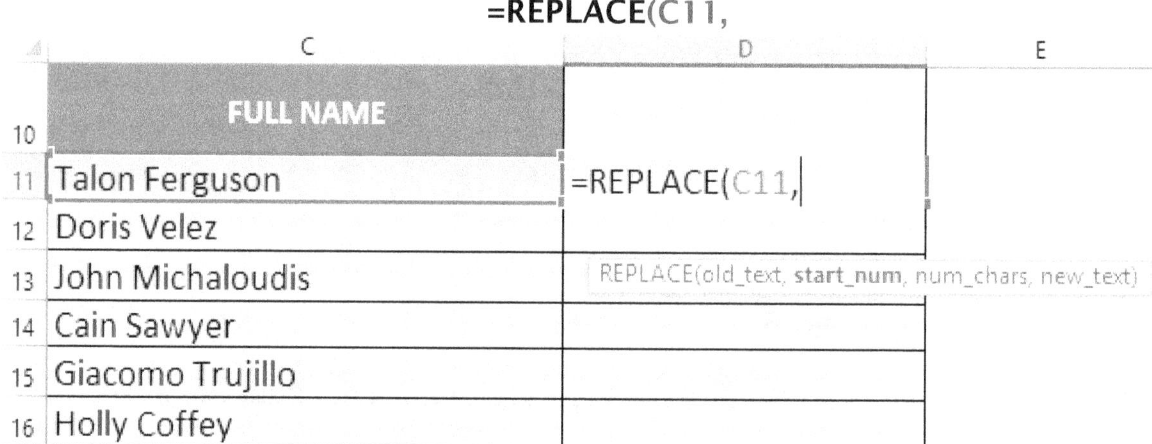

Which character do we want to start the replacement from?

We want to replace the first name, which resides on the first character:

=REPLACE(C11, 1,

	C	D	E
10	**FULL NAME**		
11	Talon Ferguson	=REPLACE(C11, 1,	
12	Doris Velez		
13	John Michaloudis	REPLACE(old_text, start_num, **num_chars**, new_text)
14	Cain Sawyer		
15	Giacomo Trujillo		
16	Holly Coffey		

num_chars

How many characters do we need to replace?

We don't have the exact number of characters, so this is where the SEARCH function comes in handy from STEP 1 above.

Search for the space character " " which tells us the end of the First Name:

=REPLACE(C11, 1, SEARCH(" ", C11),

	C	D	E
10	**FULL NAME**		
11	Talon Ferguson	=REPLACE(C11,1,SEARCH(" ", C11),	
12	Doris Velez		
13	John Michaloudis	REPLACE(old_text, start_num, num_chars, **new_text**)
14	Cain Sawyer		
15	Giacomo Trujillo		
16	Holly Coffey		

What text will serve as the replacement?

Now that we have accounted for all the characters from the First Name, we need to clear these.

We can do this by replacing it with an empty string.

This will "erase" the First Name, and leave us with the Last Name.

=REPLACE(C11, 1, SEARCH(" ", C11), "")

	C	D	E
10	**FULL NAME**		
11	Talon Ferguson	=REPLACE(C11,1,SEARCH(" ", C11),"")	
12	Doris Velez		
13	John Michaloudis		
14	Cain Sawyer		
15	Giacomo Trujillo		
16	Holly Coffey		

STEP 4: Do the same for the rest of the cells by dragging the **REPLACE** formula all the way down using the left mouse button.

Now we have all of the last names:

	C	D
10	**FULL NAME**	**SURNAME**
11	Talon Ferguson	Ferguson
12	Doris Velez	Velez
13	John Michaloudis	Michaloudis
14	Cain Sawyer	Sawyer
15	Giacomo Trujillo	Trujillo
16	Holly Coffey	Coffey
17		

GETPIVOTDATA

What does it do?

A formula that extracts data stored in a Pivot Table

Formula breakdown:

=GETPIVOTDATA(data_field, pivot_table, [field1, item1], [field2,item2],...)

What it means:

=GETPIVOTDATA(return me this value from the Values Area, any cell within the Pivot Table, [and return me the value that pertains to this Field name, and this Field item],...)

Example:

=GETPIVOTDATA("SALES",A1,"SALES REGION","AMERICAS","FINANCIAL YEAR",2013,"SALES QTR","Q1")

The GETPIVOTDATA function in Excel returns data stored in a Pivot Table. So essentially it extracts the Pivot Table data to enable a user to create customized reports.

Think of the Pivot Table like your data source, so anything you see in the Pivot Table report can be extracted with the GETPIVOTDATA function and put into a cell within your worksheet.

The GETPIVOTDATA function becomes powerful when you reference cells to create shell reports.

NB. *Only the Fields and Items that are included in the Pivot Table report (Row/Column Labels and Values area) can be used to extract their values.*

Here is our current Pivot Table:

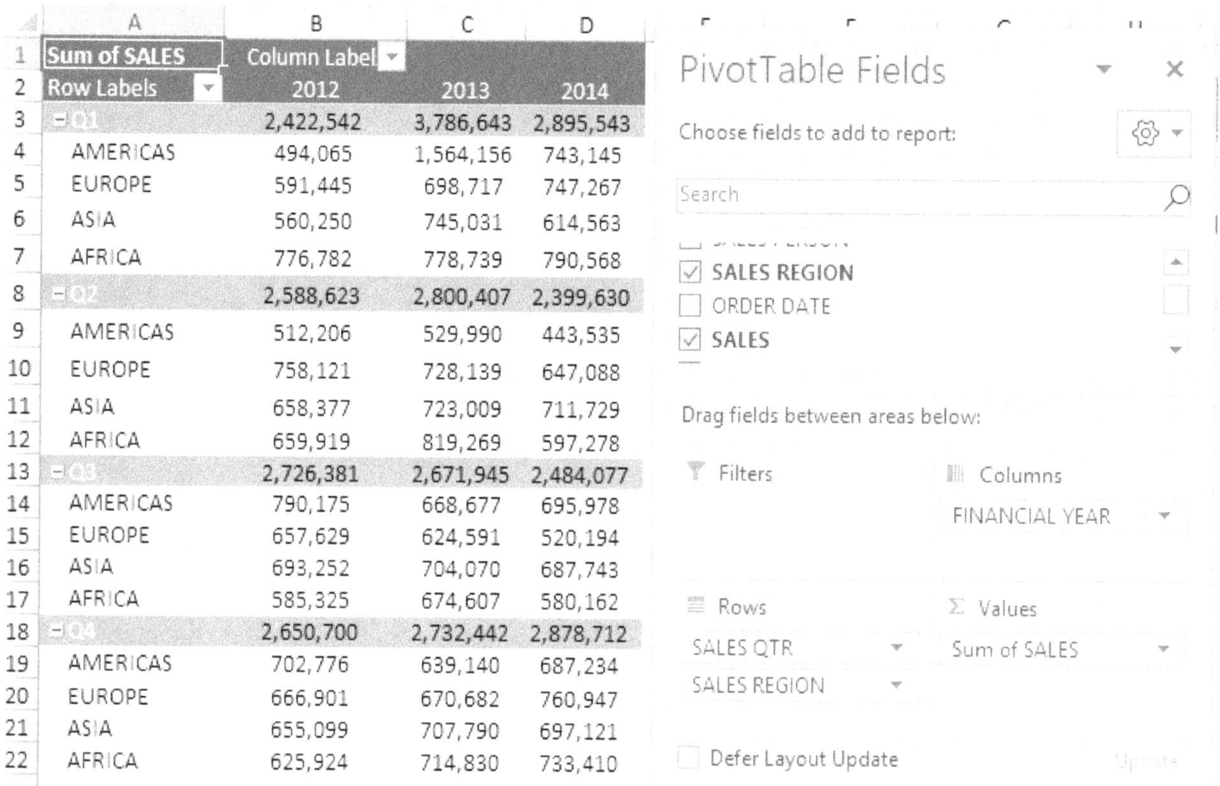

STEP 1: We need to **enter the *GETPIVOTDATA* function**:

=GETPIVOTDATA(

	A	B	C	D	E	F
25		2013	2013	2013	2013	**2013**
26		Q1	Q2	Q3	Q4	**ACTUAL**
27		=GETPIVOTDATA(				0
28	EUROPE	GETPIVOTDATA(data_field, pivot_table, [field1, item1], ...)				0
29	ASIA					0
30	AFRICA					0
31	**TOTALS**	0	0	0	0	0

data_field

What is the value that we want to return?

Type in SALES as we want to return the sales value:

=GETPIVOTDATA("SALES",

	A	B	C	D	E	F
25		2013	2013	2013	2013	**2013**
26		Q1	Q2	Q3	Q4	**ACTUAL**
27	=GETPIVOTDATA("SALES"					0
28	EURO GETPIVOTDATA(data_field, pivot_table, [field1, item1], ...)					0
29	ASIA					0
30	AFRICA					0
31	**TOTALS**	0	0	0	0	0

pivot_table

From which pivot table?

Just reference a cell in the pivot table, let's type in $A$1

=GETPIVOTDATA("SALES", $A$1,

	A	B	C	D	E	F
25		2013	2013	2013	2013	**2013**
26		Q1	Q2	Q3	Q4	**ACTUAL**
27	=GETPIVOTDATA("SALES", $A$1,					0
28	EL GETPIVOTDATA(data_field, pivot_table, [field1, item1], [field2, item2], ...)					0
29	ASIA					0
30	AFRICA					0
31	**TOTALS**	0	0	0	0	0

	A	B	C	D
1	Sum of SALE	olumn Lal ▼		
2	Row Labels ▼	2012	2013	2014
3	─ Q1	2,422,542	3,786,643	2,895,543
4	AMERICAS	494,065	1,564,156	743,145
5	EUROPE	591,445	698,717	747,267
6	ASIA	560,250	745,031	614,563
7	AFRICA	776,782	778,739	790,568
8	─ Q2	2,588,623	2,800,407	2,399,630
9	AMERICAS	512,206	529,990	443,535
10	EUROPE	758,121	728,139	647,088
11	ASIA	658,377	723,009	711,729
12	AFRICA	659,919	819,269	597,278

[field1, item1]

What are the fields that would serve as our filtering criteria?

To get our target sales figure, we will need: Sales Region, Financial Year and Sales Quarter. To do this we will need 3 field-item pairs:

=GETPIVOTDATA("SALES", $A$1, "SALES REGION", $A27, "FINANCIAL YEAR", B$25, "SALES QTR", B$26)

	A	B	C	D	E	F
25		2013	2013	2013	2013	**2013**
26		Q1	Q2	Q3	Q4	**ACTUAL**
27	=GETPIVOTDATA("SALES", $A$1, "SALES					**1,564,156**
28	REGION", $A27, "FINANCIAL YEAR",					**0**
29	B$25, "SALES QTR", B$26)					**0**
30	GETPIVOTDATA(**data_field**, pivot_table, [field1, item1], [field2, item2], [field3, item3], [field4, item4]
31	**TOTALS**	**1,564,156**	**0**	**0**	**0**	**1,564,156**

	2013	2013	2013	2013	2013
	Q1	Q2	Q3	Q4	ACTUAL
AMERICAS	1,564,156				1,564,156
EUROPE					0
ASIA					0
AFRICA					0
TOTALS	1,564,156	0	0	0	1,564,156

STEP 3: Do the same for the rest of the cells by copying the
GETPIVOTDATA formula to the rest of the cells.

	2013	2013	2013	2013	2013
	Q1	Q2	Q3	Q4	ACTUAL
AMERICAS	1,564,156				1,564,156
EUROPE					0
ASIA					0
AFRICA					0
TOTALS	1,564,156	0	0	0	1,564,156

Now your new set of data is ready!

	2013	2013	2013	2013	2013
	Q1	Q2	Q3	Q4	ACTUAL
AMERICAS	1,564,156	529,990	668,677	639,140	3,401,963
EUROPE	698,717	728,139	624,591	670,682	2,722,129
ASIA	745,031	723,009	704,070	707,790	2,879,900
AFRICA	778,739	819,269	674,607	714,830	2,987,445
TOTALS	3,786,643	2,800,407	2,671,945	2,732,442	11,991,437

IF Combined With The AND Function

What does it do?

It returns a value that you set if a condition is met, and a value if it is not met

Formula breakdown:

=IF(AND(Logical Test),Value if True,Value if False)

What it means:

=IF((Sales are bigger than $3000 & in the North region),"Bonus","No Bonus")

Example:

=IF(AND(1092>3000,"North"="north"),"Bonus","No Bonus")

="No Bonus"

When combining (or nesting) the AND function with the IF function, it allows you to add more than one condition to your formula, something that is not possible with the IF function by itself.

So you can show the results of Sales Reps that have made more than $3,000 of sales AND who are part of the North region, as explained below...

We want to show a Bonus value if sales are bigger than $3000 and comes from the North region, and No Bonus is shown if this condition is not met.

=IF(

	A	B	C	D	E	F	G	H
9	Example:	If a SALES REP has sold more than $3,000 in						
10		the NORTH region, then give them a BONUS!						
11								
12								
13								
14		Sales Rep	Region	Sales	Bonus?			
15		John	North	$1,092	=IF(			
16		Paul	South	$9,951	IF(logical_test, [value_if_true], [value_if_false])			
17		Ringo	East	$2,006				
18		George	West	$8,738				
19		Ana	North	$3,185				
20		Marie	South	$1,661				
21		Wayland	East	$5,594				
22		Helen	West	$457				
23		Paula	North	$4,935				

STEP 2: The **IF** arguments:

logical_test

What is your condition?

Sales Rep has sold **more than 3000 dollars** and comes from the **North Region.** Let us use the **AND function** to accomplish this.

=IF(AND(D15>3000, C15="North"),

	B	C	D	E	F	G	H
14	Sales Rep	Region	Sales	Bonus?			
15	John		=IF(AND(D15>3000, C15="North"),				
16	Paul	South	$9,951				
17	Ringo	East	$2,006				
18	George	West	$8,738				
19	Ana	North	$3,185				
20	Marie	South	$1,661				
21	Wayland	East	$5,594				
22	Helen	West	$457				
23	Paula	North	$4,935				

What value should be displayed if the condition is true?

We want "Bonus" to be displayed

=IF(AND(D15>3000, C15="North"), "Bonus",

	B	C	D	E	F	G	
14	Sales Rep	Region	Sales	Bonus?			
15	John		=IF(AND(D15>3000, C15="North"), "Bonus",			
16	Paul	South	$9,951				
17	Ringo	East	$2,006				
18	George	West	$8,738				
19	Ana	North	$3,185				
20	Marie	South	$1,661				
21	Wayland	East	$5,594				
22	Helen	West	$457				
23	Paula	North	$4,935				

What value should be displayed if the condition is not met?

We want "No Bonus" to be displayed

=IF(AND(D15>3000, C15="North"), "Bonus", "No Bonus")

	B	C	D	E	F	G	H
14	Sales Rep	Region	Sales	Bonus?			
15	John	=IF(AND(D15>3000, C15="North"), "Bonus", "No Bonus")					
16	Paul	Sou IF(logical_test, [value_if_true], [value_if_false])					
17	Ringo	East	$2,006				
18	George	West	$8,738				
19	Ana	North	$3,185				
20	Marie	South	$1,661				
21	Wayland	East	$5,594				
22	Helen	West	$457				
23	Paula	North	$4,935				

Apply the same formula to the rest of the cells by dragging the lower right corner downwards.

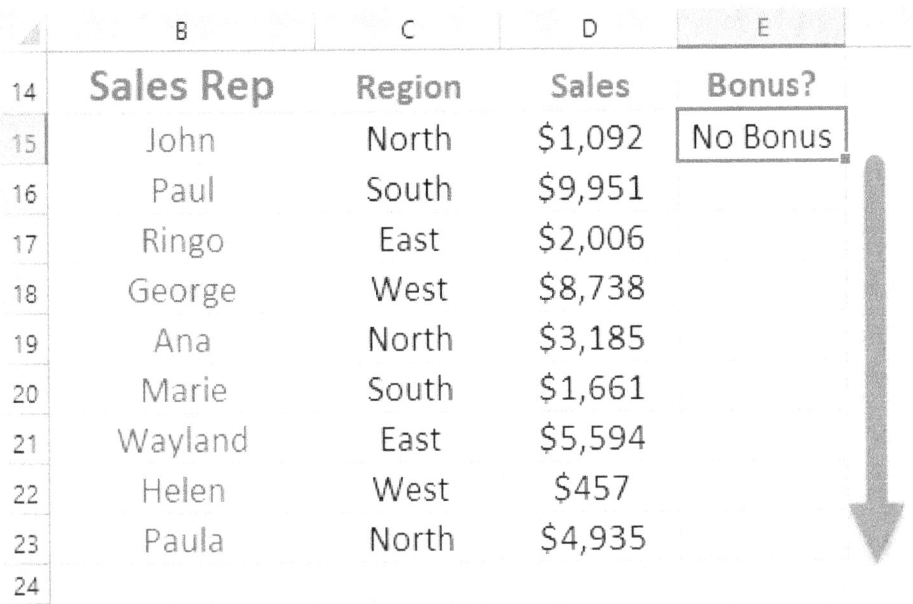

You now have all of results!

	B	C	D	E
14	**Sales Rep**	Region	Sales	Bonus?
15	John	North	$1,092	No Bonus
16	Paul	South	$9,951	No Bonus
17	Ringo	East	$2,006	No Bonus
18	George	West	$8,738	No Bonus
19	Ana	North	$3,185	Bonus
20	Marie	South	$1,661	No Bonus
21	Wayland	East	$5,594	No Bonus
22	Helen	West	$457	No Bonus
23	Paula	North	$4,935	Bonus
24				

INDEX-MATCH 2 Criteria with Validation

What does it do?

Searches the row position of a value/text in one column (using the MATCH function) and returns the value/text in the same row position from another column to the left or right (using the INDEX function)

Formula breakdown:

=INDEX(array, MATCH(lookup_value, lookup_array, [match_type])

What it means:

=INDEX(return the value/text, MATCH(from the row position of this value/text))

Example:

=INDEX(INDIRECT("Table1["&$H$14&"]"),MATCH(G14,Table1[SALES REP],0))

We can use the **INDEX-MATCH** formula and combine it with Data Validation drop down menus to return a value based on 2 criteria.

This is a little advanced so you will need to drop what you are doing and really focus. Let's go...

First we need to convert our data into an Excel Table by pressing Ctrl+T

We then create drop down menus for our *Sales Rep* column and another one for our *Units/Sales/Avg Sale* column names

Once the above are done we need to create our formula.

STEP 1: We need to nest an **INDIRECT** function within the **INDEX** function and reference the Metric cell name (H14) with our Table name (Table1):

$$=INDEX(INDIRECT("Table1["\&H14\&"]"),$$

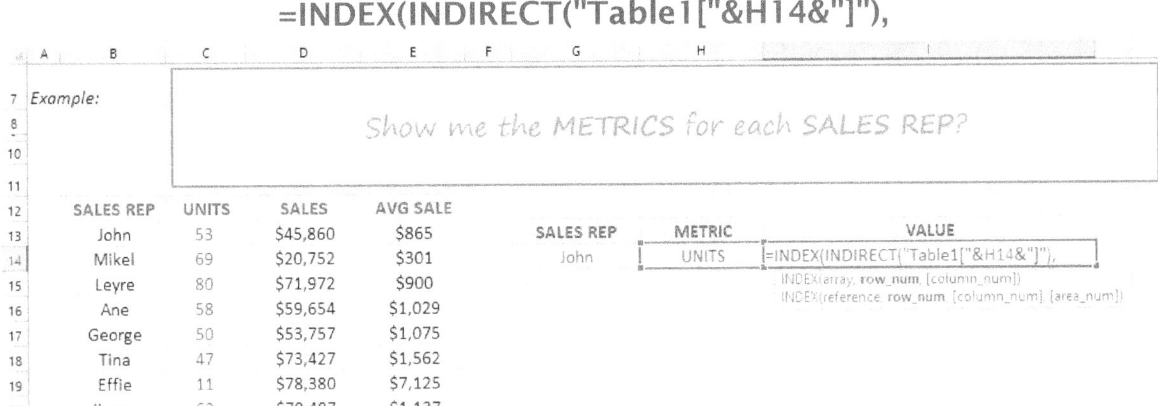

This will give us our dynamic column name within the Excel Table.

STEP 2: We need to lookup our **Sales Rep** within the Sales Rep column table:

$$=INDEX(INDIRECT("Table1["\&H14\&"]"),$$

$$MATCH(G14,Table1[SALES REP],0))$$

So by combining these formulas we can choose two criteria (Sales Rep & Metric name) to return the respective value.

Match Two Lists With MATCH Function

What does it do?

It returns the position of an item in a range

Formula breakdown:

=MATCH(lookup_value, lookup_array, [match_type])

What it means:

=MATCH(lookup this value, from this list or range of cells, return me the Exact Match).

Example:

=MATCH(C12,list2!C12:C21,0)

I am sure that you have come across many occasions where you have two lists of data and want to know if a specific item in **List1** exists in **List2**.

Well I have!

With the MATCH function you can verify if a cell´s item in **List1** exists in **List2**.

The function will return the row position of that item in **List2** hence confirming that it exists. If you get a #N/A it means that the cell´s item does not exist in **List2**.

You can then go ahead and filter your *List 1* with either the values returned or the #N/As.

Here are our 2 Lists:

STOCK LIST 1	PRICE	MATCH
Tel2154	$3,449	
Lap5468	$5,664	
Tab4577	$5,830	
Mon45657	$2,496	
Dro424	$9,553	
Tel2135	$9,644	
Lap5456	$8,600	
Tab4598	$2,990	
Mon45645	$6,282	
Dro4255	$7,760	

STOCK LIST 2	COST
Tab4577	$565
Tel2154	$515
Lap000	$574
Dro000	$984
Mon45645	$899
Tel2135	$646
Lap5456	$524
Tab000	$503
Mon45657	$933
Dro4255	$904

STEP 1: We need to enter the **MATCH function** in a blank cell:

=MATCH(

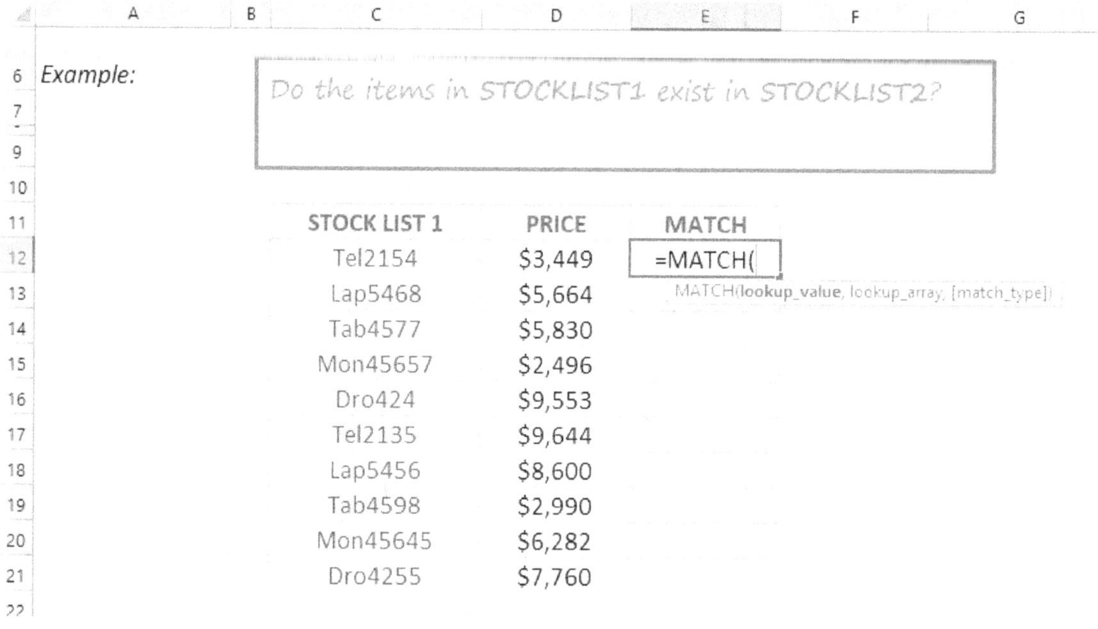

STEP 2: The **MATCH** arguments:

lookup_value

What is the value you want to check?

Select the cell containing the List1 value, as this is what we want to check against List2.

=MATCH(C12,

What is the list you want to check against?

Select the entire List2.

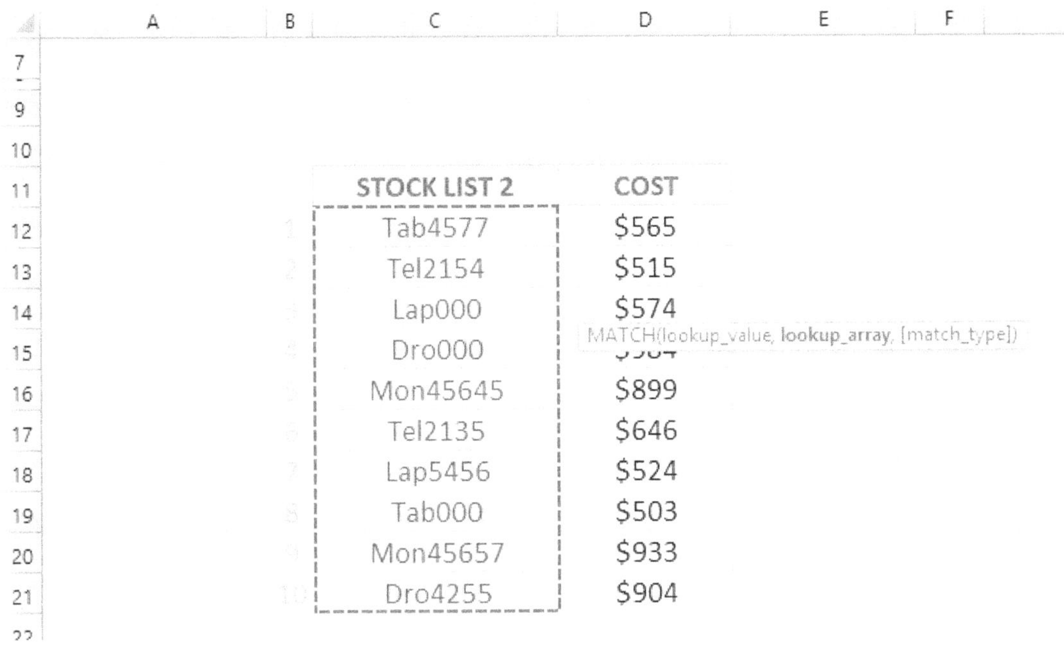

And ensure to **press F4** to make it an absolute reference.

=MATCH(C12, list2!$C$12:$C:21,

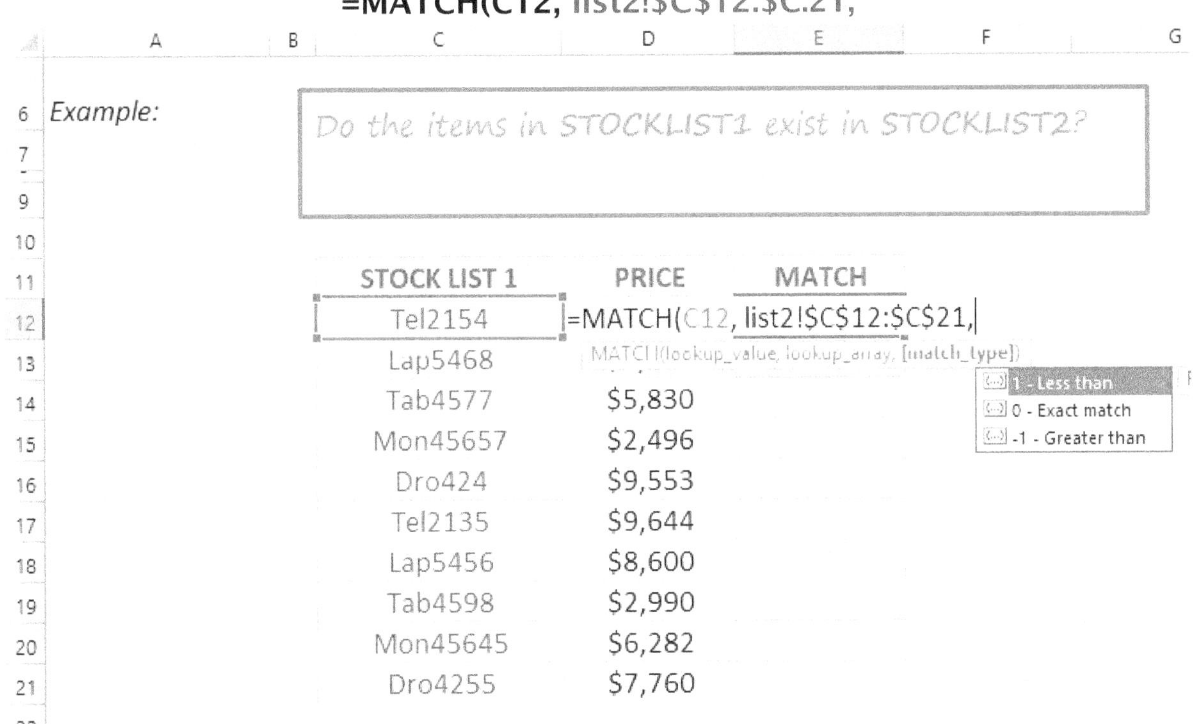

How specific is your matching?

We want an exact match so place in 0.

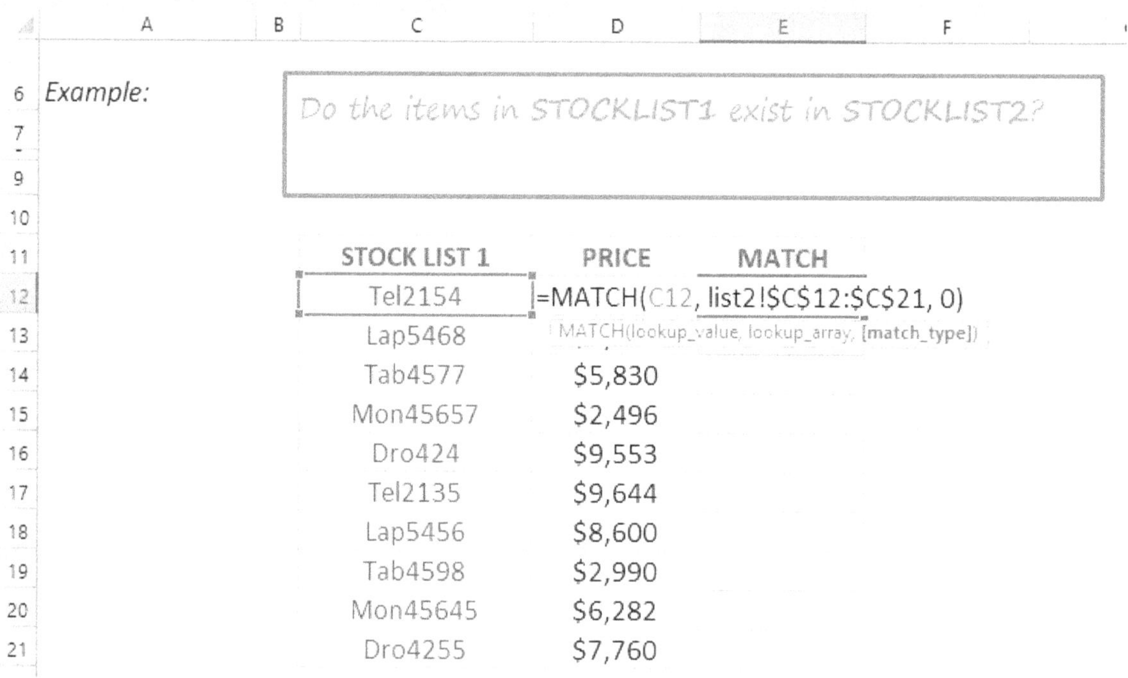

Apply the same formula to the rest of the cells by dragging the lower right corner downwards.

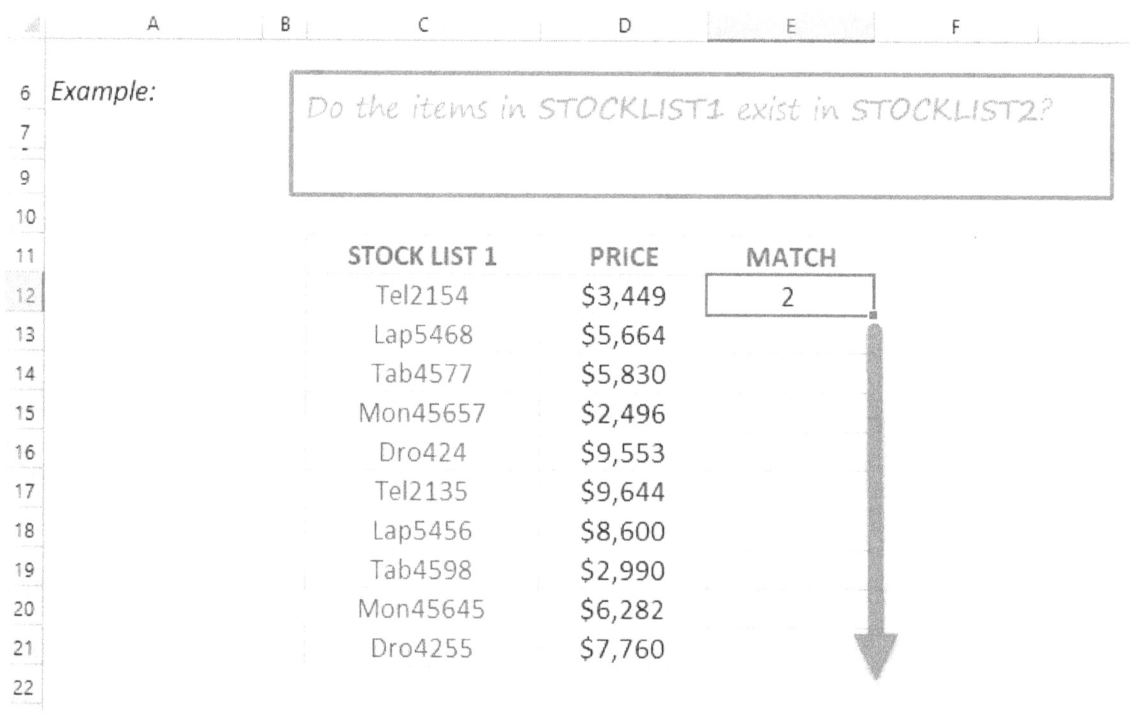

You now have all of results! You can see which row numbers the items exist in List2. For example, Mon45657 in List1 exists in List2 Row 9! If it does not exist in List2, then #N/A is displayed.

STOCK LIST 1	PRICE	MATCH		STOCK LIST 2	COST
Tel2154	$3,449	2		Tab4577	$565
Lap5468	$5,664	#N/A		Tel2154	$515
Tab4577	$5,830	1		Lap000	$574
Mon45657	$2,496	9		Dro000	$984
Dro424	$9,553	#N/A		Mon45645	$899
Tel2135	$9,644	6		Tel2135	$646
Lap5456	$8,600	7		Lap5456	$524
Tab4598	$2,990	#N/A		Tab000	$503
Mon45645	$6,282	5		Mon45657	$933
Dro4255	$7,760	10		Dro4255	$904

Named Ranges with VLOOKUP Function

What does it do?

Searches for a value in the first column of a table array and returns a value in the same row from another column (to the right) in the table array.

Formula breakdown:

=VLOOKUP(lookup_value, table_array, col_index_num, [range_lookup])

What it means:

=VLOOKUP(this value, in this Named Range, and get me value in this column, Exact Match/FALSE/0])

Example:

=VLOOKUP("Laptop",StockList,2,FALSE)

A **Named Range** makes it easier to understand Excel formulas, especially if the said formula contains an array argument.

A **Named Range** can be a cell, a cell range, a Table, a function or a constant.

STEP 1: To **define a** *Named Range* in Excel you need to select the cell/cell range/Table/function/constant and go to the **Name Box** which is located on the top left hand corner of the workbook - next to the **Formula Bar**.

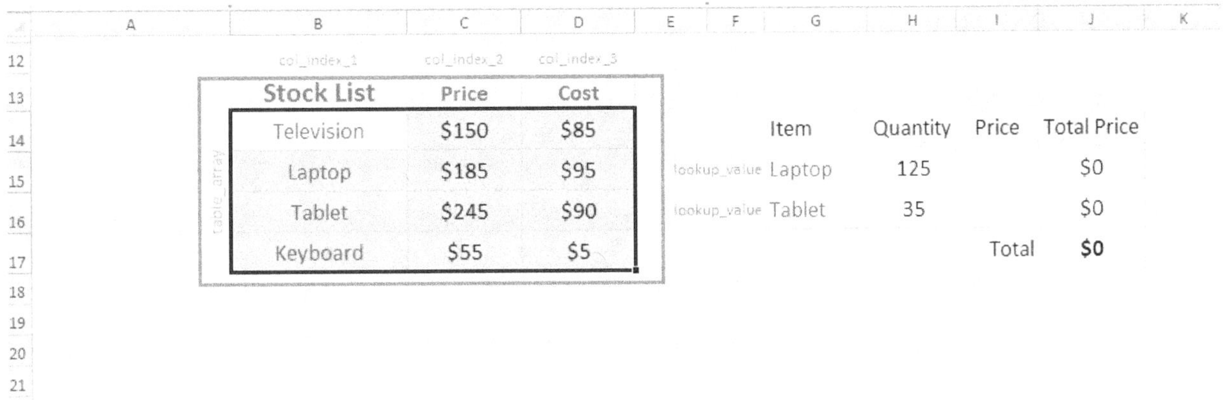

STEP 2: In here you can name your range whatever you like (make sure there are no spaces) and press **Enter.** You can view your **Named Range** by clicking on the drop down box in the **Name Box**. In our example we will give this a name of **StockList.**

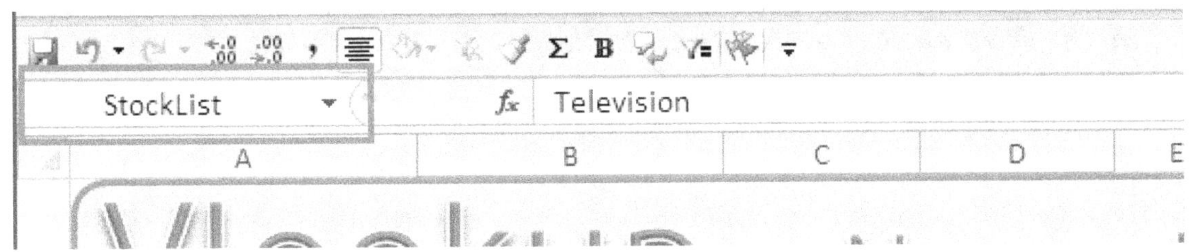

You can also **view/edit/delete your Named Range** by going to the **Formulas** tab in the Ribbon menu and selecting **Name Manager**.

STEP 3: Now that you are all set, each time you are creating a formula, like a Vlookup formula, it is best to use a **Named Range** as it makes the formula easier to understand and maintain.

We need to **enter the Vlookup function**:

$$=VLOOKUP($$

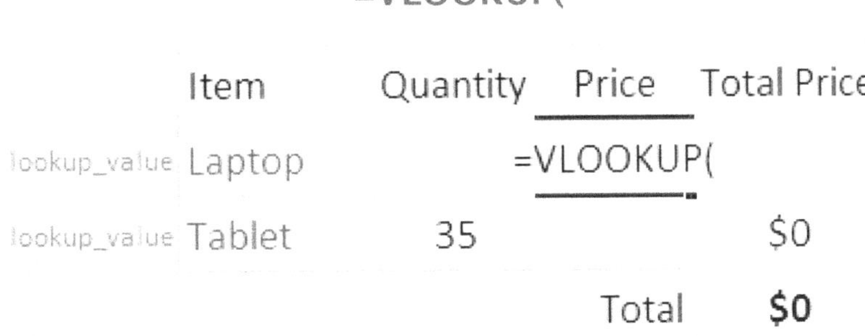

The Vlookup arguments:

lookup_value

What are we looking for?

Reference the cell that contains the text or value:

=VLOOKUP(G15,

table_array

From which list are we doing a lookup on?

Place in the Named Range of the Stock List:

=VLOOKUP(G15, StockList,

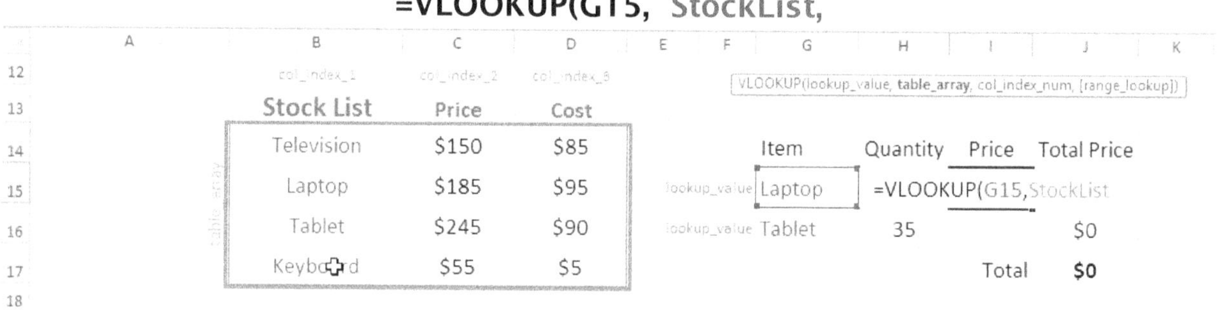

col_index_num

From which column do we want to retrieve the value?

We want to retrieve the Price which is the SECOND column from our table array:

=VLOOKUP(G15, StockList, 2,

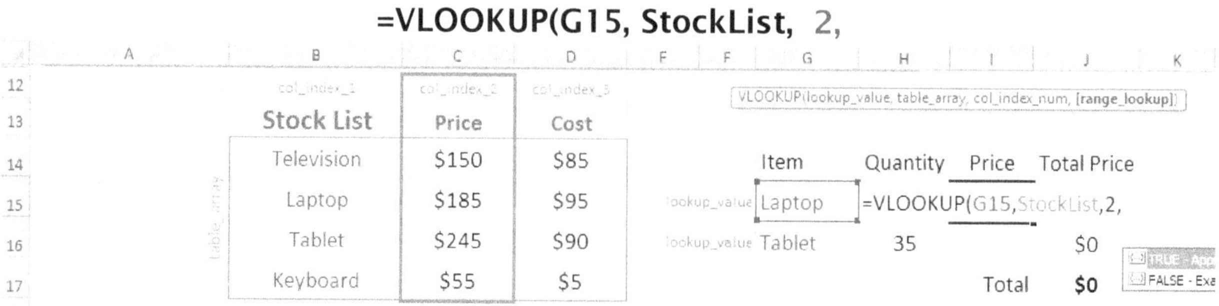

Do we want an exact match?

Place in FALSE to signify that we want an exact match:

=VLOOKUP(G15, StockList, 2, FALSE)

Item	Quantity	Price	Total Price
L		=VLOOKUP(G15,StockList,2,FALSE)	
Tablet	35		$0
		Total	$0

The price now dynamically changes based on your selection:

Stock List	Price	Cost		Item	Quantity	Price	Total Price
Television	$150	$85					
Laptop	$185	$95		Laptop	125	185	$23,125
Tablet	$245	$90		Tablet	35		$0
Keyboard	$55	$5				Total	$23,125

REPT

What does it do?

Repeats text a given number of times

Formula breakdown:

=REPT(text, number_times)

What it means:

=REPT(the text to repeat, number of times the text will be repeated)

Example:

=REPT("a", 3) ="aaa"

When you are creating an Excel Dashboard and are limited by space and do not want to insert a chart, you can easily create an in-cell bar chart using the RPT (repeat) function.

We will use the vertical bar character | as the first argument: **text** and references the value cell for the second argument: **number_times**

So it enters the vertical bar character by the amount of times of the value cell, looking something like this:

||||||||||||||||||||||||||||||||||||||||||||||||||||||||||||||||||||||||||||

Here is how it is done in just a few steps:

STEP 1: Enter the REPT function in a column next to your values

=REPT

=REPT("|")

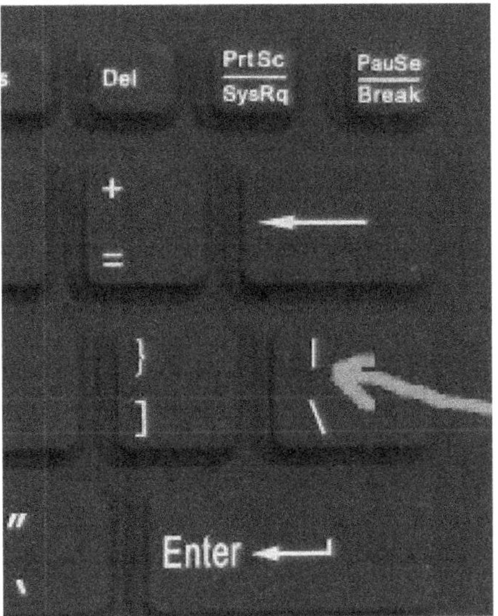

STEP 3: **Reference the value cell** for the second argument

=REPT("|", b6)

STEP 4: Highlight the formula column and **insert the** *Stencil* **font** from the Home menu and choose a font color

STEP 5: If your value cells are high, the bar will go out of your screen. To fix this, you need to enter a divisor in the second argument of your formula which will reduce the length

=REPT("|", b6/5)

MONTH	SALES	CHART
January	$125	=REPT("|",[@SALES]/5)
February	$330	
March	$161	
April	$584	
May	$455	
June	$213	
July	$345	
August	$160	

Sum a Range Using the INDEX Function

What does it do?

You can sum a range of values within a table using the INDEX function in Excel. This is valuable when you want to extract key metrics from a table and put them in an Excel Dashboard.

To make this work you firstly need to start your Excel formula with the SUM function followed by the INDEX function.

So it will look something like this:

=SUM(INDEX(Array, Row_Num, Column_Num))

The ***Array*** will be your table of data, the ***Row_Num*** will be blank and the ***Column_Num*** will be the column number where you want to SUM the values.

When we dissect the formula (by highlighting the INDEX function and pressing F9) we can see that the following is happening:
=SUM({8959;7840;7507;6690;5802;5487;3949;3836;3587;3210})

So in effect we are summing the array of values within the table. See the example below that shows you how this is done.

STEP 1: We need to place first the **INDEX** function inside the **SUM** function.

=SUM(INDEX

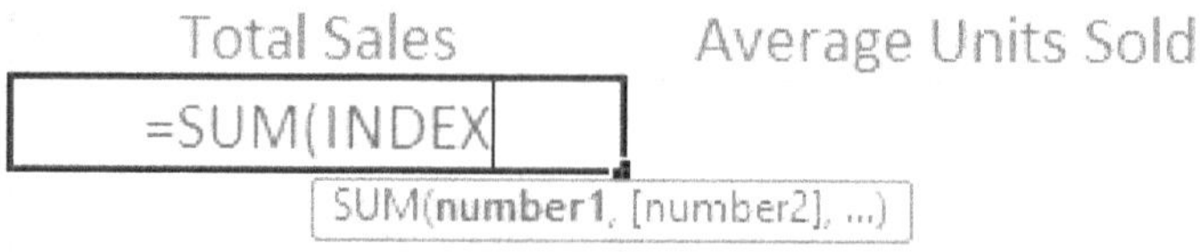

The Index arguments:

array
What is the range / table?

Reference the range of cells here that we want to get the values from:

=SUM(INDEX($C$12:$E$21,

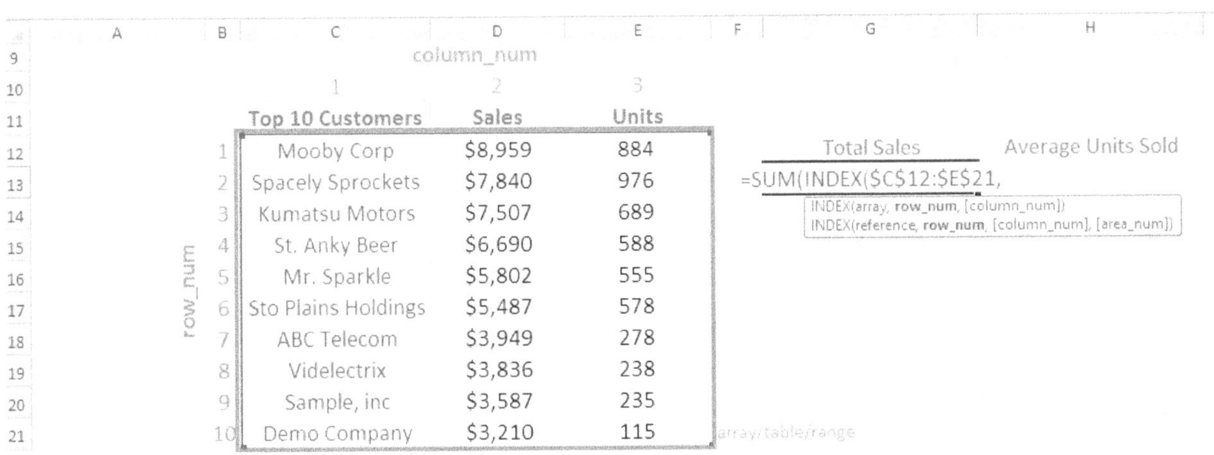

row_num
What is the row number we want to return?

We do not need to return the row, as we want to just sum all of the sales. Leave the row number blank:

=SUM(INDEX($C$12:$E$21,,

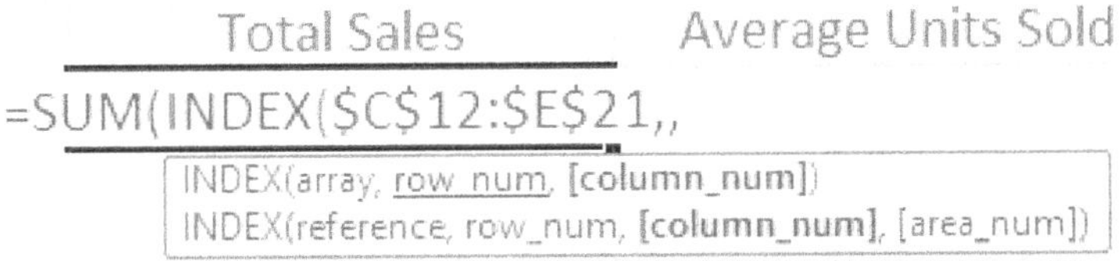

column_num
What is the column number we want to return?

Since we want the sales column, this is column number 2. So place in 2:

=SUM(INDEX($C$12:$E$21,,2))

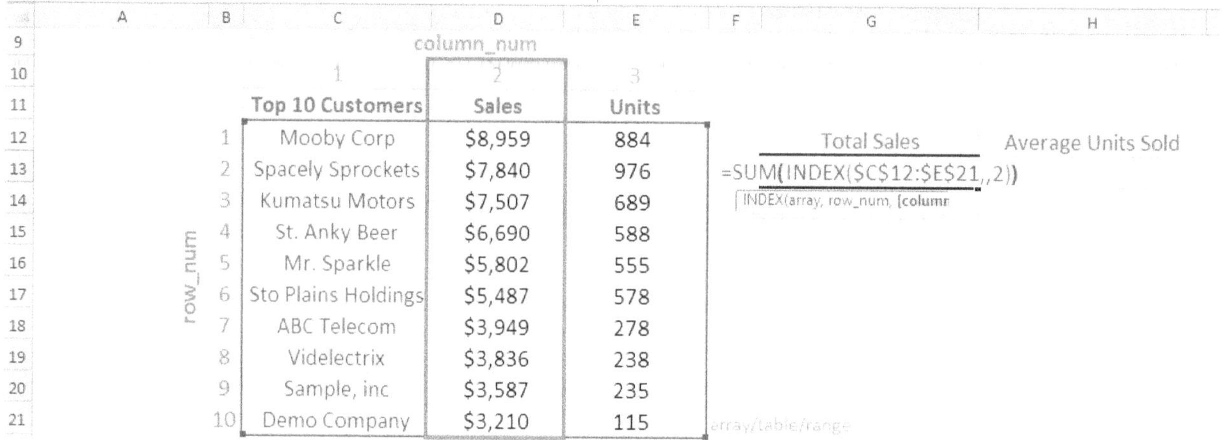

Now you are able to get the **Total Sales**:

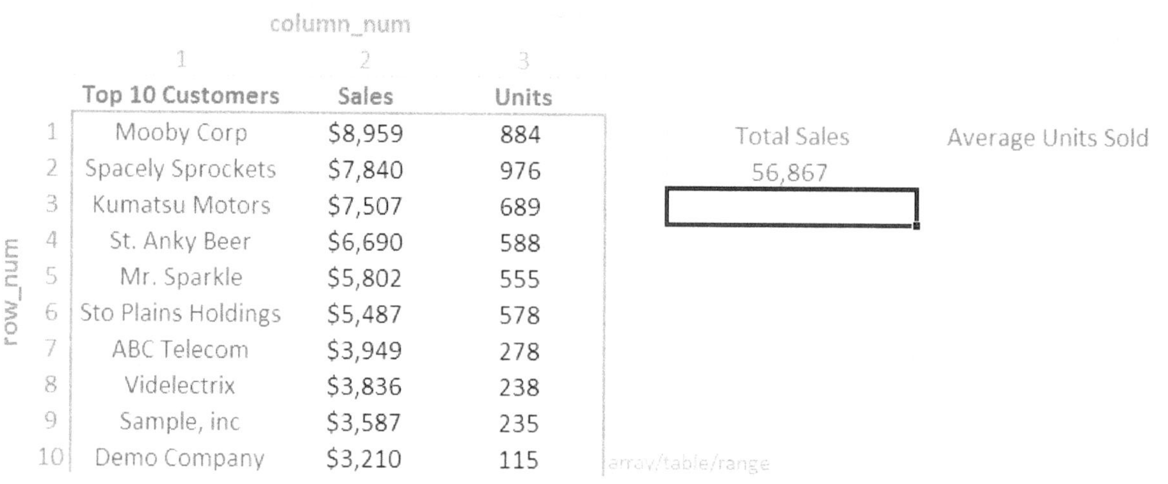

STEP 2: Now let us try how we can use this with the **AVERAGE** function. We need to place first the **INDEX** function inside the **AVERAGE** function.

=AVERAGE(INDEX

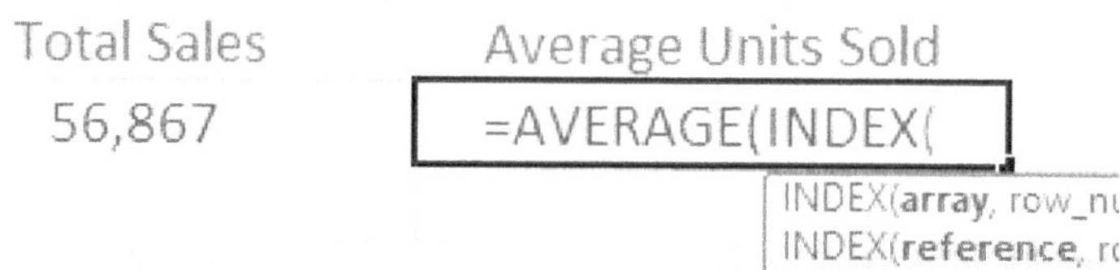

The Index arguments:

array

What is the range / table?

Reference the range of cells here that we want to get the values from:

=AVERAGE(INDEX($C$12:$E$21,

	A	B	C	D	E	F	G	H
9				column_num				
10			1	2	3			
11			Top 10 Customers	Sales	Units			
12		1	Mooby Corp	$8,959	884		Total Sales	Average Units Sold
13		2	Spacely Sprockets	$7,840	976		5	=AVERAGE(INDEX($C$12:$E$21,
14		3	Kumatsu Motors	$7,507	689			INDEX(array, row_num, [colum
15		4	St. Anky Beer	$6,690	588			INDEX(reference, row_num, [c
16		5	Mr. Sparkle	$5,802	555			
17		6	Sto Plains Holdings	$5,487	578			
18		7	ABC Telecom	$3,949	278			
19		8	Videlectrix	$3,836	238			
20		9	Sample, inc	$3,587	235			
21		10	Demo Company	$3,210	115			

row_num

What is the row number we want to return?

We do not need to return the row, as we want to just average all of the units. Leave the row number blank:

=AVERAGE(INDEX($C$12:$E$21,,

column_num

What is the column number we want to return?

Since we want the units column, this is column number 3. So place in 3:

$$=AVERAGE(INDEX(\$C\$12:\$E\$21,,3))$$

	A	B	C	D	E	F	G	H
9				column_num				
10			1	2	3			
11			Top 10 Customers	Sales	Units			
12		1	Mooby Corp	$8,959	884		Total Sales	Average Units Sold
13		2	Spacely Sprockets	$7,840	976		5	=AVERAGE(INDEX($C$12:$E$21,,3)
14		3	Kumatsu Motors	$7,507	689			AVERAGE(number1, [number2], ...)
15		4	St. Anky Beer	$6,690	588			
16		5	Mr. Sparkle	$5,802	555			
17		6	Sto Plains Holdings	$5,487	578			
18		7	ABC Telecom	$3,949	278			
19		8	Videlectrix	$3,836	238			
20		9	Sample, inc	$3,587	235			
21		10	Demo Company	$3,210	115			

Now you are able to get the **Average Units Sold**:

	column_num					
	1	2	3			
	Top 10 Customers	Sales	Units		Total Sales	Average Units Sold
1	Mooby Corp	$8,959	884		56,867	514
2	Spacely Sprockets	$7,840	976			
3	Kumatsu Motors	$7,507	689			
4	St. Anky Beer	$6,690	588			
5	Mr. Sparkle	$5,802	555			
6	Sto Plains Holdings	$5,487	578			
7	ABC Telecom	$3,949	278			
8	Videlectrix	$3,836	238			
9	Sample, inc	$3,587	235			
10	Demo Company	$3,210	115			

SUMPRODUCT: Sum Multiple Criteria

What does it do?

It returns the sum of multiple criteria from the corresponding ranges or arrays

Formula breakdown:

=SUMPRODUCT((array 1 criteria) * (array2 criteria) * array values)

What it means:

=SUMPRODUCT((find my criteria in this array) * (find my criteria in that array)
* return the values from the values array)

Example:

=SUMPRODUCT((B15:B23="john")*(C15:C23="north")*(E15:E23=1)*D15:D23)

The SUMPRODUCT function is my favorite Excel function by a stretch! You can create some powerful calculations with the SUMPRODUCT function by creating a criteria for a selected array. For example, you can see how much sales your sales rep did in a particular region and for a particular quarter without having to create a Pivot Table.

It takes some practice to get comfortable with this function but when you master it, it opens up another Excel world!

In our example, we want to get the **total sales of John in the North Region in Q1**:

Sales Rep	Region	Sales	Qrt
John	North	$2,500	1
Paul	South	$3,456	2
Ringo	North	$2,568	3
George	South	$9,854	4
John	North	$2,569	1
Paul	South	$4,125	2
Ringo	North	$2,568	3
George	South	$1,458	4
John	North	$2,562	1

STEP 1: We need to **enter the SUMPRODUCT function**:

=SUMPRODUCT(

Sales Rep	Region	Sales	Qrt
John	North	$2,500	1
Paul	South	$3,456	2
Ringo	North	$2,568	3
George	South	$9,854	4
John	North	$2,569	1
Paul	South	$4,125	2
Ringo	North	$2,568	3
George	South	$1,458	4
John	North	$2,562	1

Answer:

+SUMPRODUCT(

SUMPRODUCT(**array1**, [array2], [array3], ...)

 Create the criteria for the **Sales Rep "John"**:

=SUMPRODUCT((B15:B23="john")*

	A	B	C	D	E	F	G	H	I
13									
14		Sales Rep	Region	Sales	Qrt				
15		John	North	$2,500	1		Answer:		
16		Paul	South	$3,456			+SUMPRODUCT((B15:B23="john")*		
17		Ringo	North	$2,568	3		SUMPRODUCT(array1, [array2], [array3], …)		
18		George	South	$9,854	4				
19		John	North	$2,569	1				
20		Paul	South	$4,125	2				
21		Ringo	North	$2,568	3				
22		George	South	$1,458	4				
23		John	North	$2,562	1				

Create the criteria for the **Region "North"**:

=SUMPRODUCT((B15:B23="john")*(C15:C23="north")*

	A	B	C	D	E	F	G	H	I	J
13										
14		Sales Rep	Region	Sales	Qrt					
15		John	North	$2,500	1		Answer:			
16		Paul	South				+SUMPRODUCT((B15:B23="john")*(C15:C23="north")*			
17		Ringo	North	$2,56	SUMPRODUCT(array1, [array2], [array3], …)					
18		George	South	$9,854	4					
19		John	North	$2,569	1					
20		Paul	South	$4,125	2					
21		Ringo	North	$2,568	3					
22		George	South	$1,458	4					
23		John	North	$2,562	1					

Create the criteria for the **Quarter "1"**:

=SUMPRODUCT((B15:B23="john")*(C15:C23="north")*(E15:E23=1)*

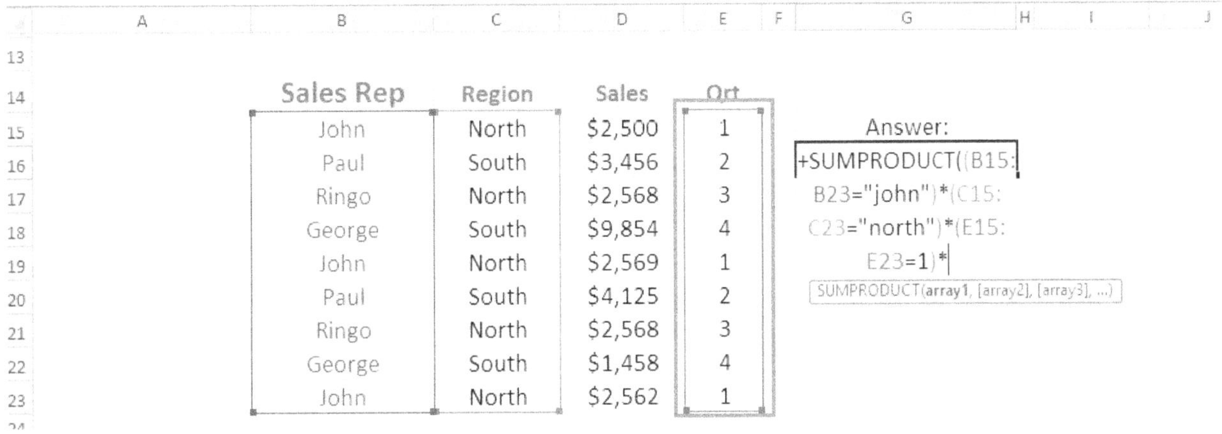

	A	B	C	D	E	F	G	H	I	J
13										
14		Sales Rep	Region	Sales	Qrt					
15		John	North	$2,500	1		Answer:			
16		Paul	South	$3,456	2		+SUMPRODUCT((B15:			
17		Ringo	North	$2,568	3		B23="john")*(C15:			
18		George	South	$9,854	4		C23="north")*(E15:			
19		John	North	$2,569	1		E23=1)*			
20		Paul	South	$4,125	2		SUMPRODUCT(array1, [array2], [array3], …)			
21		Ringo	North	$2,568	3					
22		George	South	$1,458	4					
23		John	North	$2,562	1					

Create the sum array to total the values of the **Sales** column:

=SUMPRODUCT((B15:B23="john")*(C15:C23="north")*(E15:E23=1)*D15:D23)

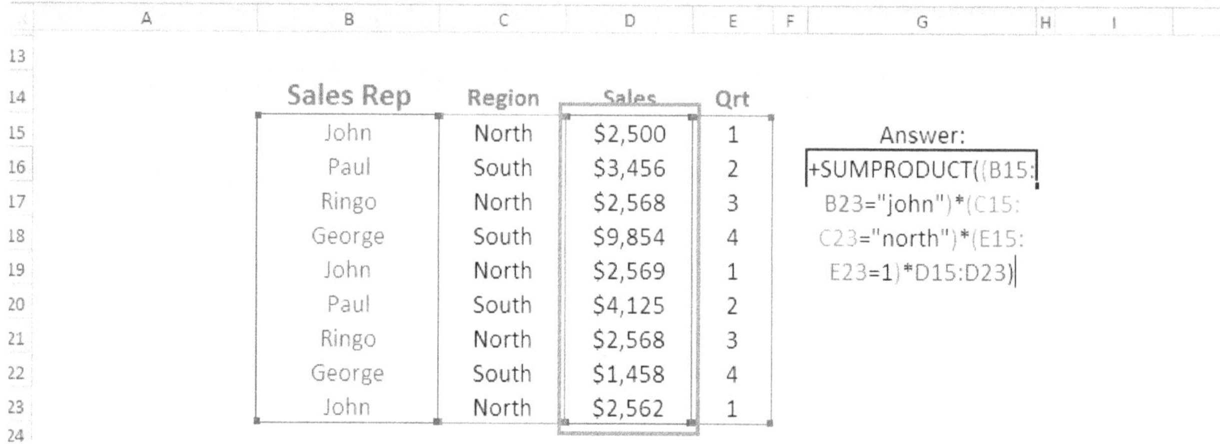

Once your formula is complete, you can see that it magically calculated the sum of the matching values!

Sales Rep	Region	Sales	Qrt		
John	North	$2,500	1		Answer:
Paul	South	$3,456	2		$7,631
Ringo	North	$2,568	3		
George	South	$9,854	4		
John	North	$2,569	1		
Paul	South	$4,125	2		
Ringo	North	$2,568	3		
George	South	$1,458	4		
John	North	$2,562	1		

SUMPRODUCT: Sum the Top 3 Sales

What does it do?

It returns the sum of multiple criteria from the corresponding range or array

Formula breakdown:

={SUMPRODUCT(Nested Formula((array 1 criteria) * array values))}

What it means:

={SUMPRODUCT(Return me the largest three values from(Region array) * Sales array)}}

Example:

={SUMPRODUCT(LARGE((C15:C23="north")*(D15:D23),{1,2,3}))}

This is probably the most advanced level a SUMPRODUCT function can reach and that is by including a nested array formula.

In our example below we want to return the 3 Largest values from the North region and sum them up. As we are asking our formula to perform multiple calculations i.e. *Get the Largest 3 values or large((array,{1,2,3})*, then an array formula is used. So to make this formula work we need to finish it off by pressing CTRL+SHIFT+ENTER

Here is our data set to get the **sum of the top 3 sales in the north region**:

Sales Rep	Region	Sales	Qrt
John	North	$2,500	1
Paul	South	$3,456	2
Ringo	North	$2,568	3
George	South	$9,854	4
John	North	$2,569	1
Paul	South	$4,125	2
Ringo	North	$2,568	3
George	South	$1,458	4
John	North	$2,562	1

STEP 1: We need to **enter the SUMPRODUCT function**:

=SUMPRODUCT(

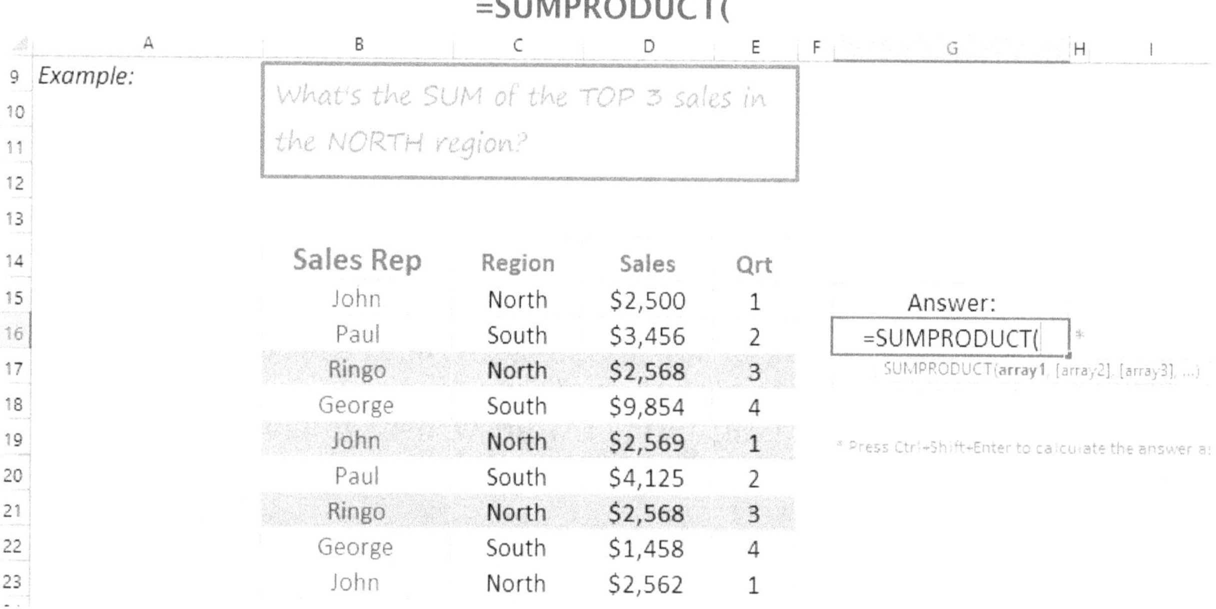

STEP 2: Enter the **LARGE function**:

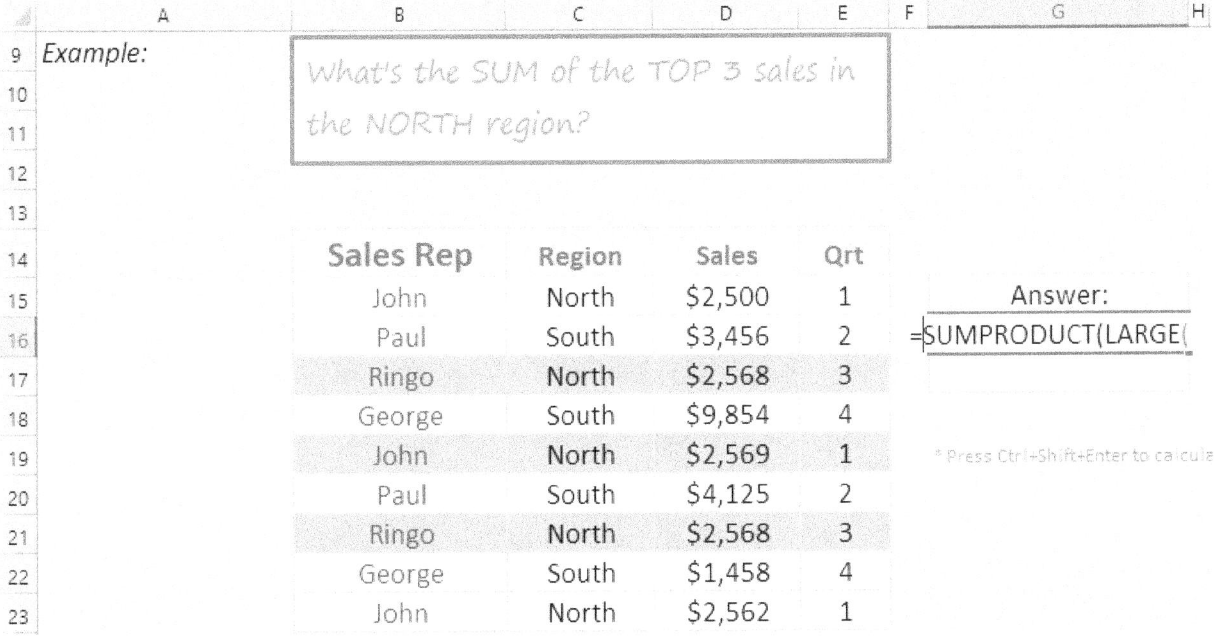

STEP 3: Create the criteria for **Region "North"**:

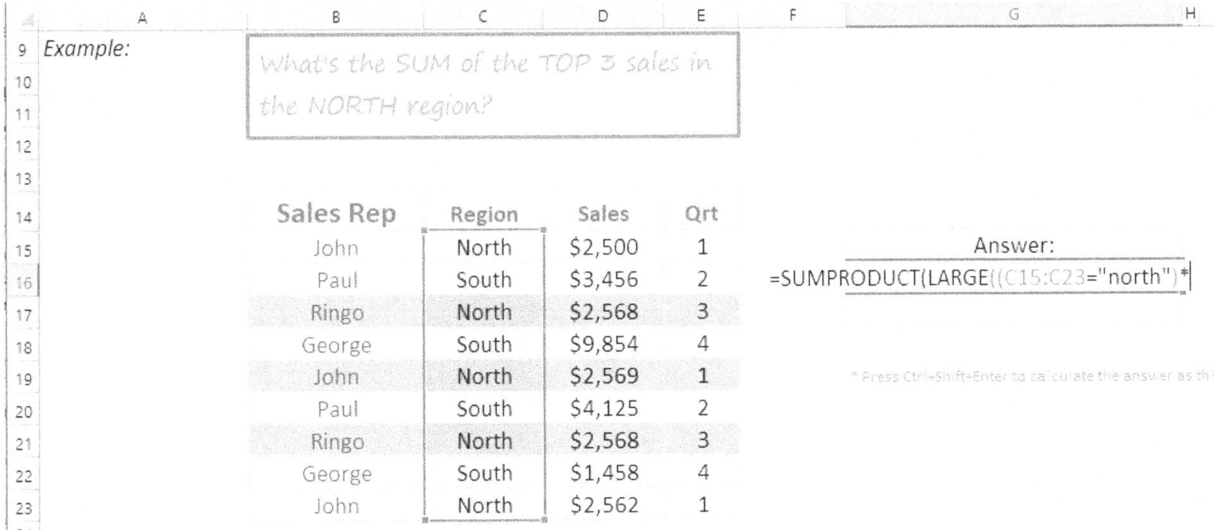

Create the **Sales Array:**

=SUMPRODUCT(LARGE((C15:C23="north")*(D15:D23),

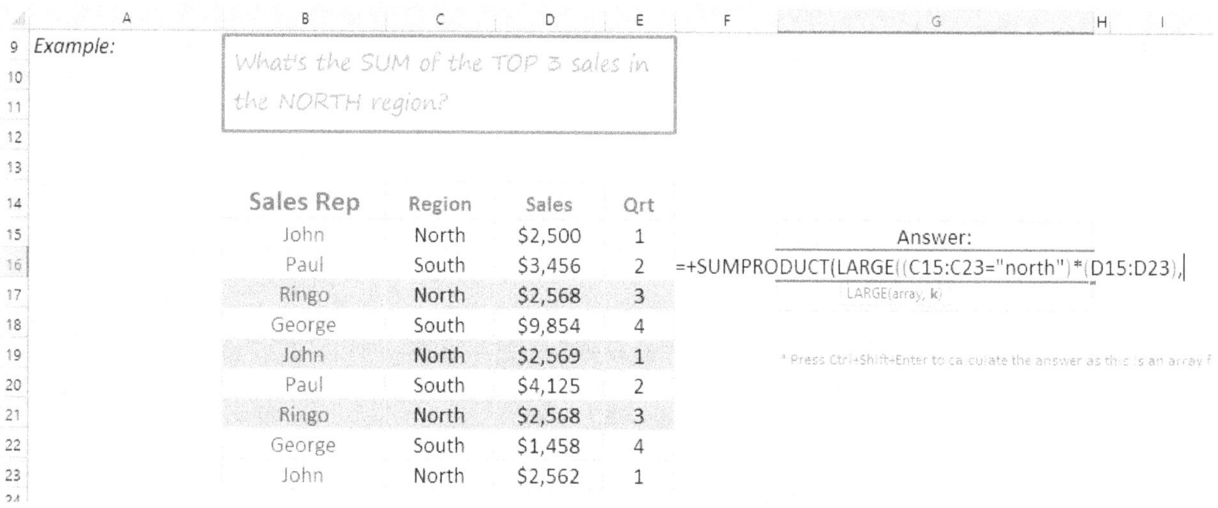

Enter the **Top 3 values {1,2,3}:**

=SUMPRODUCT(LARGE((C15:C23="north")*(D15:D23),{1,2,3}))

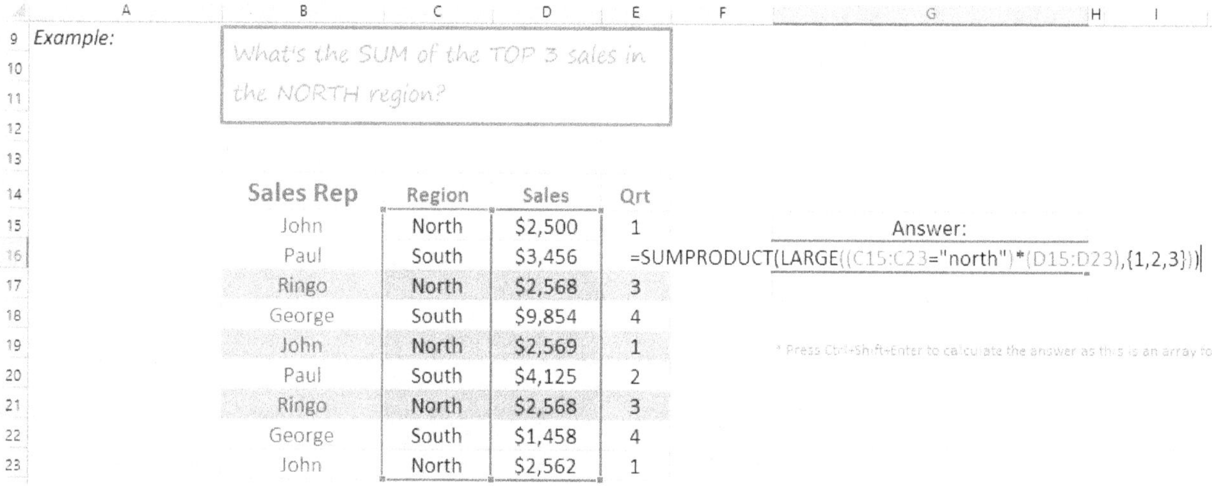

$$=\{SUMPRODUCT(LARGE((C15:C23="north")*(D15:D23),\{1,2,3\}))\}$$

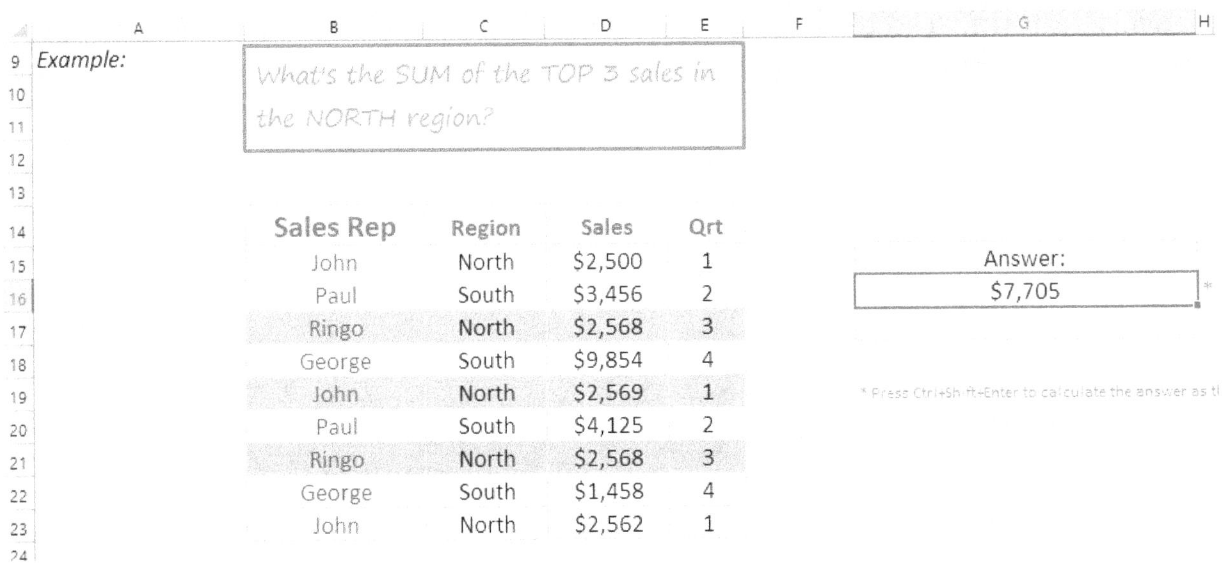

Sales Rep	Region	Sales	Qrt
John	North	$2,500	1
Paul	South	$3,456	2
Ringo	North	$2,568	3
George	South	$9,854	4
John	North	$2,569	1
Paul	South	$4,125	2
Ringo	North	$2,568	3
George	South	$1,458	4
John	North	$2,562	1

You now have the sum of the top 3 sales in the North region!

TIME – Get Elapsed Time

What does it do?

Converts a formula to text and lets you specify the display formatting by using special format strings

Formula breakdown:

=TEXT(value1 - value2, format text)

What it means:

=TEXT(formula, a text string enclosed in quotation marks)

Example:

=TEXT("1/25/2015 8.18:00 PM"-"1/24/2015 7:48:00 PM","[h]:mm")

="24:30"

When you have two points in time and you want to calculate the amount of time elapsed, then you will need to use Excel´s TEXT function

Sometimes data gets dumped into Excel with the following date & time format:

24/01/2015 19:48:00.

Using the **TEXT** function and entering a special text string can give you the time elapsed in Days, Hours, Minutes and Hours & Minutes.

See below how easy this is to implement.

We need to enter the **TEXT** function in a blank cell:

$$=TEXT(B12-A12, "dd")$$

value1 is the **end date time**
value2 is the **start date time**
format text is "**dd**" which signifies **days**

	START TIME	END TIME	Elapsed Time (Days)	Elapsed Time (Hrs)	Elapsed Time (Hrs & Mins)
			"dd"	"[hh]"	"[h]:mm"
9	Example:				
12	24/1/15 7:48 PM	25/	=TEXT(B12-A12, "dd")		
13	16/2/15 8:18 PM	26/2/15 8:25 PM			
14	18/3/15 8:18 PM	26/3/15 9:33 PM			
15	1/1/15 3:37 AM	31/1/15 4:30 AM			

STEP 2: Apply the same formula to the rest of the cells by dragging the lower right corner downwards.

	START TIME	END TIME	Elapsed Time (Days)	Elapsed Time (Hrs)	Elapsed Time (Hrs & Mins)
			"dd"	"[hh]"	"[h]:mm"
9	Example:				
12	24/1/15 7:48 PM	25/1/15 8:18 PM	01		
13	16/2/15 8:18 PM	26/2/15 8:25 PM	10		
14	18/3/15 8:18 PM	26/3/15 9:33 PM	08		
15	1/1/15 3:37 AM	31/1/15 4:30 AM	30		

STEP 3: Enter the following to get the elapsed time in hours:

We need to enter the **TEXT** function in a blank cell:

$$=TEXT(B12-A12, "[hh]")$$

value1 is the **end date time**
value2 is the **start date time**
format text is "**[hh]**" which signifies **hours**

	START TIME	END TIME	Elapsed Time (Days) "dd"	Elapsed Time (Hrs) "[hh]"	Elapsed Time (Hrs & Mins) "[h]:mm"
9	Example:				
12	24/1/15 7:48 PM	25/1/15 8:18 PM		=TEXT(B12-A12, "[hh]")	
13	16/2/15 8:18 PM	26/2/15 8:25 PM	10		
14	18/3/15 8:18 PM	26/3/15 9:33 PM	08		
15	1/1/15 3:37 AM	31/1/15 4:30 AM	30		

STEP 4: Apply the same formula to the rest of the cells by dragging the lower right corner downwards.

	START TIME	END TIME	Elapsed Time (Days) "dd"	Elapsed Time (Hrs) "[hh]"	Elapsed Time (Hrs & Mins) "[h]:mm"
9	Example:				
12	24/1/15 7:48 PM	25/1/15 8:18 PM	01	24	
13	16/2/15 8:18 PM	26/2/15 8:25 PM	10	240	
14	18/3/15 8:18 PM	26/3/15 9:33 PM	08	193	
15	1/1/15 3:37 AM	31/1/15 4:30 AM	30	720	

 Enter the following to get the elapsed time in hours and minutes:

We need to enter the **TEXT** function in a blank cell:

$$=TEXT(B12-A12, "[h]:mm")$$

value1 is the **end date time**
value2 is the **start date time**
format text is **"[h]:mm"** which signifies **hours and minutes**

	A	B	C	D	E	F
9	*Example:*					
10			"dd"	"[hh]"	"[h]:mm"	
11	START TIME	END TIME	Elapsed Time (Days)	Elapsed Time (Hrs)	Elapsed Time (Hrs & Mins)	
12	24/1/15 7:48 PM	25/1/15 8:18 PM	01		=TEXT(B12-A12, "[h]:mm")	
13	16/2/15 8:18 PM	26/2/15 8:25 PM	10	240		
14	18/3/15 8:18 PM	26/3/15 9:33 PM	08	193		
15	1/1/15 3:37 AM	31/1/15 4:30 AM	30	720		

STEP 6: Apply the same formula to the rest of the cells by dragging the lower right corner downwards. And your elapsed time results are all ready!

	A	B	C	D	E
9	*Example:*				
10			"dd"	"[hh]"	"[h]:mm"
11	START TIME	END TIME	Elapsed Time (Days)	Elapsed Time (Hrs)	Elapsed Time (Hrs & Mins)
12	24/1/15 7:48 PM	25/1/15 8:18 PM	01	24	24:30
13	16/2/15 8:18 PM	26/2/15 8:25 PM	10	240	240:07
14	18/3/15 8:18 PM	26/3/15 9:33 PM	08	193	193:15
15	1/1/15 3:37 AM	31/1/15 4:30 AM	30	720	720:53
16					

TRANSPOSE

What does it do?

Converts a vertical range of cells to horizontal, or vice versa

Formula breakdown:

=TRANSPOSE(array)

What it means:

=TRANSPOSE(the horizontal or vertical range of cells that you want to flip the orientation)

Example:

{=TRANSPOSE(A9:B13)}

Let us say you have a horizontal table, and you want to flip it to become a vertical table, did you know that there is an Excel formula that can do that for you? That's right, let us use the **TRANSPOSE Formula!**

Whenever you use this function, you should treat it as an **array formula** and it is very easy to do! You can use this to transform your horizontal table to a vertical table, or the other way around from a vertical table to a horizontal one.

STEP 1: Make sure to select your target table first with the same number of cells.

You can see we have selected a **horizontal table** that has the same number of cells (5 by 2) when compared to the original **vertical table** (2 by 5):

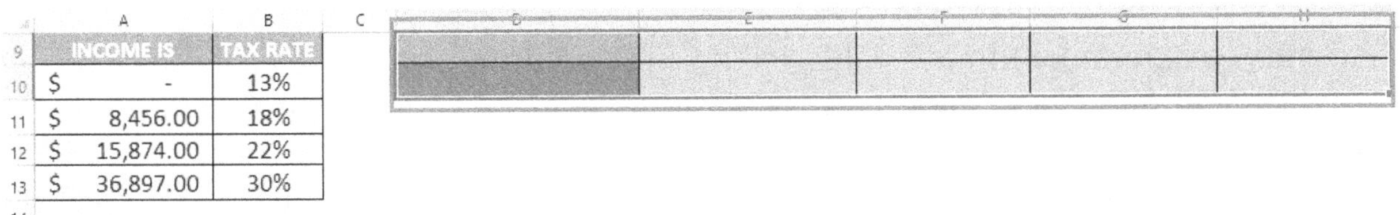

While it is selected, we need to **enter the *TRANSPOSE* function**:

$$=TRANSPOSE($$

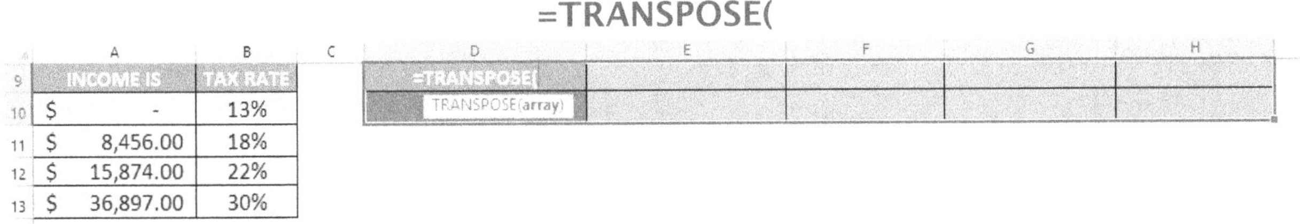

STEP 2: The **TRANSPOSE** arguments:

array

What is the range of cells that contains the data?

Select the cells containing the data that you want to flip the orientation:

$$=TRANSPOSE(A9:B13)$$

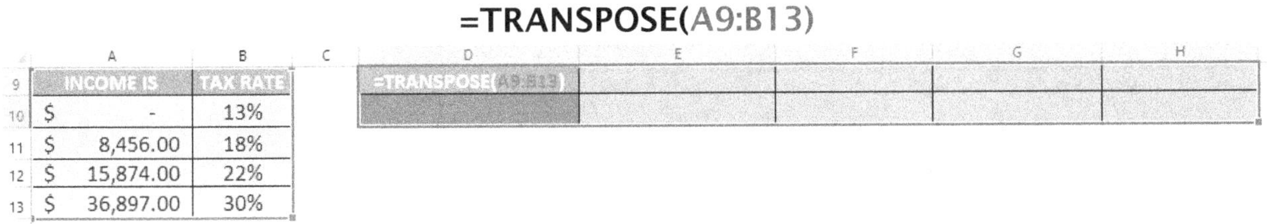

STEP 3: Once you finish typing the formula, ensure you press **CTRL + SHIFT + ENTER** for this to be treated as an **array formula:**

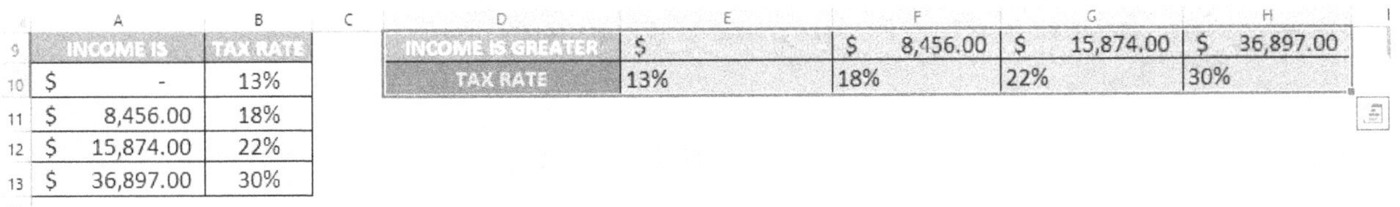

Your table now has a horizontal orientation with just the **TRANSPOSE Formula**!

VLOOKUP Approximate Match

What does it do?

Searches for an approximate value in the first column of a table array and returns a value in the same row from another column (to the right) in the table array.

Formula breakdown:

=VLOOKUP(lookup_value, table_array, col_index_num, [range_lookup])

What it means:

=VLOOKUP(this value, in this list, and get me value in this column, Approximate Match/TRUE/1])

Example:

=VLOOKUP(8500,Tax_Rate,2,TRUE)

The VLOOKUP Function in Excel is great when you want to find an exact match in your data table but what happens if you want to find an approximate match?

Approximate matches are used when you have an ascending table like **Commission Bonus Rates** or **Income Tax Rates**.

IMPORTANT: **For the Vlookup Approximate Match to work in Excel, the table_array has to be sorted in ascending order!**

So the way that this formula works is that it looks at the first value in the **Table_Array** that is greater than the **Lookup_Value** and then goes back one value.

=VLOOKUP(

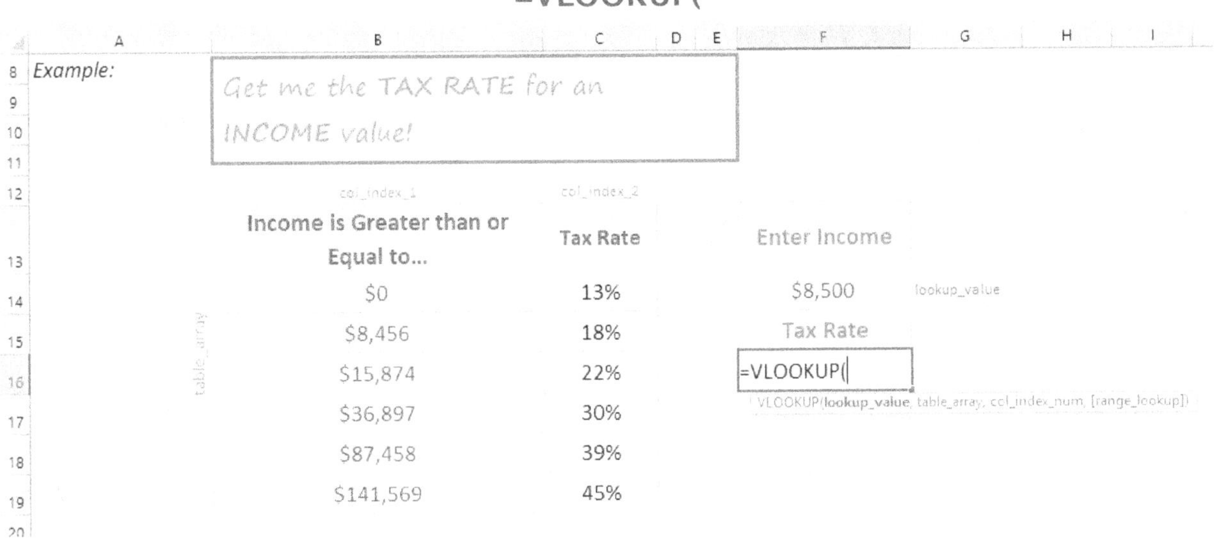

STEP 2: The **VLOOKUP** arguments:

lookup_value

What is the value to be looked up?

Select the cell that contains the income as the lookup value.

=VLOOKUP(F14,

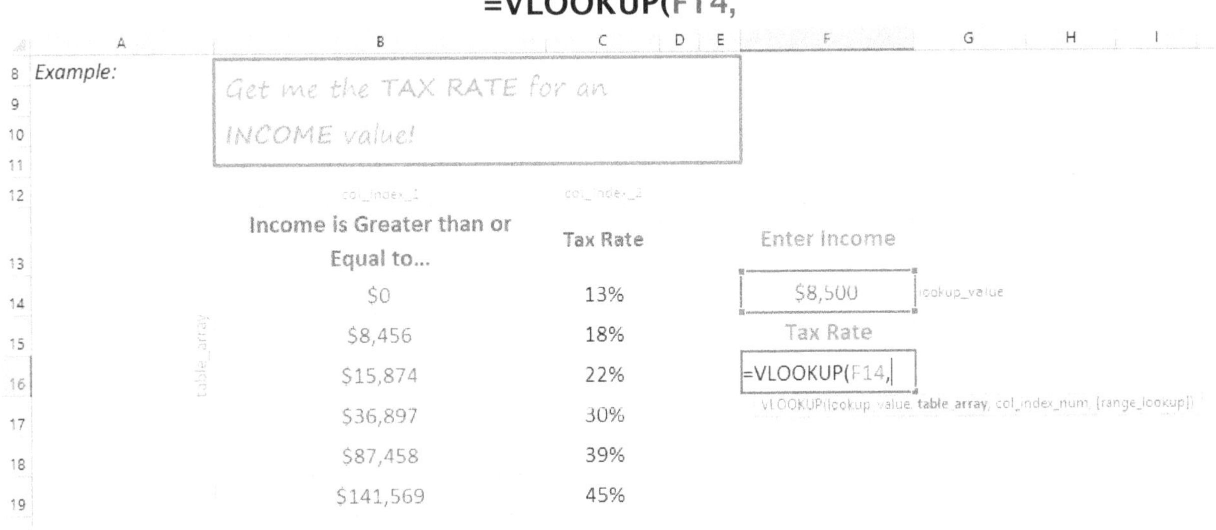

Where is the list of data?

Select the tax table, as that is where our formula is going to get the tax rate.

=VLOOKUP(F14, B14:C19,

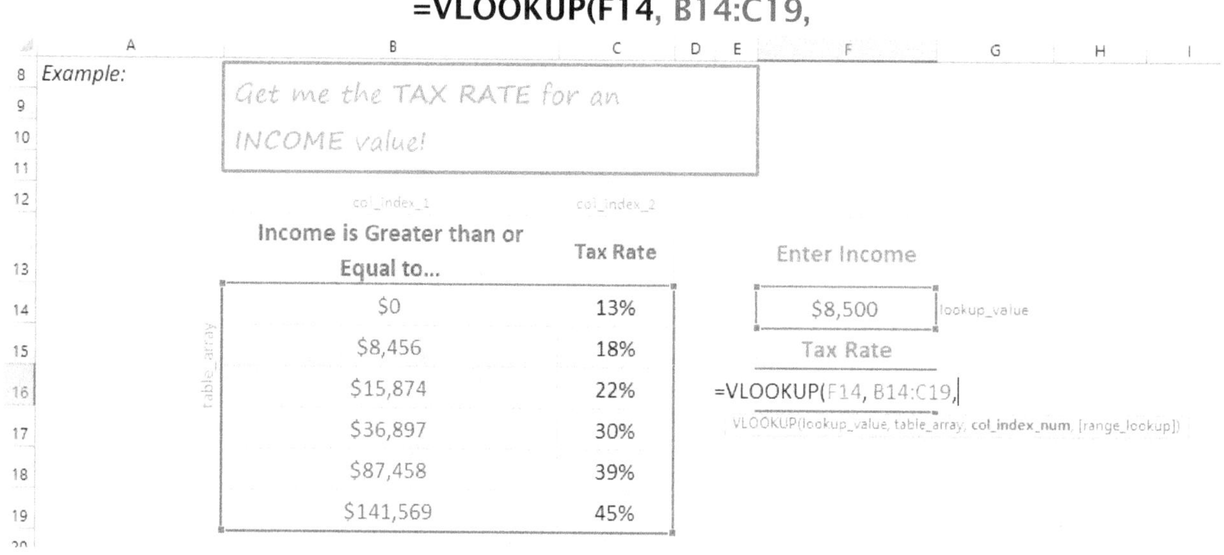

col_index_num

Which column in the table_array contains the data you want to return?

We want the tax rate which is the second column.

=VLOOKUP(F14, B14:C19, 2,

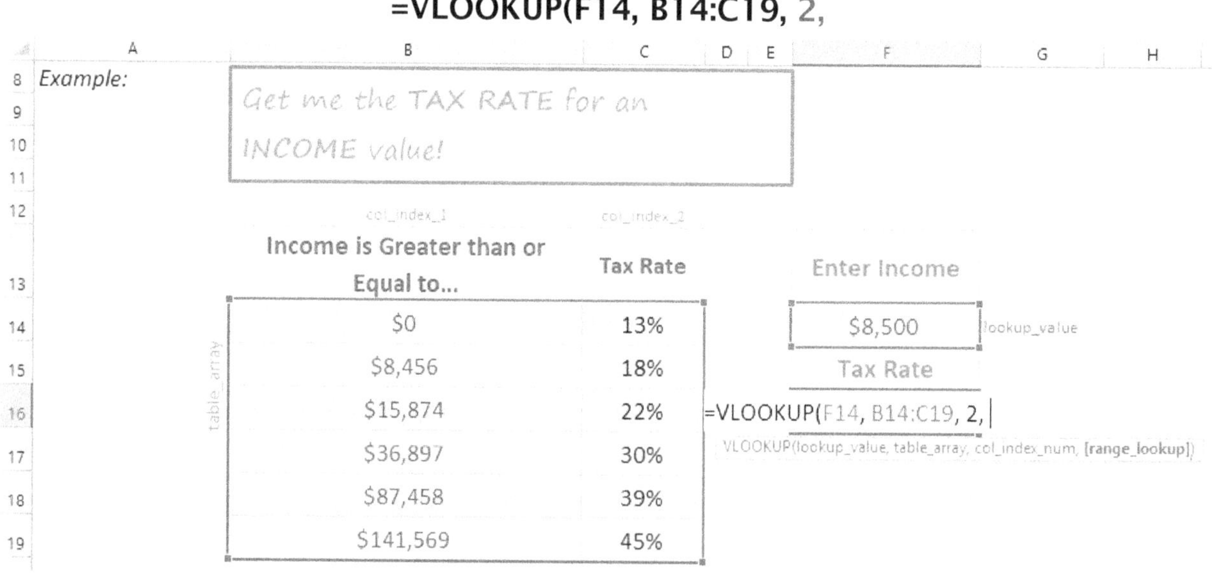

Would it be an approximate match?

Set this to TRUE as we want an approximate match.

=VLOOKUP(F14, B14:C19, 2, TRUE)

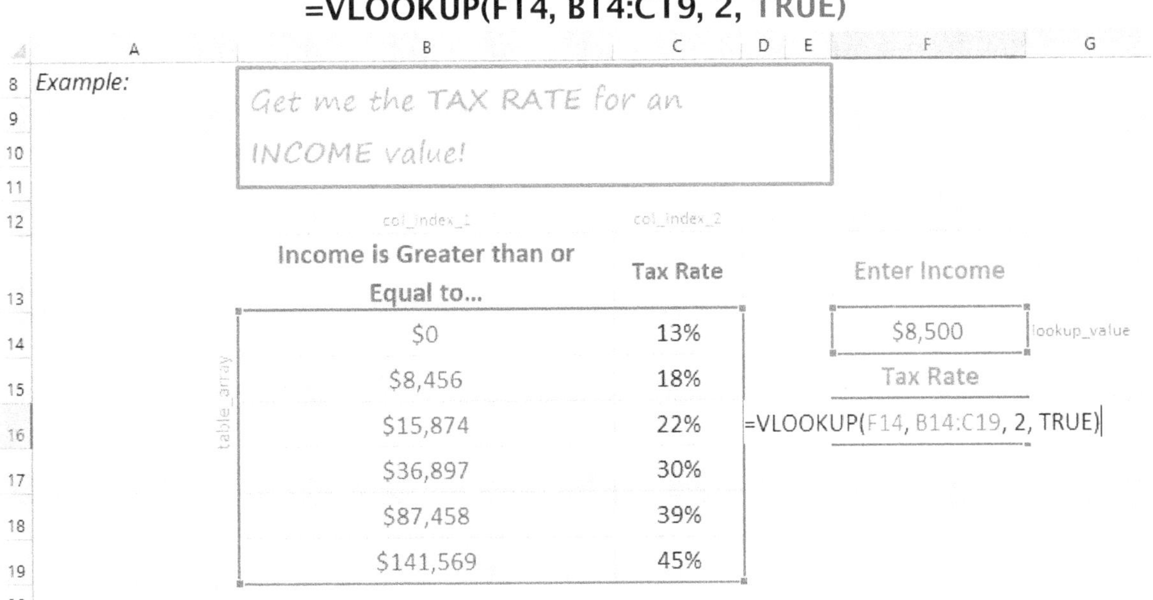

You now have your tax rate!

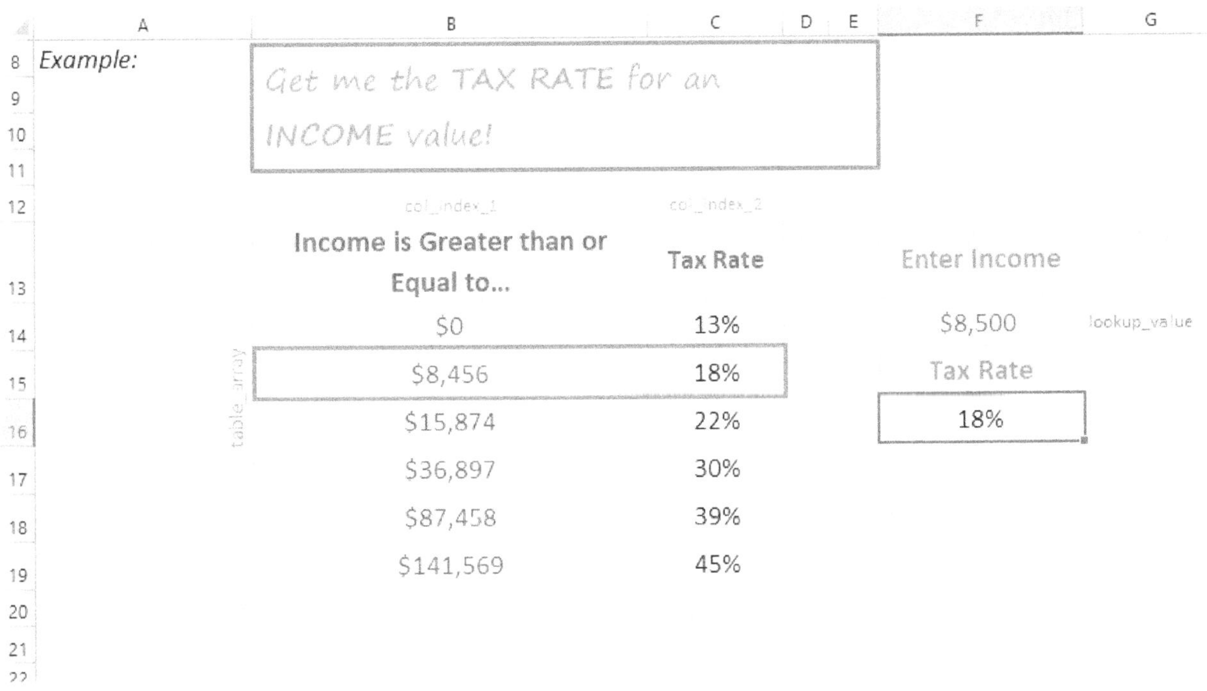

VLOOKUP with a Drop Down List

What does it do?

Searches for a value in the first column of a table array and returns a value in the same row from another column (to the right) in the table array.

Formula breakdown:

=VLOOKUP(lookup_value, table_array, col_index_num, [range_lookup])

What it means:

=VLOOKUP(this value, in this list, and get me value in this column, Exact Match/FALSE/0])

Example:

=VLOOKUP("Keyboard",B14:D17,2,FALSE)

The VLOOKUP function in Excel can become interactive and more powerful when applying a **Data Validation** (drop down menu/list) as the *Lookup_Value.*   So as you change your selection from the drop down list, the VLOOKUP value also changes.

See how easy it is to apply this with a quick VLOOKUP example below.

STEP 1: Go to **Data > Data Validation.**

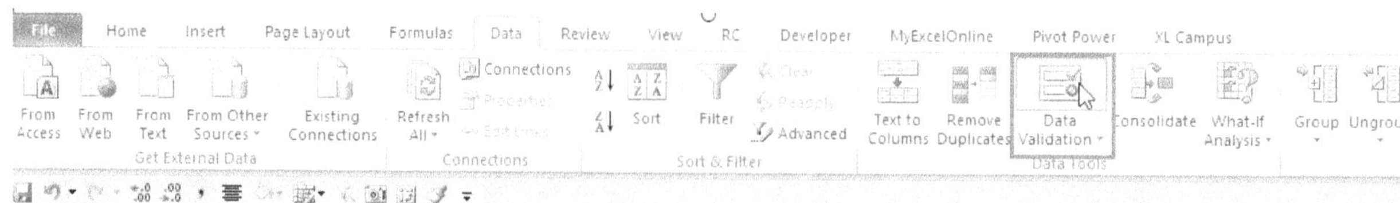

 Select **List** in the **Allow dropdown.**

For the **Source,** ensure that it has the 4 Stock List values selected. Click **OK.**

Your dropdown is ready.

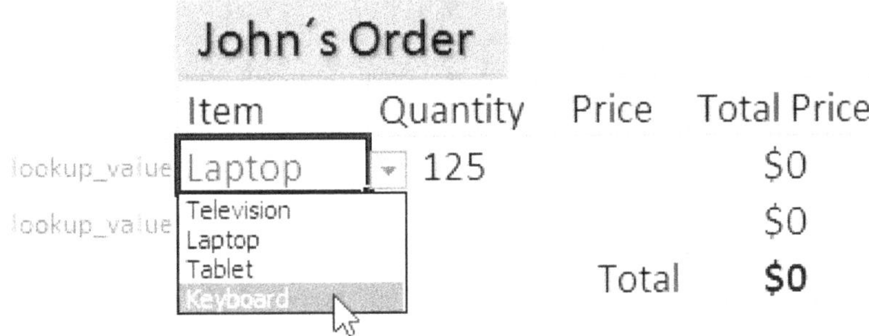

STEP 3: We need to **enter the *VLOOKUP* function**:

$$=VLOOKUP($$

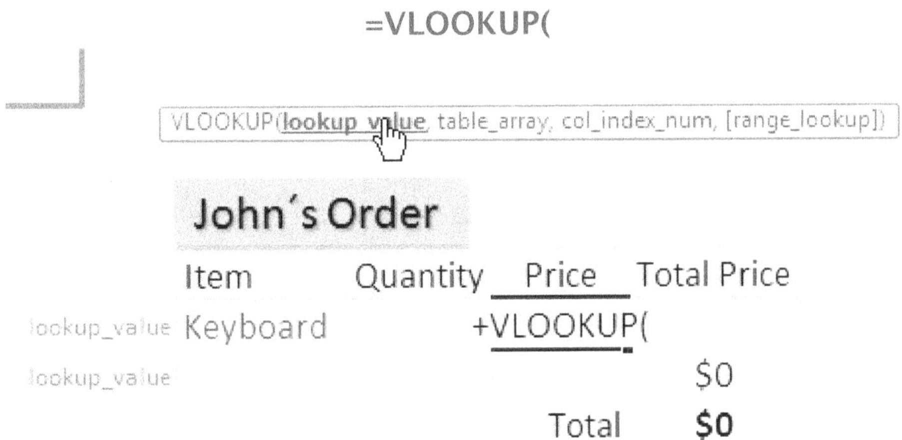

The VLOOKUP arguments:

lookup_value

What are we looking for?

Reference the cell that contains the text or value:

=VLOOKUP(G15,

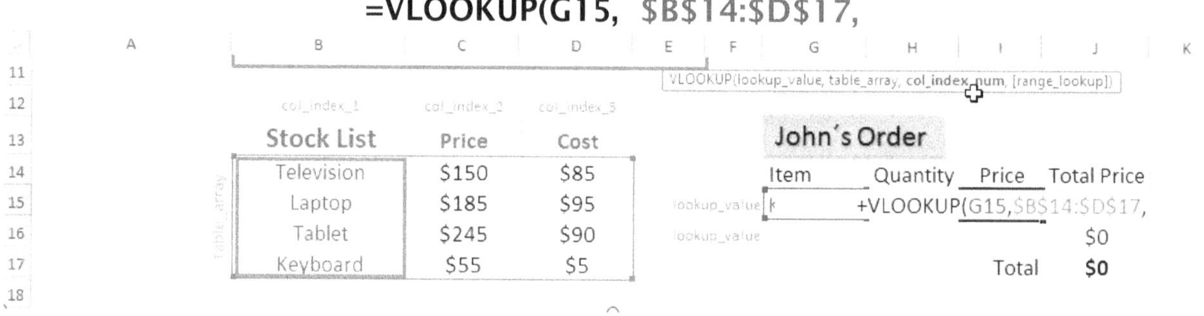

table_array

From which list are we doing a lookup on?

Place in the cell range of the Stock List:

=VLOOKUP(G15, $B$14:$D$17,

col_index_num

From which column do we want to retrieve the value?

We want to retrieve the Price which is the SECOND column from our table array:

=VLOOKUP(G15, $B$14:$D$17, 2,

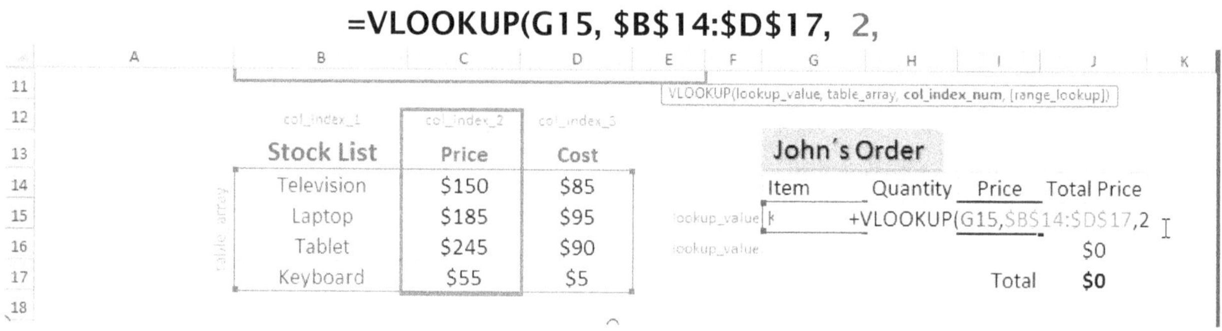

Do we want an exact match?

Place in FALSE to signify that we want an exact match:

=VLOOKUP(G15, $B$14:$D$17, 2, FALSE)

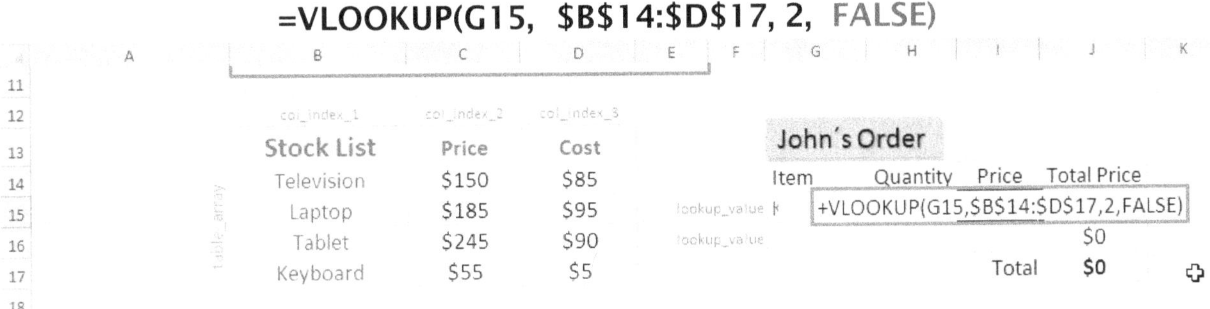

The price now dynamically changes based on your selection:

VLOOKUP Multiple Columns

What does it do?

Searches for a value in the first column of a table array and returns the sum of values in the same row from other columns (to the right) in the table array.

Formula breakdown:

{=SUM(VLOOKUP(lookup_value, table_array, {col_index_num1,col_index_num2}, [range_lookup]))}

What it means:

{=SUM(VLOOKUP(this value, in this list, {and sum the value in this column, with the value in this column}, Exact Match/FALSE/0]))}

Example:

{=SUM(VLOOKUP("Laptop",B14:D17,{2,3},FALSE))}

The VLOOKUP function can be combined with other functions such as the **Sum, Max** or **Average** to calculate values in multiple columns. As this is an array formula, to make it work we simply need to press **CTRL+SHIFT+ENTER** at the end of the formula. A very powerful feature for any serious analyst!

See how easy it is to implement in less than 1 minute with this VLOOKUP example!

We want to get the total number of units for Laptop (16,700 + 18,700 units).

STEP 1: We need to enter the **VLOOKUP function** in a blank cell:

=VLOOKUP(

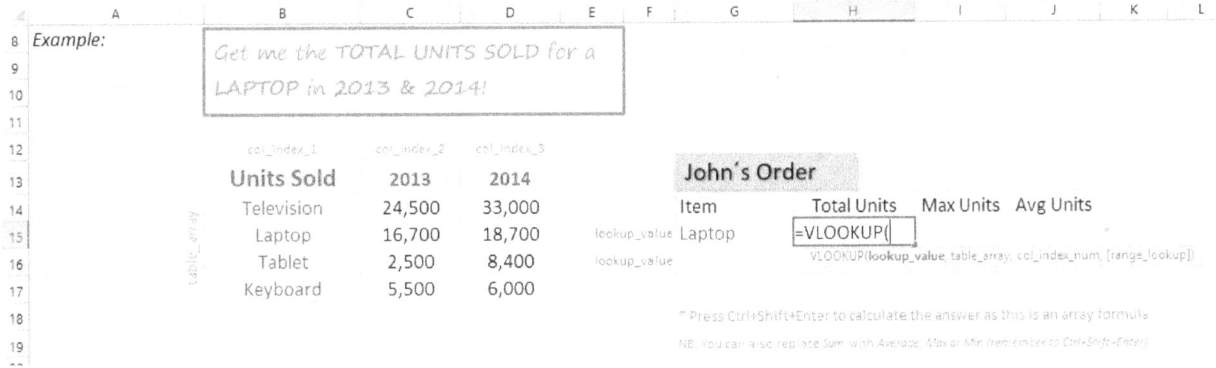

STEP 2: The **VLOOKUP** arguments:

lookup_value

What is the value to be looked up?

Select the cell that contains the item name, which is Laptop.

=VLOOKUP(G15,

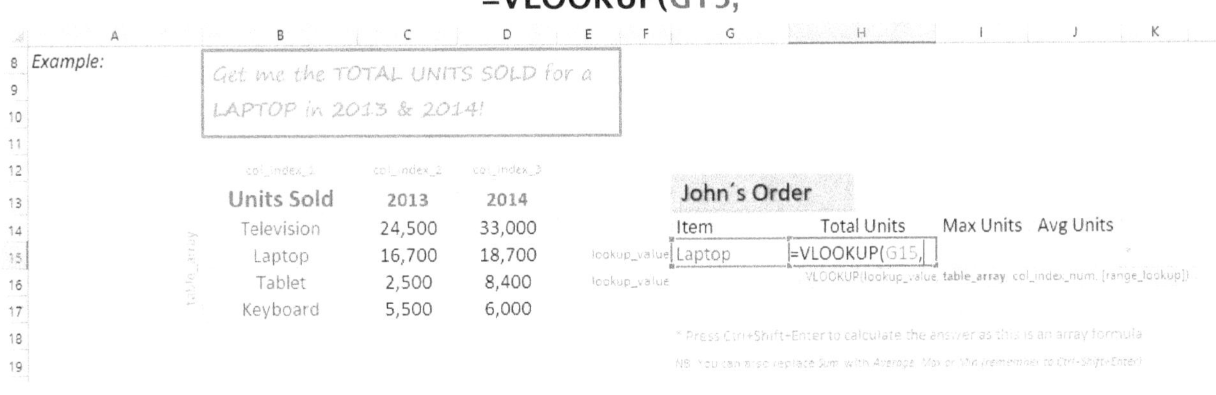

table_array

Where is the list of data?

Select the Units Sold table, as that is where our formula is going to get the unit numbers.

=VLOOKUP(G15, B14:D17,

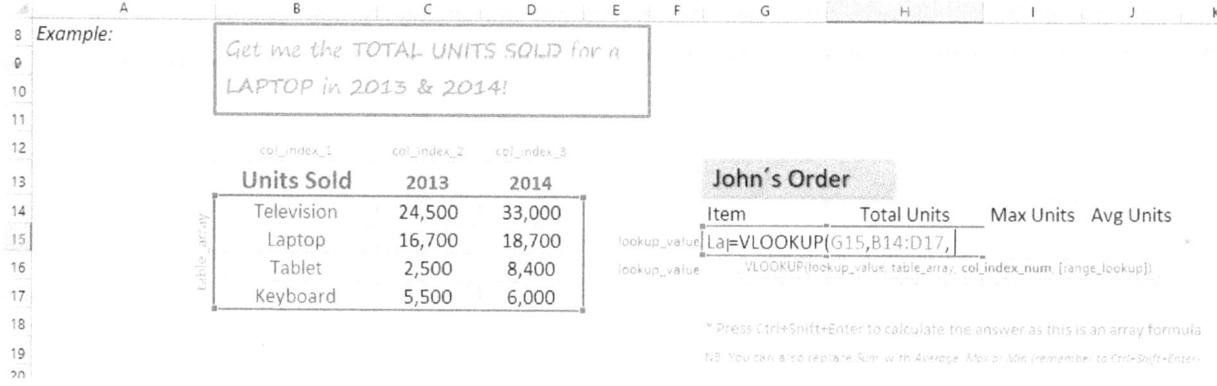

{col_index_num1, col_index_num2}

Which columns in the table_array contains the data you want to return?

We want to get the unit numbers of Years 2013 and 2014. So that will be columns 2 and 3.

$$=VLOOKUP(G15, B14:D17, \{2,3\},$$

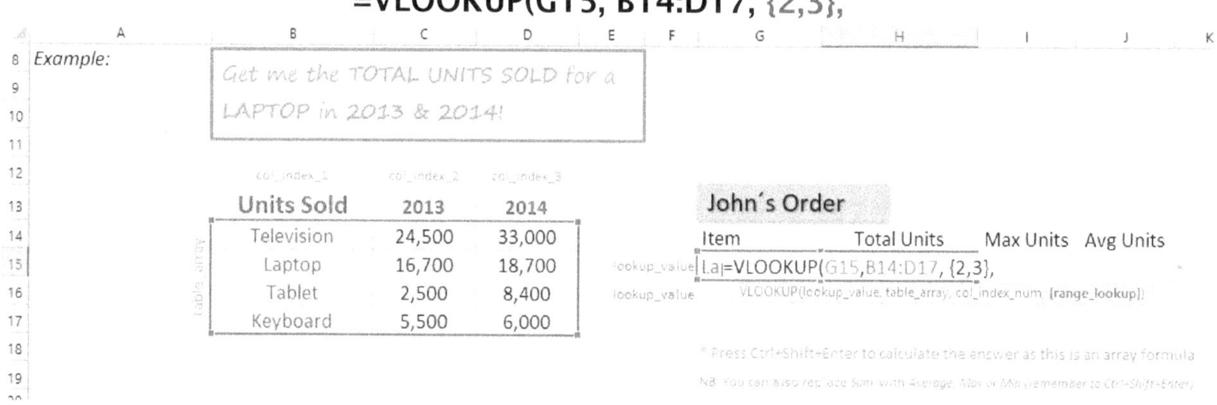

[range_lookup]

Would it be an approximate match?

Set this to FALSE as we want an exact match for Laptop.

$$=VLOOKUP(G15, B14:D17, \{2,3\}, FALSE)$$

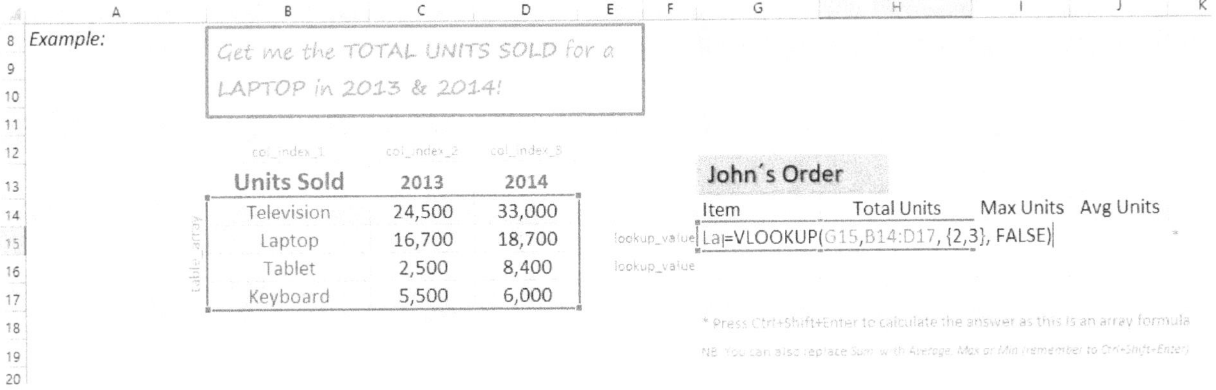

STEP 3: Now wrap the formula with the **SUM formula** as we want to get the total number of sold units for Laptop.

$$\text{=SUM(}\textbf{VLOOKUP(G15, B14:D17, \{2,3\}, FALSE)}\text{)}$$

Ensure you are pressing **CTRL+SHIFT+ENTER** as we want to calculate this as an array formula.

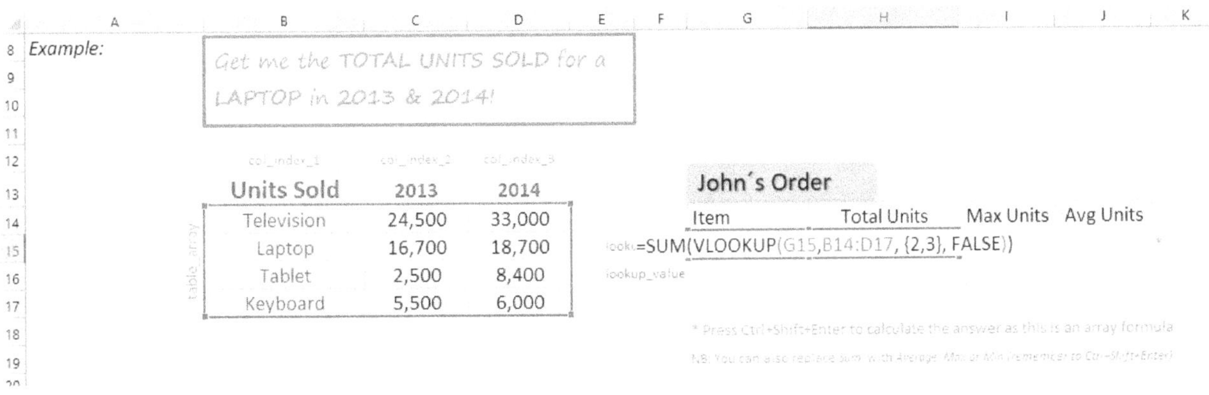

Do the exact same formula for **Max Units** and **Average Units**, by changing the **SUM Formula** with the **MAX Formula** and **Average Formula** respectively.

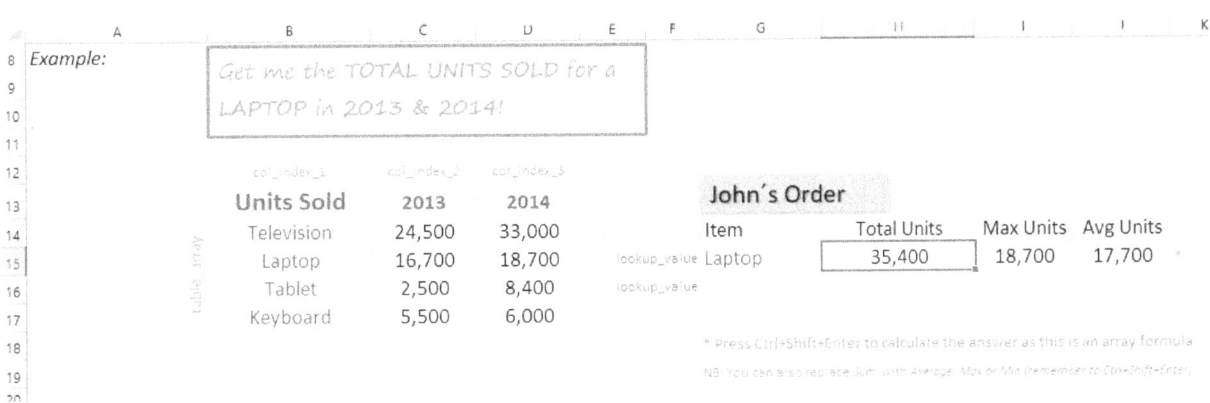

VLOOKUP with Multiple Criteria

What does it do?

Searches for a value in the first column of a table array and returns a value in the same row from another column (to the right) in the table array.

Formula breakdown:

=VLOOKUP(lookup_value, table_array, col_index_num, [range_lookup])

What it means:

=VLOOKUP(this value, in this list, and get me value in this column, Exact Match/FALSE/0])

Example:

=VLOOKUP("Nate Harris"&"HR",C:D,2,FALSE)

The challenging thing with VLOOKUP, is we are unable to **add more than one 'criteria'** to search for our value. For example, if we would be searching for 'Nate Harris' in our employee table, we would not want to search the entire table.

Instead, we want to search for 'Nate Harris' but only in the 'Sales department' of the company. This means that we have **two criteria for the search** ('Nate Harris' and 'Sales department').

VLOOKUP cannot do this if you do this the normal way! Thankfully, we can **concatenate the different criteria** so you can use them as a single lookup value.

The concatenation will be done with the **ampersand (&)**. We can get creative and create a helper column for this!

The game plan is to make a separate column that joins the data from the '**Full name**' column and the '**Department**' column, as seen in our table below.

	A	B	C
1	Full name	Department	Salary
2	Abigail Aalderink	Sales	$ 60,569
3	Sanford Bartolo	Sales	$ 81,603
4	Samuel Bartnick	Sales	$ 86,281
5	John Dumas	IT	$ 84,186
6	Kristi Hines	Production	$ 85,775
7	Apple Lyn	IT	$ 75,144
8	Lee Nazal	HR	$ 82,162
9	Lindsy Kline	Marketing	$ 98,915
10	Vicky James	HR	$ 83,207
11	Bradley Sack	IT	$ 64,717
12	Steven Lamar	Sales	$ 64,931
13	Tom Briones	IT	$ 70,988
14	Mike O'Neil	HR	$ 72,254

See how easy it is using our VLOOKUP example.

STEP 1: Let us create our helper column. Insert a column after the Department Column.

Enter this into **cell C2** and copy it down to the rest of the rows in the data.

=A2&B2

	A	B	C	D
1	Full name	Department	Helper column	Salary
2	Abigail Aalderink	Sales	=A2&B2	$ 60,569
3	Sanford Bartolo	Sales		$ 81,603
4	Samuel Bartnick	Sales		$ 86,281
5	John Dumas	IT		$ 84,186
6	Kristi Hines	Production		$ 85,775
7	Apple Lyn	IT		$ 75,144
8	Lee Nazal	HR		$ 82,162
9	Lindsy Kline	Marketing		$ 98,915
10	Vicky James	HR		$ 83,207
11	Bradley Sack	IT		$ 64,717
12	Steven Lamar	Sales		$ 64,931
13	Tom Briones	IT		70,988

 We need to **enter the *VLOOKUP* function**:

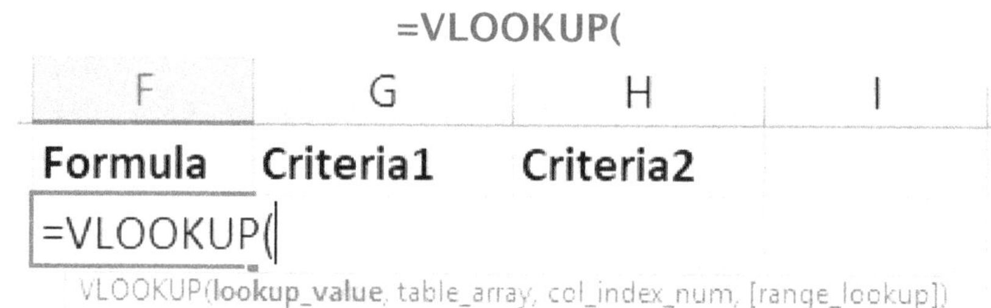

The VLOOKUP arguments:

lookup_value

What are we looking for?

Reference the cell that contains the text or value. Since we are looking in our helper column, ensure your lookup value is a combination of the full name and department:

=VLOOKUP(G2&H2,

	F	G	H
	Formula	**Criteria1**	**Criteria2**
	=VLOOKUP(G2&H2,	Nate Harris	HR

table_array

From which list are we doing a lookup on?

Place in the cell range of the helper column and the salary list:

=VLOOKUP(G2&H2, C:D,

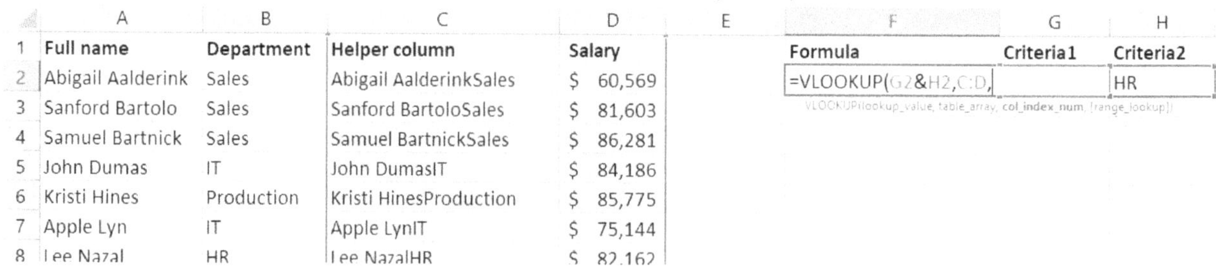

	A	B	C	D	E	F	G	H
1	Full name	Department	Helper column	Salary		Formula	Criteria1	Criteria2
2	Abigail Aalderink	Sales	Abigail AalderinkSales	$ 60,569		=VLOOKUP(G2&H2,C:D,		HR
3	Sanford Bartolo	Sales	Sanford BartoloSales	$ 81,603				
4	Samuel Bartnick	Sales	Samuel BartnickSales	$ 86,281				
5	John Dumas	IT	John DumasIT	$ 84,186				
6	Kristi Hines	Production	Kristi HinesProduction	$ 85,775				
7	Apple Lyn	IT	Apple LynIT	$ 75,144				
8	Lee Nazal	HR	Lee NazalHR	$ 82,162				

col_index_num

From which column do we want to retrieve the value?

We want to retrieve the Salary which is the SECOND column from our table array:

=VLOOKUP(G2&H2, C:D, 2,

	A	B	C	D	E	F	G	H
1	Full name	Department	Helper column	Salary		Formula	Criteria1	Criteria2
2	Abigail Aalderink	Sales	Abigail AalderinkSales	$ 60,569		=VLOOKUP(G2&H2,C:D,2,		HR
3	Sanford Bartolo	Sales	Sanford BartoloSales	$ 81,603				
4	Samuel Bartnick	Sales	Samuel BartnickSales	$ 86,281				
5	John Dumas	IT	John DumasIT	$ 84,186				
6	Kristi Hines	Production	Kristi HinesProduction	$ 85,775				

[range_lookup]

Do we want an exact match?

Place in FALSE to signify that we want an exact match:

=VLOOKUP(G2&H2, C:D, 2, FALSE)

	A	B	C	D	E	F	G	H
1	Full name	Department	Helper column	Salary		Formula	Criteria1	Criteria2
2	Abigail Aalderink	Sales	Abigail AalderinkSales	$ 60,569		=VLOOKUP(G2&H2,C:D,2,FALSE)		HR
3	Sanford Bartolo	Sales	Sanford BartoloSales	$ 81,603				
4	Samuel Bartnick	Sales	Samuel BartnickSales	$ 86,281				
5	John Dumas	IT	John DumasIT	$ 84,186				
6	Kristi Hines	Production	Kristi HinesProduction	$ 85,775				
7	Apple Lyn	IT	Apple LynIT	$ 75,144				

With this, you are now able to get the salary using multiple criteria (full name and department)!

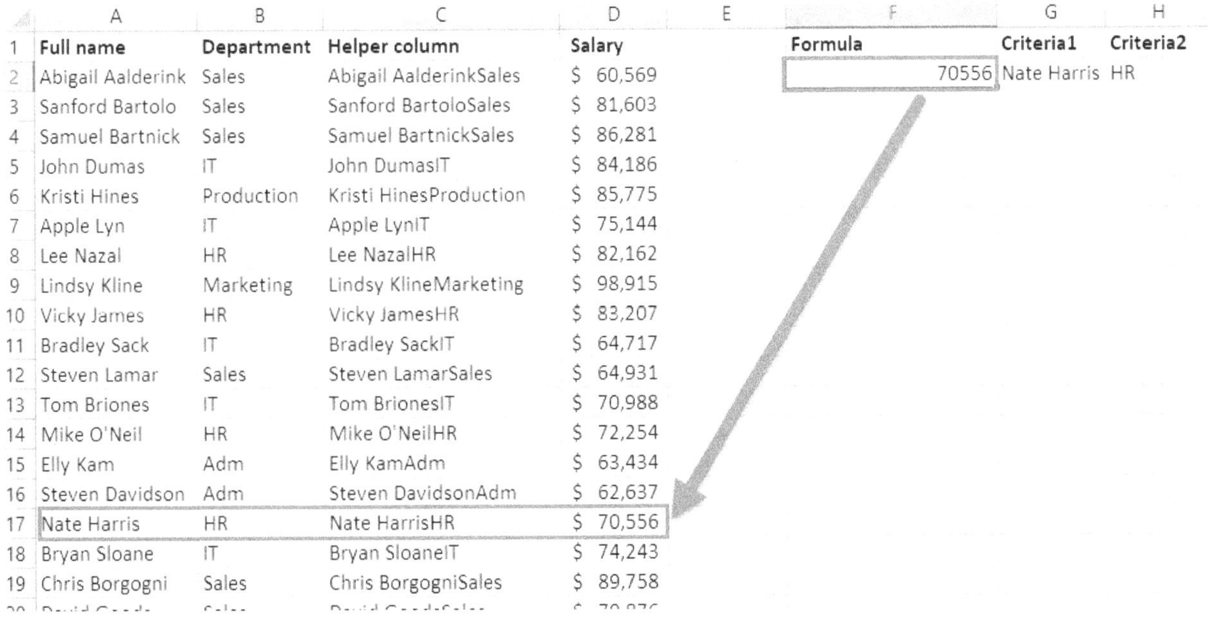

	A	B	C	D	E	F	G	H
1	Full name	Department	Helper column	Salary		Formula	Criteria1	Criteria2
2	Abigail Aalderink	Sales	Abigail AalderinkSales	$ 60,569		70556	Nate Harris	HR
3	Sanford Bartolo	Sales	Sanford BartoloSales	$ 81,603				
4	Samuel Bartnick	Sales	Samuel BartnickSales	$ 86,281				
5	John Dumas	IT	John DumasIT	$ 84,186				
6	Kristi Hines	Production	Kristi HinesProduction	$ 85,775				
7	Apple Lyn	IT	Apple LynIT	$ 75,144				
8	Lee Nazal	HR	Lee NazalHR	$ 82,162				
9	Lindsy Kline	Marketing	Lindsy KlineMarketing	$ 98,915				
10	Vicky James	HR	Vicky JamesHR	$ 83,207				
11	Bradley Sack	IT	Bradley SackIT	$ 64,717				
12	Steven Lamar	Sales	Steven LamarSales	$ 64,931				
13	Tom Briones	IT	Tom BrionesIT	$ 70,988				
14	Mike O'Neil	HR	Mike O'NeilHR	$ 72,254				
15	Elly Kam	Adm	Elly KamAdm	$ 63,434				
16	Steven Davidson	Adm	Steven DavidsonAdm	$ 62,637				
17	Nate Harris	HR	Nate HarrisHR	$ 70,556				
18	Bryan Sloane	IT	Bryan SloaneIT	$ 74,243				
19	Chris Borgogni	Sales	Chris BorgogniSales	$ 89,758				

MYEXCELONLINE ACADEMY COURSE

We are offering you access to our online Excel membership course – The MyExcelOnline Academy – **for only $1 for the first 30 days!**

Copy & Paste this $1 Trial URL to your web browser to get access to this special reader offer:

☞ https://www.myexcelonline.com/$1trial

Here is the **download link** that has all the workbooks covered in this book (copy & paste this URL to your web browser):

☞ https://www.myexcelonline.com/formulas-download

Here is the **link and password** to the Free 20-Hour Microsoft Excel Course (copy & paste this URL to your web browser):

☞ https://www.myexcelonline.com/free-excel-course

☞ Password: **101excel**